IMAGINING THE CHILD IN MODERN JEWISH FICTION

Johns Hopkins Jewish Studies
Sander Gilman and Steven T. Katz,
Series Editors

IMAGINING THE CHILD IN MODERN JEWISH FICTION

Naomi B. Sokoloff

The Johns Hopkins University Press
Baltimore and London

© 1992 The Johns Hopkins University Press
All rights reserved
Printed in the United States of America

The Johns Hopkins University Press
701 West 40th Street
Baltimore, Maryland 21211–2190
The Johns Hopkins Press Ltd., London

The paper used in this book meets the minimum requirements of the
American National Standard for Information Sciences—Permanence of Paper
for Printed Library Materials, ANSI Z39.48-1984.

Library of Congress Cataloging-in-Publication Data

Sokoloff, Naomi B.
    Imagining the child in modern Jewish fiction / Naomi B. Sokoloff.
        p.   cm. — (Johns Hopkins Jewish studies)
    Includes bibliographical references and index.
    ISBN 0-8018-4373-1 (hard : alk. paper)
    1. Jewish fiction—History and criticism.   2. Jewish children in literature.
3. Children in literature.   4. Holocaust, Jewish (1939–1945), in literature.
I. Title.   II. Series.
PN842.S6   1992
809.3'9352054—dc20   91-45940

To Rachel and Michelle

CONTENTS

PREFACE

This book examines pieces of modern Jewish fiction written in Hebrew, Yiddish, and English, all of which explore a child's view of the world.

Scant serious attention has been paid to the representation of children's voices and consciousness in adult literature. Though numerous articles have dealt with individual child characters in poetry and fiction, little overall theoretical work and few surveys have been dedicated to the literary treatment of the very young. A handful of studies have dealt specifically with the language of the child, notably with linguistic features of children's expression or speech behavior as they are incorporated into imaginative writing. Nonetheless, a potentially broad area of inquiry dealing with childhood remains largely *terra incognita*. The child's voice invites consideration in terms of stylistics, phenomenology, semiotics, psychoanalytic or cognitive studies, and assessments of changing historical trends in the ways people have conceived of childhood. My remarks in the following pages aim at helping to define this area of critical debate by concentrating on narrative voice, Bakhtin's theories of utterance, and the challenges to narration posed by texts that feature a child's perceptions.

This approach effectively sheds light on a narrative strategy I call the discourse of childhood. My concern is with the child's voice, which does not speak for itself but which is necessarily constructed by an adult narrator. The same young figures, though, who inevitably serve as an expression and extension of their authors' views, are also ones who interpret adult meanings. In the narrated events, the child character filters the words and actions of grown-ups around it through the prism of its own understandings. In short, these texts imagine a child's imaginings, and in both the plot actions and the act of storytelling the imagination of the child involves dynamic interactions between mature and immature voices. The result: oscillating perspectives that bring about an exploration of clashing cultural codes.

These qualities grant the narrative of childhood particularly rich possibilities for modern Jewish writing, which has responded to so many changes in political circumstance and collective values in the past one hundred fifty years. Indeed, the unusual exercises in narrative voice requisite for depicting a child's perceptions have been instrumental in generating outstanding works of twentieth-century Jewish fiction across a spectrum of situations. The formal problem of representing the consciousness of the child has proven inseparable from thematic attention to cultural displacements and shifting meanings, and my efforts here suggest how and why focusing on the novelty of a young character's outlook can yield texts that felicitously capture the newness of new worlds or of worlds made strange through the breakdown of previous custom and understanding.

To illustrate these ideas I have concentrated on two clusters of thematic material: texts that depict shifts away from the Torah-centered world of tradition and texts that deal with the Holocaust. Within these categories my selection has been guided by a desire to discuss a few texts in some depth. The narratives chosen impressively harness the energies available to fiction that privileges a child's view. Given these organizational priorities, the limits of space permit me to mention only in passing a wealth of other Jewish fiction also concerned, at least in part, with childhood: in Hebrew and Yiddish, works by I. J. Linetski, S. Y. Abramovitch, S. Ben Zion, M. Z. Feierberg, Yehuda Steinberg, S. Y. Agnon, Bella Chagall, and, more recently, Uri Orlev, Hayim Be'er, Yehoshua Knaz, David Shahar, Shulamit Hareven, and Amos Oz; in non-Jewish languages, Abraham Cahan, Michael Gold, Ludwig Lewisohn, Philip Roth, André Schwarz-Bart, Clara Asscher-Pinkhof, Elie Wiesel, and others. Were this group of names to include authors of autobiography and memoirs, the list could be extended on and on. A host of different questions might be formulated on the basis of such texts—for instance, how did post-Haskalah Hebrew writers or second-generation Americans, as a group, perceive their youth? Why have Israeli writers engaged more and more in reassessing their own early years as an exploration of the early years of statehood? How have attitudes toward children been transformed by changes in the social circumstance of various Jewish populations? How have depictions of girlhood differed from depictions of boyhood? These questions would call for a foregrounding of different sources and methods of analysis than the ones emphasized here, and each of these matters merits attention. My goals, however, have been other than those of a comprehensive historical survey. Not attempting to posit a school of writing, to conduct sociological inquiry, or to present exhaustive commentary on the image of children in Jewish fiction, I offer instead a mode of reading invited by the texts examined, as it illuminates and works toward defining a subgenre of the Bildungsroman.

One of the primary assumptions underlying this project is the conviction that modern Jewish fiction may, and should, be read increasingly as comparative literature. There is no such phenomenon as a monolithic modern secular Jewish literary tradition. Instead, a constellation of Jewish literatures in the nineteenth and twentieth centuries has emerged in various languages, all evolving within their separate traditions. Each must be appreciated on its own terms. Still, after considering individual texts within the context of the language in which they were conceived, it becomes imperative to put them back in comparative view in order to grasp the similarity of concerns shared among the writers, to better understand different treatments accorded and solutions proposed to common problems, and to gauge the accomplishments of Jewish writing and the impact it has had on modern fiction as a whole. In view of the intercultural underpinnings of the texts examined here, it makes little sense to read them in isolation. Each follows a character's transition from one language, culture, or country to another. Too little work has been done by way of considering such texts jointly, and part of my purpose here is to pose the possibility and encourage future efforts in this direction.

The fundamental preoccupation these fictions share is the children's discovery of Jewishness or their determination of what that heritage means for their own lives. Recognition of this focus is crucial, too, in determining the province of Jewish literature to be compared here. It is always problematic to decide what kinds of texts fall under the rubric of "Jewish" writing in twentieth-century literature. The issue is most acute in non-Jewish languages. The Jewishness of the text cannot be designated solely because the author happens to be of Jewish origin. At the same time, it is equally meaningless to deny Jewish impact entirely, simply on the basis of the author's linguistic orientation or on the basis of a loyalty to one literary approach or another. The definitional problems are not absent in the case of Jewish languages, either. Anton Shammas's novel, *Arabesques* (1986), puts the point into relief. Focusing on childhood and dual identities, but from the perspective of an Arab boy growing up in Israel, this text demonstrates clearly that literature is not a priori Jewish by virtue of having been written in Hebrew. Indeed, the author's choice of artistic medium was designed to discomfit, to deny the Jewishness of the Jewish national language and hence also of the Jewish state. My inclination is to agree with Gershon Shaked, one of the outspoken advocates and practitioners of a comparative approach to Jewish writers. He argues in his book *The Shadows Within* that the most important characteristic of Jewishness in modern literature is the very struggle with the issue of identity itself. Narratives of childhood, concerned with a young figure's search for a personal voice, are keenly attuned to such matters and contribute to a wider phenomenon in modern Jewish literature of restless seeking for self-definition.

While wrestling with these matters, I hope that this work will prove of interest to readers outside the sphere of Jewish studies. Fictional childhood, a compelling topic, commands special attention as it finds powerful expression in the extraordinary vitality and inventiveness of the texts singled out for discussion here.

The first section of this book presents introductory material; Chapter 1 considers the child as a marginalized Other and as a voice usually suppressed in adult literature, one that has emerged from heightened silence to heightened recognition in Jewish texts. Chapter 2 then sets out more detailed theoretical discussion of narrative voice and presents the specialized terminology that recurs in subsequent essays. Chapters 3–8 are divided under the headings "The Shtetl and Beyond" and "The Holocaust and Afterward." Each chapter focuses on a particular author and a specific narrative that attempts to inhabit the singular perceptions of a young protagonist. Chapter 9, by way of contrast, briefly analyzes Albert Memmi's *The Pillar of Salt* so as to put into relief the distinctiveness of the childhood narrative. Though this novel delves into many issues germane to the rest of the texts examined (multilingual childhood, a crisis of assimilation, and a struggle with definitions of Jewish identity), *The Pillar of Salt* follows classic conventions of the education novel. The narrator reminisces about the past but never attempts to forge radical access into the otherness of the child, and so the young character's voice remains subdued. In this way Memmi helps delimit the general artistic phenomenon described earlier. Chapter 10, "Others: The Silent Voice," reconsiders from another perspective the major issues raised throughout the study. Here I turn to two texts, *A Poet's Continuing Silence*, by A. B. Yehoshua, and *The Cannibal Galaxy*, by Cynthia Ozick, which invert the strategies of the preceding novels. Remaining remote from the child character's inner life, these novellas call intensified attention to the child as a mute Other who, even in its silence, can exert a powerful critique on existing discourse.

Portions of this work have previously appeared in print. A version of Chapter 8 was published in *Hebrew Annual Review* 12 (1987): 387–406 as "The Holocaust and the Discourse of Childhood: David Grossman's *See Under: Love.*" A version of Chapter 4 appears in *Hebrew Studies* 32 (1991): 19–44. Some ideas that I later reworked and adapted to the purposes of chapters 3, 4, and 9 were rehearsed in "Interpretation: Cynthia Ozick's *The Cannibal Galaxy,*" *Prooftexts* 6 (September 1986): 239–57; "Contrast, Continuity, and Contradiction: Opening Signals in A. B. Yehoshua's 'Continuing Silence,'" *Hebrew Annual Review* 5 (1981): 115–36; and "Discoveries of Reading: Childhood Stories of Bialik, Shahar, and Roth," *Hebrew Annual Review* 9 (1985): 321–42.

ACKNOWLEDGMENTS

A major impetus for the completion of this manuscript was pleasant anticipation that I would finally be able to acknowledge those who have encouraged me along the way.

This work was first undertaken while I held a Faculty Fellowship at the Jewish Theological Seminary of America in 1984–85. My time at the seminary, which allowed me access to libraries and a chance to meet with the faculty, was both productive and gratifying. I would like to express my continuing gratitude for that opportunity. My thanks go also to the University of Washington for awarding me a grant from the Graduate School Research Fund in summer of 1986, as well as released time from teaching in the spring of 1988. The Jewish Studies Program at the University of Washington provided generous financial support in 1985 through its Faculty Summer Research Fund.

A number of individuals read portions of the manuscript or discussed aspects of this research with me. For their time, their suggestions, and their critiques, their kindnesses and their skepticisms, I thank Hillel Kieval, Anne Golomb Hoffman, Gilead Morahg, Robert Alter, Gershon Shaked, David Roskies, Sander Gilman, Zilla Goodman, Alan Mintz, Shaul Stampfer, Cheryl Jaffee, Jere Bacharach, Claudia Mills, David Feldman, Ken Frieden, Edward Alexander, and Felicia Hecker. Of particular usefulness were discussions at the 1985 and 1987 annual conventions of the MLA. Two special sessions concerned with literary representations of childhood and child language brought together critics working in different traditions, but interested in parallel theoretical issues. I much appreciated the insights and enthusiasm shared on those occasions by Laurence Ricou, Mark Heberle, Elizabeth Goodenough, Mary Jane Hurst, and Mary Galbraith.

It has been a pleasure to work with the Johns Hopkins University Press and with my manuscript editor, Carol Ehrlich.

Above all I am indebted to my husband, Doug, for his patience and for his stubborn insistence that I get the work done.

REPRESENTING THE
VOICE OF THE CHILD

1 FICTIVE VOICES:
THE DISCOURSE OF
CHILDHOOD

A child is something else again. Wakes up
in the afternoon and in an instant he's full of words,
in an instant he's humming, in an instant warm,
instant light, instant darkness.

A child is Job. They've already placed their bets on him
but he doesn't know it. He scratches his body
for pleasure. Nothing hurts yet.
They're training him to be a polite Job,
to say "Thank you" when the Lord has given,
to say "You're welcome" when the Lord has taken
* away.*

—Yehuda Amihai, "A Child Is Something Else Again"

A child," writes the poet Yehuda Amihai, "is something else again."[1] In the original Hebrew, the poem reads, more literally, a child is something other (*"mashehu aher"*). In this instance the otherness of the very young consists of a capacity for wonder, an intense richness and energy that animates the child's inner life, and the sudden shifts to which that imagination is susceptible. All these, though enchanting, are perceived as foreign and incomprehensible to the adult.

Otherness always impinges in some way on treatments of childhood in adult writing. No grown writer can speak authentically in the name of childhood or in the voice of a child, for inevitably there exist disparities between grown-up narration and the experience of youthful characters. The sensations and perception of childhood are to some extent always irretrievable to memory and articulation. Youngsters, for their part, may author highly revealing and compelling texts, but they do not write mature narratives. In short, children are outsiders in large measure because of their unusual relation to language. The word *infant* signifies *one without speech,* and children in imaginative writing by their elders are by definition Others whose words must be translated into a world of mature discourse they do not yet inhabit.[2]

For these reasons, literary representations of childhood and the

3

consciousness of child characters invite examination through two kinds
of approach. First, a burgeoning critical literature on otherness which
has come into prominence in recent years emphasizes the persistence of
cultural bias, the blindness of discourse that informs a variety of texts
and so ensures the dominating vision of more powerful, hence vocal
and recognized, social orders, at the expense of less powerful classes
or groups. This brand of criticism demonstrates how respected, can-
onically accepted literary works encompass, distort, or misrepresent
the more suppressed voices of society.[3] In opposition to this line of
thought stands that critical tradition which has emphasized the potential of literature as a way to overcome otherness by depicting inner life.
This criticism observes that, through the representation of consciousness, fiction can do what human beings generally cannot. Imaginative
writing may penetrate the intimate, never communicated thoughts of
someone else and so reveal the hidden side of people or give voice to
those not readily heard by society. It is one of the special virtues of
literature to convey the feel of another person's existence, and so to
illuminate aspects of human lives that other disciplines, such as psychology and sociology, cannot.[4]

Depictions of childhood engender a series of complications in
debate about otherness. The first of these regards inner life. While representations of consciousness are by nature a highly fictive enterprise, an
as if restoration of the uncharted territory of another mind, the exploration of a child's private world is, to an increased degree, an exercise of
the imagination. This is a mysterious realm into which adults get only
occasional glimpses. Unlike suppressed voices in any given canon that
may eventually gain autonomy (women, for instance, in traditions of
writing dominated by men), use of the child's voice and perspective in
adult fiction must necessarily remain a ventriloquism and a peculiarly
literary phenomenon. And yet, the narrative presentation of a child's
mental life may often have a ring of authenticity about it that the imper-
sonation of other voices or the treatment of other private views would
not. All adult writers and readers were children once. Consequently,
there is a familiarity to this strangeness that may foster texts more likely
to persuade than those in which men adopt women's voices or privileged authors presume to take the stance of the downtrodden and
outcast. The concept of otherness proves slippery in regard to children
for another reason as well. The young make highly mutable Others.
Engaged in an accelerated process of growth and change, they find
themselves constantly in transition. The point is important because
peripheral figures appearing in literary texts usually serve to set apart a
dominant group, to define its limits and so elevate its worth by contrast
with their own devalued status. The child, though, destined one day to

usurp adult power, lives on extremely dynamic and shifting margins. Young characters may present continuing challenges to definitions of themselves and their relations to adults, thereby confusing demarcations between self and other, identity and difference.

That the child has been a creature often defined from without is a well-recognized phenomenon. Since the publication of Philippe Ariès's *Centuries of Childhood,* it has become a commonplace to observe that the very concept of childhood, and the word *child* as social label, have varied from culture to culture and from epoch to epoch.[5] Scholars have taken issue with some of Ariès's conclusions—importantly, that youngsters in medieval Europe were seen strictly as miniature adults—but his main principle still holds. Childhood, as a category distinguishable from maturity, has had a variegated history. Over time there have evolved many different ideas of what a child is.[6]

European literature, responding to changing definitions of children, took an interest in young characters primarily after Rousseau and the revolution of ideas concerning education that came about in the eighteenth century.[7] In English belles-lettres it was not till Blake and Wordsworth that childhood acquired prominence as a theme. Since that era the topic has gained increasing favor in literary work. It is enough to recall Charles Dickens' Oliver and Pip, Mark Twain's Huck Finn, Henry James's *The Turn of the Screw* and *What Maisie Knew,* James Joyce's *A Portrait of the Artist as a Young Man,* Virginia Woolf's *The Years,* and the Camera Eye sections of John Dos Passos's *U.S.A.* to recognize the visible place childhood has occupied in the Anglo-American tradition. Within this general framework, of course, writers of each period and milieu arrived at their own interpretations of child figures, depending on their own particular assumptions and priorities. Among the most widely documented of these is the romantic myth of the child unspoiled by civilization, whose purity is contrasted to corruption and who puts into relief the author's protest against contemporary cruelty. Consider Charlotte Brontë's *Jane Eyre.* There has also been a converse myth stemming from Calvinistic notions of original sin and the child as an uncivilized, satanic figure. Pearl in Hawthorne's *The Scarlet Letter* has been read this way. A more contemporary parallel is found in the evil children of William Golding's *The Lord of the Flies* or Stephen King's horror tales. In short, children have been at times idealized and sentimentalized, at other times demonized. Still other texts have presented the child as enigma and so turn this figure into a symbol of otherness itself. Such is the case with the little boy nicknamed Father Time in Thomas Hardy's *Jude the Obscure.*[8] If these interpretations seem at once familiar and contradictory, neither peculiar to children nor illuminating of traits intrinsic to the young, it is because such descriptions, with slight variations, could apply to Jews in writing by non-Jews, to Arabs in Israeli literature, and to further instances of ethnic or racial minorities within majority literatures. Each case of othering responds to a similar psychological mechanism, one that foists onto the outsider projections of one's own fears or hopes. As those feelings and perceptions shift, so shifts the assessment of the Other from vilification to glorification.[9]

In comparison to these patently adult constructions of childhood, some of which have attracted lengthy study, literary attempts to present the perceptions and understandings of young children have been much less common (and less carefully analyzed). By and large they are a product of the twentieth century, with its intense interest in psychological development and in depictions of psychic life. Still, very few writers adopt child narrators or undertake a sustained presentation of the small child's view from within. (This assertion leaves aside the matter of children's literature. Writing designed for a juvenile audience constitutes a separate and very large field unto itself.) There are a number of major authors often associated with fictional children, but many of these in actuality dispense with early years rather abruptly. Such is the case with Joyce's *Portrait* and with Thomas Wolfe's *Look Homeward, Angel*.[10] Adult texts entirely devoted to expressing the interior drama of a young figure are an exception rather than a rule.[11] The voice of the child therefore remains a subdued one, despite the modern fascination with childhood; despite, too, the appearance of the autobiography concerned exclusively with childhood and adolescence, which has become a widely popular genre in its own right. (The memoirs of Maxim Gorky and Michel Leiris are but two particularly acclaimed and celebrated examples.)[12] Certainly, there have been some noteworthy experiments with a young perspective: *Who Has Seen the Wind?* (1975), for instance, by Canadian novelist W. O. Mitchell, merits attention, as does *Celestino antes del alba* (Celestino before dawn, 1972), by Cuban writer Reinaldo Arenas. The voice presented in this last text, though, may be that of a deranged individual and not necessarily a child. The strangeness of the mad or the mentally deficient and the child are deliberately conflated, recalling William Faulkner's strategy in creating Benjy for *The Sound and the Fury* (1929). Some well-known texts featuring a child speaker prove deceptive, for they concentrate less on that figure's development than on the world around him or her. Marcel Proust's *Remembrance of Things Past* (written between 1908 and 1922) recalls childhood, but it does so primarily to provide a frame for other discussion, and so it sets an agenda distinct from that of representing the consciousness of the child. Far more writing, certainly, has attended to the adolescent's viewpoint. Since childhood has been defined differently at different times, and since demarcations between maturity and immaturity have been so fluid, it is problematic to speak of the teenager as a separate category of character. And yet, within the spectrum of young figures in fiction, those who have passed the age of puberty clearly outnumber those who have not.[13]

The oddity of adopting a tenacious focus on the small child's outlook proves indispensable in a number of outstanding works of modern Jewish fiction which are the object of this current study. Sholem Aleichem's *Motl Peyse dem khazns* (*Mottel, the Cantor's Son,* published in installments from 1907 to 1921), Hayim Nahman Bialik's *Safiah* (*Aftergrowth,* written between 1908 and 1923), and Henry Roth's *Call It Sleep* (1934) present the early encounters of a not-yet-adolescent protagonist with *heder* education, religious texts, and traditional Jewish culture. Jerzy Kosinski's *The Painted Bird* (1956), Ahron Appelfeld's *Tor hapela'ot* (*The Age of Wonders,* 1978), and David Grossman's *'Ayen 'erekh: ahavah* (*See Under: Love,* 1986) present responses to the Holocaust through the eyes of a little boy. Individually, each of these highly accomplished pieces merits attention for the way it meets artistic challenges posed in the narration of childhood. Together, the texts suggest some reasons why the voice of the child commands special attention in Jewish literature.

Predictably, as these narratives privilege a once subdued voice, they achieve a novelty of outlook. Much as would be the case in any literature, the young figure fosters an innovative angle of vision through its naiveté, its immature understandings, or its unusual perceptions. In addition, as these child characters make frequent readjustments in their views of the adult world, an emphasis on changeability, on unfolding development or nascent understanding, enlivens the upending of established ideas proffered by these texts. As elsewhere, too, the young figure always serves as the expressive vehicle for a more mature perspective, that of the adult author who constructs the child character. Imagining the child therefore may occasion sensitive exploration of juvenile thinking, but at other times it serves mainly as a pretext to promote adult ideas. Either way, the status of the child as an outsider on the margins of adult activity proves congenial for the purposes of the artist whose aim is critique or reinterpretation of a status quo.

The pairing of texts that deal with religious education and texts that deal with the Holocaust brings out the novelty of the child's view with special force. These two quite separate thematic areas both entail a breakdown of prevailing discourse. The authors in the first set challenge the values and forms of expression associated with religious observance and sacred writing. Those in the second group grapple with the problem of speaking about unspeakable horror. The element common to both is a revisioning of the world or a description of new realities that exceed old ways of speaking. Attempts to let the child speak also derive exceptional dramatic impact in this literature because these texts arise out of, over against, or in response to contexts that once clearly defined children as silent Others and as small versions of the grown-up Jew. The child, by becoming more vocal in this writing, insists on orienting the narrative to its own agenda, and so it stands in stark opposition to and defiance of a previous agenda that denied children expression or recognition as individuals in their own right.

These treatments of childhood further gain resonance as they tie in to thematic concerns with Jewish identity. Since the era of the Emancipation, Jewish writers have struggled with defining their relationship to their own religious/ethnic heritage and to the majority cultures that have surrounded them. In each of the narratives examined here a concerted effort to inhabit the otherness of the child is integral to examining the otherness of the Jew. Tensions between within and without, between marginal and central views, are at once exacerbated and enhanced by this convergence of issues. By taking a category of character once peripheral and placing it at center stage, these texts feature a figure who is (in several senses) minor and ally it with major issues of modern Jewish writing. Most importantly, as both insider and outsider to the sphere of adult Jewish activity, the child is an intimate stranger. To the extent that the Jews form a minority culture and so an Other, this figure becomes the Other of the Other. In this capacity children serve as a useful instrument for observing, criticizing, or celebrating both their elders and the non-Jewish world in its treatment of the Jews.

To understand the functions of the child in this fiction, it is important first to consider these young characters against a broader background of Jewish writing about childhood. Modern secular Jewish literatures, which have emerged most energetically since the mid-nineteenth century, often turn childhood to a privileged theme—understandably, since this writing has unfolded in response to unending social, religious, and political upheavals in the past one hundred fifty years. Nostalgia and reassessments of origins are natural stances for authors who have traveled far from their beginnings. So, for instance, as Jews have dealt with assimilation, the Bildungsroman has taken on tremendous importance. This genre, with its partial attention to childhood, emphasizes the relation of home and family to the world, the familiar Jewish environment to the wider social milieu. American-Jewish literature presents clear illustrations. To name just a few examples, Abraham Cahan's *The Rise of David Levinsky* (1917), Ludwig Lewisohn's *The Island Within* (1928), Saul Bellow's *Herzog* (1964), Alfred Kazin's memoir *Walker in the City* (1951), and even Philip Roth's *Portnoy's Complaint* (1969), contrast immigrant background with opportunities for acculturation, starting at an early age.[14] Parallel phenomena appear also in Jewish writing by German-, French-, and Spanish-speaking authors. Consider another context as well: Israeli fiction since the sixties has been heavily populated by child characters. Hebrew writing, a literature centrally concerned with national identity in a time of rapidly changing political circumstances and shifts in self-definition, had barely reached one generation after statehood before it was inundated with accounts of childhood designed to explore the past.[15] Some of these efforts represent an escapism to an earlier, more innocent or less agonizing period; others document a way of life that is no more; and still others attempt to discover the roots of present malaise or anachronistically revision the past to account for later events. Titles of note, in this connection, include David Shahar's *Heikhal hakelim hashevurim* (*The Palace of Shattered Vessels*, 1969), Hanokh Bar Tov's *Shel mi atah yeled?* (*Whose Little Boy Are You?* 1970), Shulamit Hareven's *'Ir yamim rabim* (*City of Many Days*, 1974), Amos Oz's *Har ha'etsah hara'ah* (*The Hill of Evil Counsel*, 1976), Hayim Be'er's *Notsot* (*Feathers*, 1979), and Yehoshua Knaz's *Moment musikali* (*Musical Moment*, 1980).

Of course, even when a text does not discuss a past, but supposes a child contemporary to the time of writing, young characters are necessarily shaped by an adult author's conception of the issues at hand. As such these characters can also serve to express cultural shifts. Through the young figure, for example, the narratives by Sholem Aleichem, Bialik, and Roth emphasize a growing modernization and secularization of Jewish life. The child not yet fully initiated into tradition nor fully understanding of Jewish obligation becomes an indirect spokesman for authors who had themselves moved away from the orthodoxy of their early family life. Secularized adults, the writers sought out characters capable of seeing *otherwise* the religious definition of Jewishness. This strategy works in *Mottel*, which makes no pretense of retrospection, as well as in *Aftergrowth* and *Call It Sleep*, which have a clear autobiographical component and attempt a nostalgic reconstruction of the past.

By providing the child a forum for speaking out, these texts depart from earlier literary treatments of childhood in which that voice was stifled. The problem of the child's muted voice in this group of texts stems from the legacy of the Enlightenment. Haskalah didactic and fictional texts alike frequently center on education, advocating its role in acculturating Jewish communities to Western values. The pervasive portrayal cultivated there is that of the boy treated as a little adult and grievously denied a genuine childhood. The work of S. Y. Abramovitch (better known by his pen name, Mendele the Bookseller) is a case in point. His autobiographical narrative, *Of Bygone Days,* defined the Jewish youngster as one "expected to act like a full-fledged Jew before he has learned to walk, whose childhood flits by like a dream, leaving him a gloomy old man before his time."[16] This assessment was not an idiosyncratic or isolated opinion. Part of a widespread notion of what constituted the difference of the Jews, Mendele's judgment was based on two facets of Eastern European Jewish custom: first, the sending of male children at age three or not much older to *heder,* there to study the holy books for long hours each day; second, the arranging of early marriage between children. This practice, rooted in religious conviction, served also to secure financial and social status and at times was designed to help the young avoid military service or government-enforced attendance at non-Jewish schools. The literature of the Haskalah and the Hebrew renaissance, as well as contemporaneous Yiddish writing, repeatedly calls attention to the (male) child who—up until his precipitous initiation into matrimony—is condemned to a life of all books and no play.

This kind of dreary picture obtains in memoirs ranging from Solomon Maimon's autobiography (1793) to Shmarya Levin's *Childhood in Exile* (1927) and figures prominently, as well, in fiction—for example, I. J. Linetski's *Dos poylishe yingl* (*The Polish Lad,* 1862). These texts and many others depict an onerous existence in which the boy comes under the power of the hated *melamed,* the usually incompetent and frequently malicious individual who becomes an elementary teacher because he has failed at other occupations.[17] Such a life was said to deprive children of normal joys and also of the here and now, particularly of the physical freedom to enjoy the out-of-doors. Accordingly, the idea of childhood is expressed most often through a contrast between debilitating study and a liberating, nurturing world of nature forbidden the Jewish child. Time and again the youngster is presented as someone who reads and rereads the ancient writings and who thereby transports himself and his thoughts to another world. Devoted to a long-ago era accessible only to memory, the Jewish child overlooks "things that are in front of his nose."[18] In the Western European context, what sets this conceptualization of childhood apart from familiar ideas of the young as miniature adults is, in part, its lateness. *Of Bygone Days* was written between 1898 and 1911, while Ariès's discussion refers to patterns of social life that were outmoded by the eighteenth century. Also unique is the overwhelming emphasis on textuality and entrance into the holy writ. The valorization of sacred text compounds the child's silence. Because of his studies the boy, in a remarkably literal way, is absorbed into adult discourse.

Naturally, it is important to remember the agenda that motivated these Haskalah and post-Haskalah views. These texts were devised to protest the strictures of religion. The customs accorded such a negative interpretation by the Enlightenment have lately come under reconsideration by historians, and there is reason to believe that the lives of many children, though difficult, were not necessarily so coercive of early maturity as was often supposed in the popular imagination. There exist persuasive economic grounds, for instance, to surmise that only the rich could afford early marriage. Furthermore, even after marriage the bride and groom were maintained as dependents, not as full-fledged adults, by the bride's parents.[19] Anecdotal evidence suggests, too, that Mendele's view of education is at least somewhat exaggerated. The long hours at *heder* were devoted in part to study but in large part also to games, and so the religious school in effect constituted a kind of communal day-care system.[20] More importantly, the Orthodox educational system was not entirely insensitive to the needs of children. Many customs were designed to appeal to young children and so to encourage their study of Torah.[21] *Halakha,* Jewish religious law, was keenly alert to various physical, cognitive, and emotional stages of development in the maturation of the individual, and Judaism, even in ancient times, did not mistake the child for a diminutive replica of his elders.[22] It is true, just the same, that in the traditional world of European Jewry the adult text had paramount value and children very early on were expected to deal with it. The first lines the *heder* pupil was taught to read came from Leviticus and not from primers, graded readers, or books specially designated as children's literature. Indicative of this cultural emphasis on text was folk belief in the wise infant. The baby in utero was reputed to know the Torah in its entirety. According to this legend, birth brings a forgetting, presenting the individual with a lifetime goal of recovering lost unity. The idealized image of the child, therefore, is that of a creature fully imbued with or subsumed into the sacred text, at one with God's word.[23]

Altogether, the Enlightenment with its strident attack on religion represented the Orthodox world unfairly, but it did articulate a telling point by insisting on the child's subordination to adult discourse. By calling attention to the muffling of the child's viewpoint, Haskalah literature also paved the way for the sounding of the child's voice in later fiction. That is to say, by deeming the silencing of children an objectionable phenomenon, this writing made a first move toward acknowledging that the perceptions of the young are worth heeding. Subsequently, out of the rigid typology of the child as oppressed, precocious scholar there emerged toward the turn of the century a broader, more complex attention to childhood that included explorations of consciousness.

Whereas previously the child's voice was absorbed in the holy text, now it gained power and autonomy as more writers paid attention to ways in which the child absorbs or rejects learning.

Part of the impetus for this development was a new importance attached to inner awareness as a realm for serious literary consideration. The valorization of introspection was a manifestation, in Jewish literatures, of the turning inward to psychic life typical throughout Western narrative fiction in the age of modernism.[24] More fundamentally, though, both introspection and the sounding of youth form part of a Jewish preoccupation with redefining the relationship of the secular to the holy and, hence, also of the individual to the larger social system. Children figure prominently in this literature, for what could be more unconventional, more suited to breaking old molds (or more conducive to a celebration of self) than the untrained imagination associated with creativity and artistry? The novelty of the child's view can take the form of disregard for old ways, of revisioning traditional society, or, more specifically, of reinterpreting its prime texts (scripture and other classical sources). The minds of small fry become fertile ground for challenging sacred language thanks to discrepancies between untutored or untamed young thought and the authoritative word. Altogether, in this literature the child emerges as a new voice that offers a vehicle for expressing the discovery of new worlds or the turning topsy-turvy of an old one.

In Hebrew, M. Z. Feierberg is credited with pioneering efforts in depicting the inner world of the child. He champions the young imagination as it struggles to free itself from the constraints of *heder* routine, particularly in the short story "Ba'erev" ("In the Evening," 1898) and in the opening portions of the novella *Le'an* (*Whither*, 1899). In this latter text the protagonist discovers that he cannot operate in a vacuum but, to express himself, must use the very language of faith against which he is rebelling. In this way he invests the same vocabulary with different meaning.[25] Another notable early treatment of a child's consciousness is S. Ben Zion's *Nefesh retsutsa* (Broken souls, 1904). This novella, devoted in its entirety to presenting the inner life of a *heder* boy, shows a child not yet quite of bar mitzvah age whose agile mind rages against the cramped, rote learning of his school. This character, too, deftly turns the language of the classroom back on itself in an attempt to undermine the system with its own terms. Using the lexicon of the Eighteen Benedictions, the biblical story of the binding of Isaac, and the Passover *hagadah*, the boy ponders his own life. *Heder* discipline becomes a form of bondage and cruel near-sacrifice of the young, while the Gentile boys from the village, at liberty to roam barefoot in the countryside, appear as "*bnei horin,*" free men.[26]

In *Mottel, Aftergrowth,* and *Call It Sleep,* three of the most acclaimed and sustained literary explorations of Jewish childhood, young characters similarly avail themselves of uninformed but dynamic interpretations of the adult world. The child's mind is at once open and uncomprehending, limited in its understanding but often rich in original insights. This combination of forces leads to irony and pathos, comic inversions, and exalted redefinitions of Torah-oriented language and values.[27] In the process the child's vision also assesses (sometimes celebrating and sometimes excoriating) the community that maintains those beliefs. By focusing on a child's innocence, in the sense of both ignorance and blamelessness, the texts reap various artistic benefits. As exuberance and vitality contrast with the deterioration of older cultural values, there results a more pointed condemnation of the past. On other occasions ironic contrasts make the loss of the past seem more poignant. An aura of innocence can also sweeten attacks on tradition. Young characters' disrespectful antics may elicit indulgence, because they can be viewed as mischief that does not amount to apostasy. Such actions serve as an opportunity for critique without becoming a complete disavowal of Jewish culture.

A brief overview of common traits in these narratives shows how they put the novelty of the child's outlook to distinct ends, in accordance with the authors' own values and priorities.

Set at the turn of the century, Sholem Aleichem's *Mottel* adopts a child narrator who rejects *heder* study, whimsically inverting and then abandoning it. Hastening to leave behind him the moribund patriarchal order of the shtetl, the hero joyously welcomes a move to the New World and an attendant loosening of religious obligations. Though the family emigrates to America out of necessity, because of the dire privations they have suffered, the protagonist's unconventional outlook transforms collective tragedy into comic highjinks. The child not only deconstructs destruction and recovery, as previous criticism has shown; this narrative also dismantles the very opposition child/adult. Demonstrating the flux of changing circumstances and the breakdown of stable custom and meaning, childish resilience comes to signify power, while adults, beset with new beginnings and uncertainties, are cast as childlike in their unpreparedness and vulnerability.

Bialik's main character, by contrast, resists the narrowness of his *heder* instruction but does not relinquish devotional language so freely. Instead, the child fashions the lore and legends of the Bible into his private daydreams, using these tales to impute an idyllic, glory-filled wonder to his poverty-stricken village home in late-nineteenth-century Eastern Europe. This character, like Mottel, undoes reigning assumptions of the adult world. His elders assume an opposition between individual imagination and traditional texts. Bialik's narrative, through

its exploration of the child's consciousness, blurs the boundaries between collective language and private experience. In this way it registers
the author's own struggle with poetry as nationalist and as personal
expression.

Roth, writing at a later date and from a more assimilated position
than either of his predecessors, creates a protagonist who translates a
biblical passage into his intensely intimate vision. Merging the words of
Isaiah with the technological imagery of a proletarian setting, *Call It
Sleep* elevates the quotidian and reaches a compromise, typical of modernism, between the sordid and the sublime. This move also welds
together the child's knowledge of Judaism with the Christian elements
of his environment. The main character is a little boy residing in New
York from 1909 to 1913, who tries to assess his own friendship with a
non-Jew even as he puzzles over the love affair his mother once had with
a Gentile. Struggling with competing definitions of values, he arrives at a
highly individual reconciliation of opposite views, moving far beyond
the secularization of Jewishness evident in *Mottel* and *Aftergrowth*.
Once again, as a child's voice and consciousness gain new prominence,
the text endorses the innovative vision of an outsider who dismantles the
assumptions of the adults around him, and whose novel stance coincides
with and reflects the author's own views.

Kosinski, Appelfeld, and Grossman, as they deal with the
Holocaust, also give voice to the young and allow them to speak back
against a silence once imposed on children. The characters here confront forces of obliteration, intent on rendering the Jewish child mute
through genocide. To be sure, the parallel between this fiction and the
narratives by Sholem Aleichem, Bialik, and Roth makes much more
apparent an abyss of difference separating the two sets of texts. In *The
Painted Bird, The Age of Wonders,* and *See Under: Love* the silence in
question is of incomparably greater proportion. The early narratives of
the *heder* privilege a new celebration of private consciousness, while the
later ones react against an entirely brutal, massive destruction that held
no regard for the individual. Here, as before, however, a definition of
children as little adults contributes to the suppression of voice. Nazi
ideology treated young victims as Jews in miniature, that is, as guilty
simply by the fact of having been born. Even infants, in the Nazi view,
were not innocents to be spared but the seed of the subhuman. Considering such values to epitomize the criminality of Hitler's beliefs, Elie
Wiesel and others have dwelt on the murder of babies as one of the most
horrifying of the Nazi atrocities.[28] Texts that privilege the sensitivities of
the Jewish child as they tell of the Shoah deny that murderous ideology
the last word.

Kosinski, Appelfeld, and Grossman also contend with another

dimension of silence. Treatments of the Holocaust in imaginative literature pose a fundamental dilemma: how to assimilate the unimaginable
into the imagination, how to find a language commensurate with the
enormity of events that took place during the Shoah. That these are
difficulties to be reckoned with has become an axiomatic tenet of criticism dealing with literary responses to disaster. Extensive commentary
has considered how such difficulties of expression have left their mark
on art, and how art continues despite the pressures against it. Less
attention, though, has gone to another phenomenon: the number of
narratives that have adopted a child's point of view and limited perception of historical events when struggling with these issues. Such fiction
as Clara Asscher-Pinkhof's *Sterrenkinder* (*Star Children*, 1946), Ilse
Aichinger's *Die Grössere Hoffnung* (*Herod's Children*, 1948), Uri Orlev's *Hayalei 'oferet* (*The Lead Soldiers*, 1967), Louis Begley's *Wartime
Lies* (1991), portions of André Schwarz-Bart's *Le dernier des justes* (*The
Last of the Just*, 1959), and even, to some extent, the opening pages of
Elie Wiesel's *La nuit* (*Night*, 1958) are oriented to a child's outlook.
Some of these are autobiographical fictions, others are by individuals
who were not children at the time of the war. All, however, attempt to
enter into the consciousness of children and to speak for them as they
record Holocaust events that affected the lives of children.[29]

Engagement with a child's vision and inner life, always problematic in fiction, is in some ways well suited to narrative concerning the
Holocaust. Focus on a child's partial understanding helps alleviate
the adult narrator's struggle with language and artistic expression, for
the young character's incomprehension serves to indicate the incomprehensibility of the catastrophe. For example, when children fail to
understand what occurs in their surroundings, their confusions highlight the madness about them. Their misunderstandings of words, in
particular, can lodge a protest against the ways grown-ups speak and
against the inadequacies of language in explaining what has happened.
Children's clouded understandings of events can also act as a filter,
allowing the author to forestall disclosure of overly horrifying fact. In
other cases, faced directly with brutality, the children view events in an
immature way that buffers them and makes persecution more bearable.
One of Clara Asscher-Pinkhof's young girls beams with pride the day
she first gets to wear a star on her jacket. She interprets the badge in her
own terms, as a decoration and as a new outfit to wear to school. Uri
Orlev's boys explain away the death around them as a game and see the
effects of war as an extension of their play with toy soldiers. These young
characters take privation for granted; it is what they have known most of
their lives. (Historians of the Holocaust have recently turned to the topic
of children, documenting evidence that lends credibility to this kind of

fictional portrait. Of particular interest are the games devised and played in the ghettos and camps that helped children to cope with terror as an everyday occurrence.)[30]

Disparities that necessarily remain between child characters and adult narration create rich opportunity for the contrasting of different perspectives. When a young figure accepts as matter-of-fact what the adult reader would consider wrenchingly sad or inconceivable atrocity the result is an irony that defuses pathos. Conversely, a juxtaposing of evil with the innocence of childhood often produces, for the reader, a heightened awareness of cruelty and destruction. In either case the narrative contrasts the character's unknowing stance with the reader's knowledge of history after the fact and so highlights the unfathomable nature of the disaster. These factors in large measure account for the impact of Anne Frank's diary and operate, too, in the reception accorded other works written during the Shoah (e.g., the poems by children gathered from the Teresienstadt concentration camp and collected under the title *I Never Saw Another Butterfly*).[31] Finally, fictional accounts of childhood can easily give rise to self-conscious considerations of these issues. Making evident that the child's understanding is limited, such writing announces that it attempts to convey something beyond what the character can express, and in this way the text gestures toward the inexpressible.

To be sure, the complexities fostered by entrance into the thoughts of a child persist and in some ways are exacerbated in this thematic domain. Retrospective narration and the representation of a child's consciousness are paradoxical phenomena, for it is impossible to recapture in a verbal act the nonverbal reality of past experience or of an antecedent state of less articulate understanding. Retrieving the long ago becomes more acutely problematic when the past in question has suffered violent destruction. The severing of former self from later narratorial voice is magnified many times over in works by authors who, having experienced the Shoah themselves, try to depict their earlier lives. This is writing that often reaches over a chasm of time to invoke an age of naiveté irrevocably altered by subsequent trauma. In addition, for such writers as Wiesel, Orlev, and others, the later transformations in their lives included the adoption of a new country, culture, and language. Orlev relinquished his native Polish for Hebrew, and Wiesel, who grew up with Yiddish, Hebrew, and Hungarian, writes primarily in French and English. Consequently, theirs is an art that at many levels emerges out of and reflects radical disjunction of circumstance. Advantages and disadvantages result. Childhood as a remote, foreign territory is in some ways simply irretrievable. In other ways the very foreignness of childhood and the difficulty of depicting the long ago can help indicate a pervasive experience of loss. For the writer who did not experience the Shoah personally, there exists a separate set of problems. The obstacles to imagining the unimaginable are in this case that much greater, and these writers run the risk of trivializing or of evoking accusations of bad taste or sentimentality. To explore the alien, in some ways unknowable, world of Holocaust destruction by entering into the mind of a child is doubly risky. Twice removed from the writer's own voice, narrative experiment with inhabiting these two kinds of otherness presents a literature grounded in disjunction even as does the writing of the displaced survivor.

It is within the peculiar parameters outlined here—of a special freedom or aperture onto artistic expression, together with an intensified sense of anomaly and artifice—that fictional treatments of childhood and the Holocaust have often played themselves out. *The Painted Bird, The Age of Wonders,* and *See Under: Love* provide unusually strong examples, as they all call direct attention to the problem of silence, even as they emphasize the child's capacity for revisioning a world of horror. At the same time, these works emerge from distinct contexts and put the child's perspective and altering views to different purposes.

Kosinski and Appelfeld write from personal experience. Though many details of these novels are not to be construed as accurate descriptions of incidents in the authors' lives, *The Painted Bird* and *The Age of Wonders* are responses to an autobiographical impulse and are accounted for by a Holocaust childhood. As he shows the torments and misfortunes of a small boy wandering through villages and forests, Kosinski turns unremitting brutality to self-evident norm. The child contributes to this emphasis of the text because the protagonist's credulous imagination, shaped by the language of fairy tales and superstition, places his understandings outside common sense norms. Though he witnesses cruelty of surreally gargantuan proportions, the boy accepts quite naturally that human beings are capable of perpetrating inhuman violence. The boy's ahistorical perceptions also help the narrator cast the tale as a universal parable of evil, and so *The Painted Bird* disavows the distinctiveness of the Jews. The child, then, is a device that discredits the precepts of his enemies who define the Jew malignantly and fanatically as Other.

In *The Age of Wonders* the child also achieves novel perception, but he does so as a naive insider who puts into relief the failings of adult Jews. The narrative does not bring him face to face with horror. It concentrates on Austria before the war, where the protagonist observes the craving for assimilation, which renders the grown-ups helpless, either unable or unwilling to foresee the coming disaster. The partial occlusion of events through the child's faulty, foggy comprehension of conversations makes for a blurred line between the said and the unsaid, interpretation and enigma. As a result the world becomes strange, making eerily unbelievable the approaching destruction. In this way the use of the child character melds a critique of Jewish self-hatred with a more sympathetic acknowledgment that events will turn out disastrously, beyond anything the grown-ups could have imagined.

Grossman's child protagonist is the son of survivors—unlike the author—and so is less of an autobiographical fiction. Born after the war, this child struggles to uncover the secrets of his parents' past. He arrives at a troubled grasp of the Shoah and lapses into a silence that signals an inability to conceive of so much suffering. In the process the child also dismantles the opposition between heroes and victims cherished in Israel during the fifties (the scene of his growing up). Wishing to see his parents in idealized terms appropriate to his cultural setting, he imagines for them acts of strength and courage. Then, learning more about the humiliations and pain the survivors suffered, he becomes confused, both inebriated with and repelled by power and its effects. Grossman's uncomfortable questioning of an earlier heroic ideal is, in significant measure, a product of the political climate in which this novel was written. Published in 1986, this tale expresses an uneasiness over the uses of military force in Israeli society. The result is both a reappraisal of the survivors as an Other marginalized in Israeli life and, in general, a greater identification with victims.

As this last point suggests, the child's views in this fiction, no less than was the case with *Mottel, Aftergrowth,* and *Call It Sleep,* reflect the authors' outlooks. Most importantly, in *The Painted Bird, The Age of Wonders,* and *See Under: Love,* the perspective of the child undoes distinctions between the plausible and the implausible, reflecting the adult's retrospective knowledge that unimaginable violence did take place during the Nazi period. In *The Painted Bird* Kosinski imagines the child in keeping with his theory of art as a loosening of boundaries between the possible and the improbable. Appelfeld's cultivation of the child's muted voice illustrates his own convictions about expressive difficulties in art that deals with the Shoah and so is based on tensions between the sayable and the unsayable. Grossman relies on the child's fantasies, daydreams, and speculations as a tool to overturn hierarchies of established values.

Constructed out of their authors' hindsights and insights after the fact of the Holocaust, the young figures in these novels represent an impulse to come to terms with the Jewishness so deeply threatened by the Shoah. (This move is carried out in a variety of ways: in a positive sense, by commemorating the past; in a negative sense, by evading the

distinctiveness of that past; in an equivocal sense, by questioning definitions of Jewishness.) None of the writers turns to definition of Jewish
culture from within traditional terms of custom and covenant, but they
do portray characters acutely self-conscious of their affiliation with the
Jews as a people. In this regard it is significant that the main characters
are conceived as outsiders to the Jewish community, figures too young to
know much about the Jews and/or children highly assimilated into
secular European or Israeli norms. As they encounter anti-Semitism,
then, they become preoccupied with Jewishness, but they maintain a
critical distance and a critical eye that coincides with the author's own
stance toward the Shoah. Kosinski's boy, for example, is an exception,
an Other to the Other, in a very elemental way. Though persecuted as a
Jew, he survives when most of the Jews are killed. Consequently, he is in
a position to record his observations and his judgments of his tormen-
tors. Appelfeld's protagonist understands even less than the adults in his
family do and so can see clearly their self-defeating denials of Jewishness. Grossman's second-generation character is neither fully of the
survivors nor of the sabras, and he juggles two models of Jewishness
against each other.

In their attention to the emergence and suppression of a child's
voice, *The Painted Bird, The Age of Wonders,* and *See Under: Love* offer
instructive contrasts and counterparts to *Mottel, Aftergrowth,* and *Call
It Sleep.* Most important is the success or failure of the young voices to
assert themselves. The texts by Sholem Aleichem, Bialik, and Roth ex-
ploit the child's limited understanding to allow an invigorating misreading and renewal of old social codes and meanings. In the texts dealing
with the Holocaust the children also bring imagination and energy to a
new reality that exceeds old codes and means of expression. The results,
however, differ as these characters respond to far more ghastly events.
The children do not so much devise new, alternative interpretations as
acknowledge the inadequacy of their attempts to make sense of the
Shoah. Kosinski's protagonist loses his ability to speak. In Appelfeld's
semi-hushed world the child character suffers incomprehension and
deep mistrust of words. As the little boy in Grossman's narrative comes
to learn more and more about the Shoah he approaches mental breakdown and the text arrives at an exhaustion of the child's voice. Altogether, while the first set of texts homes in on discarding or recasting specifically Jewish language, the second set concentrates on a closing out of
language in general. The thematic domains are in some ways opposites.
As they portray Jewish accommodations to modernity and modern
Europe's rejection of the Jew, they naturally engage different emphases
of optimism and despair. In both cases, though, the child provides a
source of renewed artistic vision, and these two groups of texts, precisely

because they are disparate, illustrate the versatility that has made the imagination of childhood a significant contribution to modern Jewish fiction.

Each of the narratives discussed in this study achieves its construction of childhood through its own distinctive prose style and mode of composition. Though they exhibit a constellation of related concerns and narrative strategies that may all be classified as a discourse of childhood, these texts are not to be construed as sharing a narrowly defined technique nor a common approach to characterization. Making no pretense at depth in psychological portraiture, Sholem Aleichem presents Mottel as a contrivance. He is clearly neither a child nor an adult, but an artistic device devoid of inwardness. This narrative has more in common with the picaresque than with probing, modernist explorations of consciousness. As it, too, bears affinities with the picaresque, *The Painted Bird* provides a macabre counterpoint to Mottel. More an emblem of self-preservation than a being of complex inner life, the protagonist of this novel continually evades a series of adversaries as any good picaroon does. However, Sholem Aleichem's boy plays the successful naif, not unlike Huck Finn, and demonstrates irrepressible good spirits. Kosinski's Boy survives as he can. Faced with ever-present threats of extinction, he manages to get by through harrowing exertions of will and magical thinking that makes his agony more bearable. *Call It Sleep* and *See Under: Love* provide a very different treatment of childhood, achieving a rich, multifaceted, and psychologically penetrating representation of a child's inner world. The two novels emphasize the most troubling, least easily articulated workings of their characters' psychic lives. Roth concentrates on a rough setting that can be filled with wonder through the child's perceptions. Grossman presents a world of more profoundly disturbed social relations, where the child's fanciful interpretations of events prove, painfully, to be but wishful thinking. *Aftergrowth* and *The Age of Wonders,* for their part, combine individual reminiscences and reveries with anecdotal, episodic treatment of a range of figures. The two texts thereby give an overview of collective values along with a sketch of the protagonist's personal musings. Again, these texts show, first, that the imagining of childhood does not restrict itself to a particular type of character and, second, that character type is not necessarily indicative of the valence placed on youth. Comparable figures can serve a variety of purposes to convey differing conceptions of childhood. Bialik's Shmulik is a powerless, neglected boy who combats his helplessness through escape into an interior realm of lyrical sensibility. He exemplifies the idealized, romantic notion of the child as repository of innocence and fancy. Appelfeld's protagonist, even more bereft of power, discovers purpose if not solace through witness and memory. In contrast to Bialik's text, Appelfeld presents a moving tribute to childish innocence that has been grimly diminished, metamorphosed into merely a renunciation of understanding. Each narrative springs from separate concepts about childhood and is motivated by diverse factors, ranging from romanticism's idealizations of innocence to modernist or postmodern celebration of unstable meanings.

The chapters that follow examine more closely the specific ways in which these texts show the child's view of the world. In each thematic cluster discussion progresses from less complex to more complex representations of consciousness. First in each section is fiction that clearly uses the child as a device; last comes the narrative that most seriously considers children as psychological beings rather than merely as a pretext for advancing adult views. At stake in all cases, though, are the details of how each text is animated by issues of otherness. As a matter of narratorial voice, each demonstrates a concerted effort to experiment with dual perspectives. As a matter of plot the child is presented as the source of an alternative vision, an ability to see otherwise. As a matter of the literary historical circumstances of its writing, each imagined childhood reflects the author's own frame of understanding. In each case, through its skewed, creative angle of vision, the child becomes an instrument for demonstrating the restless play of identity and difference in which Jews, as Others, have perceived themselves. The novelty of outlook made possible through inhabiting the otherness of the child offers an effective vehicle of expression for a people repeatedly unfamiliar with itself and at pains to define its own difference.

2 NARRATIVE VOICE AND THE LANGUAGE OF THE CHILD

Mikhail Bakhtin's concept of the dialogic imagination provides an effective theoretical model for understanding several key aspects of the narrative of childhood.[1]

First of all, fiction presenting ways in which a child's mind attempts to come to terms with adult meaning necessarily bases its plot in a confrontation between contrasting frames of reference. In such texts a young character meets and challenges the words and views of an adult environment. By the same token, peculiar difficulties of narration arise from the hybrid nature of writing that features the imagined outlook of a child. In this prose a youthful voice or vision is appropriated by and transformed within another, more mature discourse. This means that narration and narrated events alike rely on an intersection of adult and child perspectives. Both levels of these texts therefore supply prime examples of the double-voicing and interanimations of language that Bakhtin has shown to be such a crucial part of narrative art. That oscillating perspectives govern both dimensions of this fiction makes for a notable cohesion of formal and thematic concerns. Above all, these qualities assure that this writing will be the nexus for shifts of meaning. Reinterpretations of values take place clearly in several directions in narratives of childhood.

Bakhtin's Dialogic Imagination and the Child

Bakhtin's theories, expounded in his work *The Dialogic Imagination,* stem from the basic premise that language is never unitary, except as an abstract grammatical system of normative forms. As a vital social phenomenon, it is dynamic and plural. Composed of the distinct kinds of idiom specific to varying groups in society, any language encompasses differences of expression determined, for example, by class, ethnicity, profession, age, formality of situation, and—though Bakhtin egregiously ignored this possibility—also by gender.[2] All these multiple linguistic stratifications vary from one historical period to another and are constantly in a state of change. In addition, every individual brings private connotations to certain words. Not only dialects, jargons, and specialized lingoes but also time, distance, and disparities of outlook or assumed reference contribute to the polyphonic quality of language; each brings new valuations and nuances to every particular act of speech or writing. It follows that, in the vast plenitude of discourses that make up any cultural setting, many varieties of language will come into contact with one another. They may present competing definitions for the same things or, conversely, use the same words, marked by differences of connotation, to different purposes. One discourse may subsume another, reinterpret it, or question its assumptions. Each thereby deprivileges and relativizes the other, and this process of mutual modification is deemed to be *dialogic*. Indeed, all utterances can be seen to constitute a matrix of social forces. The notion of *heteroglossia*, that is, the collision of different meanings and valuations in any given word, leads to the primacy of context over text in Bakhtin's thinking. According to this view, each time a word is uttered it will have an impact uniquely its own, depending on the conditions in which it is pronounced. By the same token, the word is not a neutral medium but a social practice "populated with the intentions of others" (294).

These ideas apply in a number of ways to the silencing and sounding of child characters. Most immediately, the child represents an instance of alien words not often cited or heard in adult fiction. When it is featured centrally in a narrative, the child's voice adds to the interaction of speakers which Bakhtin finds most visible in, and characteristic of, the novel. This he considers a privileged genre, because of its ability to represent a spectrum of social groups. Conjoining disparate and disruptive voices and views, such fiction becomes a site of struggle. The child's vocal self-assertion brings yet another expressive force to the polyphonic text, which, as it incorporates a range of stances and outlooks, foregrounds a series of conflicts collective in nature.

Bakhtin explores the impact of these matters in a more intimate realm by asserting that psychic life consists of a complex amalgam of words spoken or written by others and selectively appropriated by the individual. People continually assimilate, reevaluate, and so redefine the words of those about them. According to this model, ideas develop through "an intense struggle within" for hegemony among various points of view, directions, and values (345). Narratives of childhood not only illustrate but elaborate on this understanding, for they provide an acute case of psychic life dependent on the words of others. First of all, children are unusually susceptible to absorbing, uncritically, what others say. As Bakhtin notes, "the ability to distinguish between one's own and another's discourse, between one's own and another's thought, is activated rather late in development" (345). At the same time, less encumbered by preconceived notions than adults, children often bring a special openness to conventional expressions. As a result, they may wrest words free from some of their usual semantic burden, or they may recontextualize words more fluidly than do other individuals. This point is particularly important in texts that associate children's views with intensely private perception. Finally, narratives of childhood are often narratives of development that highlight a character's progressive casting off of earlier ideas. As such they may supply keen examples of independent thinking which occurs less as a smooth process than as a kind of strenuous effort at liberating oneself from reified, authoritative dictates or received opinion. For a number of reasons, then, narratives of childhood bring heightened attention to ways in which characters process a world of alien discourses in order to make them "internally persuasive" (that is, to acknowledge and transform ideas into one's own).

In fiction this is a dynamic that may serve the purposes of psychological portraiture, showing children who arrive at genuinely creative thought or who wrestle with the difficulties of achieving intellectual autonomy. The same narrative elements, though, may serve other artistic purposes as well. For example, the child's capacity to parrot adult views becomes useful in satiric texts. The youngster who overhears what adults say and presents their words—as if naively—to the reader is indispensable in writing that mocks those adult formulations. In either case the words of adult others are essential as background against which the child's thoughts are to be understood by the reader. This kind of counterpoint is an integral part of the dual voice phenomenon central to writing that features the imagined outlook of a child.

In each of these capacities, the representation of the child's consciousness confirms those of Bakhtin's insights that tie in matters of theory with the history of the novel. From its beginnings this genre has frequently featured figures of incomprehension, stupidity, and naiveté: the fool, the picaroon, and the hero of the Bildungsroman who is not yet assimilated into normative societal roles. All these characters, through their ignorance and unknowing, may cast an ironic light on previously established social conventions.[3] Incomprehension in the novel always carries a polemical function, as it interacts "with an intelligence whose masks it tears away" (403). Sustained representation of children's perspectives, a very modern literary experiment, makes possible the same uncomprehending presence the fool once provided. Therefore, far from being a marginal phenomenon concerned with a negligible Other, the representation of the child's mind facilitates a highly effective extension of major trends that have defined the novel as a genre from its inception. Literary studies have observed that the ironic structures of the novel grant it a subversive quality and make it singularly suited to questioning prevailing ideologies. Young figures, close in nature to Walter Benjamin's view of the child as the best revolutionary, can similarly unleash transformative and critical energies as their immature premises clash with social fact and conventional wisdom.[4] In the process, emphasis on the child's view can also demonstrate pointedly how dialogic in-comprehension leads to a metanarrative or metalinguistic awareness. That is to say, such fiction cultivates a distinct attention to language per se. Bakhtin remarks that "a failure to understand languages that are otherwise generally accepted and that have the appearance of be-ing universal teaches the novelist how to perceive them physically as objects, to see their relativity, to externalize them, to feel out their boundaries, that is, it teaches him how to expose and structure images of social languages" (404). Words do not serve merely as a medium for extralinguistic experience. Instead, because of their dialogic rela-tions, their own rhetoric and the intentions inherent in it are put into relief.

It is important to distinguish between childhood narratives, as they are being considered here, and the Bildungsroman.[5] The latter, which traces its protagonist's growth into adolescence and young adult-hood, demonstrates its character's accommodation to society. This gen-eralization holds true whether that acquiescence is total or partial and even if there results a complete rebellion, such as Stephen Daedalus's refusal to conform to expectations of nation, church, and family. In any event, a code of understanding to be entered into or reacted against exists in more crystallized, reified form than that available to child characters in Sholem Aleichem's *Mottel*, Bialik's *Aftergrowth*, Henry Roth's *Call It Sleep*, Kosinski's *The Painted Bird*, Appelfeld's *The Age of Wonders*, and Grossman's *See Under: Love*. In these cases the young-ster's openness sets him apart. The character's as yet undefined or fluid grasp of the world is more extreme, and this quality in the narrative often leads to an emphasis on discovery. Predictably, then, the child's apprehension and reworking of grown-up understandings are of partic-ularly intense potential as instruments for dismantling preconceived notions.

Of course, there are no hard and fast rules for defining when this age of revisioning ends. All the texts in this study concern children less than thirteen years of age, and so, in their conceptions of the childlike view, the novels also conform to the traditional Jewish definition of manhood as beginning at the age of bar mitzvah. By attempting to dwell within that perspective, such writing foments what the Formalists would consider the essence of literariness: the development of an aes-thetic that questions ordinary perceptions of reality.[6] The aim of belles-lettres, in this view, is to defamiliarize, to deform the usual—creatively—and so counteract the process of habituation fostered by routine modes of seeing the world. In one degree or another attracted to "the inchoate as literary strategy,"[7] these authors all focus on young figures as a way to undo the assumptions expressed around them and so provide a paradigmatic instance of literary "making strange."[8]

Yehuda Amihai's poem "A Child Is Something Else Again" (a portion of which appears as the epigraph to Chapter 1) comments incisively on many of these issues. Intent on domesticating the child's inner vision, that locus of novelty at once most alien and most admired by the poet, adults are presented in the poem as attempting to educate the young into mature language. Seeing the child as something still unfinished, incomplete and in need of guidance, they impart to him the usual expressions of polite address and train him "to say 'Thank you' when the Lord has given, / to say 'You're welcome' when the Lord has taken away." The child, however, possesses his own distinctive perceptions and world of discourse; he is "full of words," "instant light, instant darkness," and his otherness puts into relief the limits and incompletions of the very adult words he learns to pronounce. In comparison to the wealth of experience and wonder the child embodies, the courtesies favored by grown-ups (and the religious pieties these phrases suggest) seem inadequate to account for the depth and complexities of human life. The poet, accordingly, recalls the story of Job. Soon to be visited by travails and misfortunes not of his own making, the child will be left with explanations that are insufficient or not humanly comprehensible. The speech provided by adults offers but a very partial entrance into understanding, and it does not suffice to arm this young life with tools to master the world or express it fully.

In short, two worlds of discourse on a collision course prove each other to be limited. Admittedly, this poem accords the child special sympathy and admiration. Still, the youngster's absorption of adult polite expression shows him to be uneducated, and their education to be marked already by failure. This kind of confrontation is typical, too, in narratives of childhood, with an important difference. Amihai remains aloof, a commentator evaluating a child's situation from without. Of prime interest for this current study are texts that attempt to sound the child's own voice or to illuminate children's lives from within. To discuss those texts calls for a closer examination into the unusual exigencies of narration that purports to speak for a child.

Bivocal Narration

Bakhtin points out that novels implement dialogic interactions in a number of ways. Dialogue, in the ordinary sense of directly transcribed verbal exchange, is but one possible form. Other possibilities at the level of narrated events include interpretations of one character's words by another, reports of another's speech, and parody of statements by others. Even simple juxtapositions of characters can lead two distinct kinds of idiom to expose their contrasting assumptions and so reveal each other's ideological underpinnings. Giving rise to another, extensive set of dialogic relations are all those strategies of narration that allow the authorial figure to coordinate his or her voice with that of a character. Sometimes the result is to underscore boundaries between the two kinds of voices, and sometimes the effect is to blur them or leave room for doubt and indistinctiveness.

Bakhtin does not present a subtle, highly developed scheme of classifications for such narrative techniques. His strength derives instead from his vigorous, precedent-setting insistence on bonds between reported utterances and reporting contexts.[9] Studies by a variety of other thinkers may supplement and complement his accomplishments, making his ideas more manageable as finely tuned analytic tools. Work, for example, by Gerard Genette, Dorrit Cohn, Brian McHale, Shlomith Rimmon-Kenan, and Meir Sternberg can amplify his insights. Their approaches thereby also allow discussion of overarching thematic matters to be combined and coordinated with scrutiny of more properly aesthetic issues. That is to say, dialogic interactions within a plot (the child's interpretation of adult meaning, his readings, reportings, and reformulations of the world in a way commensurate with his youth) can be shown to be intimately linked with formalisms of narrative voice, represented speech, and fictional modes for presenting consciousness—other aspects of this art also governed by dialogic relations.

There exist many different ways in literature that a child may speak for itself or be spoken for through an adult. A spectrum of possibilities from more to less vocal, more to less perceptible authorial intervention, determines whether the views of characters and narrators will clash or coincide. It should be noted first that my concern is with texts that feature a child whose perspective orients the narrative. In Genette's terms, this figure is a "focalizer," as distinct from the narrator, who composes the words actually constituting the text.[10] Moreover, in the fiction discussed here, the focus is generally closer to the represented actions than to the narrating agent, and emphasis rests significantly, too, on the child's world within. Where the character lacks inwardness (for instance, in Sholem Aleichem's *Mottel*), his grasp of events becomes paramount. This character's perceptual apparatus looms large as the filter that subjectively interprets the outside world.

Inevitably, since story must be cast into words by an adult, narrative orientation will always be wrested away in part from the child. And, naturally, shifts between adult and child focalization will modulate the amounts and kinds of information available to the reader, affecting any number of issues. Prime among these are temporal factors. Restricting the orientation of a text to a child's view may increase suspense and a sense of immediacy or identification with narrated events. A mature narrating figure, reminiscing, would allow opposite benefits. Drawing on memory and a long-term assessment of events, this kind of figure can make a survey of time for the reader. Similarly, in terms of cognitive issues, both adult and child views allow a privileged angle. Though working with limited understandings, the child may perceive the world as a magic place or may bring more sensitive and felicitous insights to a variety of experiences. In opposition, the adult who is more knowledgeable or is equipped with information after the fact may contribute irony, compassion, humor, or bitter wisdom to an appraisal of the past.

Because the representation of a child's mind as a matter of course encourages narrative strategies that conflate perspectives, equivocation and duality are hallmarks of many fictional depictions of childhood. It is not surprising that in Shlomith Rimmon-Kenan's *Narrative Poetics,* a concise handbook of narratological principles, many of the examples that illustrate ambiguous focalization and complex narrative voice come precisely from texts that feature child protagonists.[11] Here, for instance, is a section from Rimmon-Kenan's discussion of Joyce's "Araby":

> In this narrative, an adult narrator tells about himself as a child (of unspecified age). His language is sometimes "coloured" by his perceptions at the time of narration (external focalization), sometimes by those of his younger self (internal focalization) and sometimes remains ambiguous between the two. A sentence like "I had never spoken to her, except for a few casual words, and yet her name was like a summons to all my foolish blood" (p. 28) betrays the adult narrator as focalizer through the evaluative adjective "foolish." Similarly, although the lexis and syntax of "I forget whether I answered yes or no" (p. 29) could easily be attributed to a child by virtue of its simplicity, forgetting can only be recognized in retrospect. The words "I forget" thus point to an external focalizer by signalling temporal and cognitive distance from the events. On the other hand, the comparison of the silence of the deserted bazaar to that of a church—"I recognized a silence like that which pervades a church after a service" (p. 32)—reflects the child's association between the world of religion within which he was brought up, with the world of the bazaar which he endowed with a quasi-religious dimension. For the child, the disappointment is similar when both rituals are over.
>
> . . . Perhaps most interesting are those cases where choice between an external and an internal focalizer is problematic or impossible. Take, for example, "I imagined that I bore my chalice safely through a throng of foes" (p. 29). The language is that of the narrator, but the

focalizer can be either the narrator or the child. As the vision of the narrator, the stress is on the cliché-nature of the child's imagination and the tone is ironic. (83–84)

As is evident from these remarks, the relation of narrator to protagonist may vary considerably within one text. The spectrum of possibilities is even wider within a series of texts that all explore children's perceptions. In every case, however, bivocality or a two-in-one effect is characteristic of the discourse of childhood in imaginative writing. The otherness attendant on this brand of narrative is ineradicable whether the stance adopted by the author is one of third-person or first-person narration. The self looking back retrospectively presents no less an instance of superimposed voice than does a separate narratorial figure pretending to record a child's thoughts, or the invention of a child narrative persona speaking a language concocted by an older author.

Dissonant and consonant relations between adult narratorial figures and child protagonists depend a great deal on gaps between adult verbal capacity and what a child can put into words. Therefore it becomes important to gauge ways in which narratives of childhood document the outlook of their protagonists by emphasizing or deemphasizing representations of speech. In this regard it is useful to note that depictions of consciousness generally rely on three categories of narration, classifiable according to Dorrit Cohn's terminology as quoted monologue, narrated monologue, and psychonarration.[12] The first concept refers to direct transcription of the character's words, whether those words are expressed openly or confined to inner speech. The second approach, Cohn's term for free indirect discourse, renders the character's thoughts in his or her own idiom while maintaining the third-person technique and basic tense of narration. In the third approach an authorial voice is clearly present and perceptible, telling about the inner life of a character. Each narrative mode offers advantages and disadvantages for creating a discourse of childhood.

To begin with direct citation: some authors attempt to infuse their texts with the language of children as described by psycholinguistics. Salient features may include special vocabulary such as diminutives, onomatopoeia, or deviant lexical forms. Improper handling of pronouns, vague uses of *it,* and childish syntax (such as run-on sentences) can also indicate immaturity. Children's rhymes, songs, or word games are eminently quotable as markers of young speakers. There are, however, notable pressures against extended citation of child speech. The language of actual children rarely makes for coherent narrative directed to an older audience. And, to the extent that a writer could approximate a child's voice and manner of narrating, there would still ensue a struggle with essentially incompatible possibilities: striving to make the text mimetically genuine or making it artistically effective.[13]

Consequently, narrated monologue frequently serves as a more natural choice for rendering child thought. As Cohn notes, this kind of writing often proves both flexible and complex. Suspended between the "immediacy of quotation," on the one hand, and, on the other hand, mediation of one figure's thinking by another's, such prose tends to fluctuate when in proximity with other techniques (106–7). That is to say, it sometimes exhibits qualities proper to other categories of narration. For instance, a midway point between psychonarration and narrated monologue might fit under the rubric of "stylistic contagion." Clearly told by a figure other than the focalizer, narrated monologue would in this case absorb features of the character's speech, whether in the form of an occasional word or in terms of longer segments of narrative. It is possible to devise additional distinctions as well to describe represented speech. Brian McHale suggests a number of useful differentiations, which span the spectrum from a simple report that a speech act has occurred, to a paraphrase of reported remarks, to indirect discourse proper which closely reproduces the wording of the original utterance.[14] Of course, these concepts may aid not only in showing how an adult relays a child's words but also in detailing how a child relays adult words.

It is crucial to keep in mind that representations of speech conforming to linguistic criteria are not the only or necessarily the most effective form of co-presence that may exist between authorial views and views of a character. Artists have conceived of children's thinking in highly imaginative ways that do not aim at transcription of actual utterances. A study of Canadian author Clark Blaise, for instance, notes that in the novel *A North American Education,* the author's prose displays preponderant use of infinitives to indicate the child register.[15] Although not the form any flesh-and-blood child would actually use in this way, the infinitive creates sentences that have beginnings but no endings, and so it suggests potential for starting over: "To leave Montreal for places like Georgia and Florida; to leave Florida for Saskatchewan, to leave the prairies for places like Cincinnati and Pittsburgh and finally to stumble back to Montreal a middle class American from a broken home after years of pointless suffering had promised so much" (155). This stylistic device, repeated frequently enough, becomes an analogy for childlike qualities. It gestures toward both the vulnerability and the hope of individuals who, like children, are constantly beset with new beginnings.

In a study of Dos Passos's *U.S.A.,* McHale further complicates matters as he questions the very notion of mimetic rendition of speech.[16]

Pointing out how far from authentic children's expression are those parts of the Camera Eye sections that have always been understood as a child's words, this account argues that readers are willing to overlook or disregard many overtly contrived details. Linguistic features of a text, it turns out, are read as markers of children's speech primarily due to the context of surrounding narrative. This means that even when some of the features proffered as a child's clearly do not correspond to genuine speech, or when they might be attributable to the speech of other classes of characters, these passages are apprehended as specifically childlike because the reader *expects* to associate them with young figures. Coordinate syntax, for example, the long strings of "and" typical of Camera Eye passages, could be interpreted as an element of that informal diction known as "restricted code."[17] They are not, however, mistaken as such, for authenticity in transcription of speech is not an exclusive, determining factor in establishing the illusion of mimesis in narrative.

There is another reason that the discourse of childhood in art relies only partially on represented speech. Often what characters say aloud to others, or even silently to themselves, is not as perceptive as what the narrator may say about their deepest thoughts or psychic tensions. Varieties of nonverbal thought, as they reveal relations between what is articulated and what is not, take on fundamental importance in fiction about children. An appreciation of the child's language is virtually impossible without a simultaneous understanding of its limits, its referential capacities, and its blind spots—that is, what the child can and cannot verbalize.

As semioticians have rallied to point out, voice is in no simple sense synonymous with verbal expression, spoken or unspoken. The self is always several, for it is fragmented into conflicting impulses: some conscious and some not. This insight has led poststructuralist critics to speak of "subjects" and not "individuals."[18] Moreover, by viewing language as a network of social relations and as a code into which the speaker is co-opted, these critical stances have further undermined the notion of coherent voice. Language is said to speak through the person, rather than the other way around, and people are seen to constitute a matrix of criss-crossing ideologies. Accordingly, words contain significations hidden to speakers who not only unknowingly disclose deep motivations and secret desires but also reveal unarticulated assumptions and collectively defined values. Child characters make for pointedly pertinent examples of this phenomenon. Such figures often speak naively and do not appreciate what their statements imply, either psychologically or as an expression of broad social circumstance.

To be sure, there is a distinct risk in endorsing this brand of semiotic thinking to approach literary childhoods. Such ideas have been used primarily to deconstruct what are perceived as powerful discourses. By contrast, the ineluctably contrived nature of fictional child language makes this voice far from an authoritative Word with presumptions to unassailable truth. The imagined child is unavoidably a highly divided construct, its voice a hybrid of youth and maturity. Fundamental skepticism toward the notion of voice, then, can foster too harsh an assault on the idea of the individual and so prove counterproductive for examining a perspective already defined as fragile and difficult to identify.

An instructive precedent comes from the field of feminist criticism. The radical decentering and the prospect of political dispossession implicit in much of the poststructuralist enterprise has caused rancor among critics eager to celebrate women's self-expression. It may be desirable, then, to strike a cautious balance: to keep in mind that it is useful to conceive of the child as voice or focalizer in order to posit the revisioning power of childhood narratives, but to remember also that the voice represented is a peculiarly ununified one. Temporary and mutable, given to accelerated changes and growth, it is also always susceptible to coloring both by the language of the surrounding social environment (in the narrated events) and by the adult narrative voice that mediates it. This is a voice that must strive arduously if it is to assert a measure of autonomy, whether thematic or formal. In light of these matters, Bakhtin's theories are more congenial tools of analysis than the work of his successors (such as Kristeva, Foucault, and Derrida) who claim to have superseded his views.[19] Bakhtin's work played a seminal role for semiotics as it launched investigations into the layeredness of voice. However, precisely because it does not dismiss such concepts as intentionality, the importance of the author as organizing center, and the possibility that the individual may be an active producer of meaning, the dialogic imagination suggests a useful critical framework for exploring narratives of childhood and the interpenetrations of utterances, the intertextualities and the double-voicedness typical of those texts.

Semiotic Thematics

As childhood narrative features clashes between the youngster's imagination and accepted convention, a number of semiotic issues find a natural thematic focus in such writing. These include challenges to referentiality, consideration of ways in which context affects determinacy or indeterminacy of meaning, and debate about the nature of signs. The theory of the dialogic imagination would predict that any juxtaposition of discourses will lead to a metalinguistic emphasis and point to contrasts between those various kinds of expression. Texts that emphasize representations of consciousness and inner life amplify that phenomenon and make for an art that homes in on the relationship between linguistic code and individual speakers: how they interact, how each shapes and influences the other. The recasting of social codes takes on special valence in narratives where the child is a figure conceived as beyond the usual boundaries of language—that is, seen either as *infans*, the preverbal creature, or as someone who is not yet a fully articulate speaker. Texts that associate young views with intensely private, unconventional perception construct the child's experience as one that defies communicative expression. The result is therefore not only to highlight the limitations and blind spots of individual speakers but also to examine the relation of verbal formulations to nonverbal experience.

This is an important point, since semiotic criticism often holds that there are no meaningful experiences nor objects of knowledge outside of signs and codes of interpretation. Bakhtin in notable measure set the precedent for such a stance. Concerned with higher psychic functions, he discounted interest in lower sensation because he deemed it to be devoid of the verbal qualities that would endow it with ideological structure. However, to suppress to an extreme any consideration of the extralinguistic realm can lead to an overextended notion of textuality. Robert Alter, objecting to the excesses of such thinking, rightly observes that to see a tiger is to interpret it, but to suppose that tigers cannot exist apart from human thought is foolish. He quips that, although readers may decenter, deconstruct, decode, and reencode a tiger in a text, "even the hardiest structuralist would not step inside the cage with the real beast, whose fangs and claws, after all, are more than a semiotic pattern."[20] To supplement such observations, it should be recognized that not all sensory information is equally highly codified and structured. Acknowledging those activities of mind which by gradation remain more remote from verbal formulation might correct a still fashionable overemphasis on language as an infinite play of signs isolated from referentiality. This change of emphasis might also allow studies on the representation of consciousness to ask a new set of questions: what role does linguistic process play in preserving or modifying cognitive boundaries? What, by contrast, is the role of nonlinguistic perception, and what are the limitations of language in thinking? How do people grapple with instabilities of meaning to deal with changing circumstances in their physical world?

These matters often come to bear on fictional rendering of the child's mind or they underlie basic thematic preoccupations of childhood narratives. Children frequently cannot articulate as much as they perceive. The young grapple arduously with the physical world at a nonverbal level, arguably in a less mediated way than do adults. Furthermore, their language, one in the process of being learned, is given to continual change and dramatic transformations. For these reasons a focus on young characters may be ideally suited to narrative that challenges the primacy of denotation by depicting a fluidity of changing codes in relation to extralinguistic reality.

The texts studied here clearly direct attention to discrepancies between actualities, the characters' apprehensions of them, and the characters' verbal formulations of their understandings. This mandate is not always (indeed, most often not) carried out in terms of psycholinguistic verisimilitude. Rather, the child as agent of plot creates opportunities to gesture toward a fundamental issue: to what extent do events lead to expression, and to what extent do preexisting frameworks of meaning determine the child's ability to perceive? Among the authors I examine, Roth and Grossman come closest to dealing with these matters in a psychologically convincing way. Kosinski and Sholem Aleichem illustrate the opposite pole of artifice. Bialik and Appelfeld fall somewhere on the continuum between those two possibilities and mull over the problem of words and things, how language refers and for whom, with varying degrees of interest in rendering the interiority of their characters. In each case, though, to insist on narrative voice and the language of the child is not to diminish the social implications of the works or to reduce discussion to a narrow focus on text defined as signs in relation to signs. On the contrary, it is meant to signal that attention to language in these fictions is a part of the characters' attempts to interpret concrete experience as well as the meanings others assign the world.

It is not only in the plot that the child, conceived as Other and in some ways remaining outside language, takes on a highly charged role. There are ramifications, too, for the narration. Even as the imagining of the child's imagination shows that experience may exceed the usual norms and means of reference, so this fiction evinces related questions about the mimetic capacities of art. The narrator who wishes to convey perceptions outside of conventional formulation must stretch storytelling techniques to indicate an inaccessible realm of being, especially in texts that attempt to express extraordinary wonder or inexpressible horror. The breaking or recasting of linguistic/social codes therefore may operate in tandem at two levels in these texts; the thematization of estrangement from language or the breakdown of meaning is matched by innovations of narration and literary convention. In both style and content these texts provide keen examples of defamiliarization or "making strange."

Dialogic Interaction and Modern Jewish Literature

Bakhtin's theories prove particularly attractive as they describe literary historical circumstances conducive to interactions of voice. The heteroglossia of the novel as a genre can manifest itself most evidently in texts that deal with polyglot milieus and with eras of social transition. Similarly, in Bakhtin's estimation, the most intensely dialogic style is forged in times of upheaval. These allow for a convergence and mutual acknowledgement of diverse social idioms. Thus, Bakhtin argues in *The Dialogic Imagination,* the novel arose under optimal conditions. Most notably, Cervantes' *Don Quixote* emerged at the time when the Renaissance destroyed "the verbal and ideological centralization of the Middle Ages." As separate languages and levels of diction meet in that text, defying "the enclosed quality of the old universe," no word can exist in a state of "being for itself" (414–15). Instead, the various tongues and registers are coordinated to reveal one another's presence as "an ideologically based act" (365).

Such issues have special resonance for Jewish literature, since instability of setting, periods of transition, and interpenetrations of language have been staple features of Jewish literary circumstance and subject matter in the modern period. Multilingualism has been endemic to Jewish life in the Diaspora, stemming naturally from the minority status of Jewish communities and also from internal Jewish bilingualism. Typically, Hebrew has functioned as the holy tongue of liturgy, while a Jewish vernacular (Yiddish, Judaeo-Espanol, or Judaeo-Arabic, for instance) has served everyday purposes. Both, in turn, existed along with the language of a surrounding majority population. To this has been added another brand of multilingualism, due to the various kinds of religious, social, and political upheaval characteristic of Jewish history in the past one hundred years. Displacements of Jewish populations and massive migrations resulting from persecution, economic hardship, and war have often led to the adoption of new lands and new languages. Even in the Jewish state, where a Jewish language has come to coincide with national language and where there is no fundamental, a priori division of secular and religious life into separate languages, a polyglot milieu is the norm rather than the exception. Many individuals speak a native tongue other than Hebrew, and many authors write in Hebrew not as a matter of second nature but as a deliberate act of will. All these factors contribute to make modern Jewish literature especially equipped as a laboratory of the dialogic imagination.

Indeed, in the tales discussed in this book, the immigrant or minority status of many of the characters heightens the polyphonic components of the narrative. Often the multilingual, multiethnic settings intensify the generational conflicts of central concern to the young protagonists. This sociolinguistic complexity results, too, in a marked self-consciousness and attention to the theme of semiotic initiation (i.e., the youngster's awakening grasp of received models of interpretation). Sholem Aleichem describes Eastern European immigrants to America, as does Henry Roth. Both place special emphasis on their characters' struggles with new languages, much as David Grossman describes the milieu of Yiddish-speaking newcomers, Holocaust survivors, to Israel after World War II. Kosinski, for his part, thematizes barriers of dialect, though he does not dramatize them stylistically.

Appelfeld and Bialik suppress overt mention of multilingualism in the settings they describe, but language shift is integral to their art because of their own adoption of a new language as their artistic medium. These cases put a general principle into relief. At the level of narration, as well as at the level of narrated events, language choice and language shift have important implications, for they indicate transformations of outlook and divisions between the author and his characters. For example, Sholem Aleichem's pioneering of a secular Yiddish narrative tradition represents a choice against the Hebrew in which he first composed and which was at that time the language of prestige. Opting to return to the mother tongue of his childhood, in *Mottel* he makes a significant move to dissociate his prose from the sacred connotations so prominent in the holy tongue. Like Mottel, the author represents the voice of a new order more accepting of secular ethnic Jewish identity and more intent on protecting the vitality of the people than on preserving the pieties of the past. Bialik, in contrast, adopts Hebrew as the language of his art, and this choice allows him proximity to that same sacred tongue, which his main character challenges but finally accommodates. Revived as part of a national movement, intended to reinvigorate the Jewish people by recalling ancient strengths, Hebrew permits this writer an elevated diction peculiarly suitable for endorsing the child's exalted vision of an impoverished world. Bialik's move away from his native Yiddish, however, also distances the narrator from his remembered past, making childhood that much more irretrievable.

Roth, too, writes in a language other than his native tongue. Never schooled in that first language, Yiddish, he quite naturally wrote in English. All the same, linguistic distance from early childhood is no less crucial a generating force in *Call It Sleep* than in *Aftergrowth*. Here, as there, it creates tensions between a present world and a world that is no more. The Yiddish-speaking characters inhabit an English-speaking world that views them with disdain, but the author, from his own vantage point later in time, uses his medium to make an elevated impression of the Jewish immigrants. He extols a warmth and nobility of expression found in Yiddish, through his craft as a writer of English. Kosinski and Appelfeld, for their part, share a common background of linguistic dislocation and relocation. Kosinski, born in Poland, wrote his novel in English after his 1954 arrival in the United States. Appelfeld, born in Bukovina, spent much of his childhood hiding in the forests of Eastern Europe. Early on he spoke a smattering of three or four languages but was schooled in none. Later he received a Hebrew education in Israel and began to write in that tongue. For each of these authors the use of an adopted language provided distance from the horrors of the Shoah. Turning linguistic obstacles to their advantage, they created a prose curiously divorced from the context to which it refers. This move, then, forms part of the struggle to describe the indescribable and to produce a fictional world unmoored in horrific reality. Their creation is an in-between realm of the imagination, able to traverse past and present yet not fully part of either one.

Interactions, then, between the language of narration and the language of narrated events add to the complexity of these texts. To examine this kind of phenomenon in more detail from a technical angle, it is useful to turn to Meir Sternberg's typology of narrative methods for representing multilingual discourse.[21] Though fiction is normally unilingual, it can render other languages through a variety of techniques. These range from direct citation to homogenizing conventions that simply ignore linguistic difference. There exist, too, a number of possibilities in between these extremes. Examples include selective quotation of a second language; orthographic signals or lexical modifications that register features of the second language; prose that retains some of the semantic scope of a foreign culture, though not its exact verbal expression. Charting the uses of such techniques in fictions of childhood reveals more than simply technical virtuosity on the part of the authors. These concepts can help indicate how the child's voice emerges out of and is implicated in the linguistic milieu that surrounds him.

Indeed, the narratives explored here are not solely private accounts. On the contrary, the child—de-automatizing the varieties of expression in his environment—allows the author to capture changes and transformations of the social setting. By the same token, those shifts in themselves create or magnify many of the conflicts and opportunities in the child's world, including the need for the child to define Jewishness and arrive at an understanding of his own relation to his heritage. Certainly, many of the characters' discoveries are of a highly personal nature. The encounters with or glimpses of wonder, awe, terror, love, sex, and death are the very stuff of any childhood. Here, however, these experiences are clearly inscribed within the larger context of shifting societal values. It is not just that their growing up hinges on the abiding

concerns of twentieth-century Jewish writing: readjustments and reap-
praisals of faith, redefinitions of community, and responses to catastrophe. In addition, there is a particularly intense collision of social forces
in these fictional figures. The intersection of child and adult understandings in the plot is grafted onto the intersection of child and adult voice in
the telling of the story. This circumstance helps explain the centrality of
such texts within the corpus of modern Jewish literature. Because it is so
ineluctably contrived, because it revisions and is revisioned at every step,
the child's consciousness serves as a congenial instrument for capturing
instabilities of meaning. The child's voice in fiction is an invention that
can at once capture imaginative, unfamiliar views but also remain
moored in matters of communal concern. Shifts in understanding, reap-
propriations of meaning, and reinterpretations of Jewishness evidently
and simultaneously take place in several dimensions of the narrative.

In part the slipperiness of this character is effective because it
conveys the elusiveness of Jewish identity. While all narrative can be read
as an amalgam of discourses and a site of struggle among conflicting
values, Bakhtin's alertness to the layeredness of every utterance proves
exceptionally apposite in the case of modern Jewish fiction. Jewishness
is never simply a matter of language, country, or religion, and indeed,
these three common components of identity often do not coincide in the
case of Jews. In this literature, very clearly, self-expression for both
characters and narrators represents a convergence of forces that defy
any sense of unified self. Problems of filiation and affiliation, as they
intensify and complicate intergenerational dialogue, in some measure
set these texts apart from non-Jewish counterparts in other novelistic
traditions.

To be sure, the definition of certain texts as Jewish is troubled, and
made more urgent, because this writing emerges from overlapping cultural contexts. All are a combination of Jewish and non-Jewish elements. While these authors grapple with Jewish languages and/or contexts, the very fact that these are texts composed within the Western
literary tradition places them at a remove from the pious past and from
more properly Jewish genres of writing. An important corollary of this
observation is that these conceptions of childhood may best be explicated in terms of Western notions. Familiarity with Western ideas about
children contributes importantly to the amalgamation of discourses
that comprises each author's own artistic voice. Accordingly, mention of
the picaresque, the fairy tale, Wordsworth, Freud, Lacan, Vygotsky, and
other influences in the history of understandings about childhood is
integral to an analysis of these texts.

As the authors, like their fictional children, grapple with Jewish
identity, yet also distance themselves in varying measures from Judaism,

Jewish language, Jewish nationality, or Jewish collective values, questions of limits inevitably arise. Were a Jewish writer to renounce all the usual measures of identification—religion, language, ethnicity—would anything remain to define that writer or the writer's art as Jewish? Just as pertinent is the question, will such a person continue to be seen as a Jew by others? Such questions do not admit easy answers. The discourse of childhood, however, with its peculiarly fictive voice and its acts of literary ventriloquism, becomes an apt forum for inventing and sounding new self-conceptions, and for bringing those ideas into dialogue with Jewish traditions and historical transformations.

THE SHTETL AND
BEYOND

3 SHOLEM ALEICHEM— MOTTEL, THE CANTOR'S SON

God has pity on kindergarten children.
He has less pity on schoolchildren,
And on grown-ups he has no pity at all.

—Yehuda Amihai, "God Has Pity on Kindergarten Children"

*T*he conventional Haskalah portrayal of the *heder* boy as a miniature adult, old before his time, often relied on an opposition between the world of books and the world of nature. The little Jew, immersed in holy writ, was seen as having been deprived the delights of the outdoors and so denied a child's fundamental need for play. In his autobiographical narrative from the turn of the century, *Of Bygone Days*, S. Y. Abramovitch (known by his pen name, Mendele the Bookseller) moves a step toward liberating the child from the study hall. Speaking on behalf of the boy he once was, the narrator voices the sensibility and perceptions of childhood long silenced by religious tradition. Significantly, the decisive moment of self-assertion and self-definition for the child protagonist is that time when, leaving the *heder* behind, he suddenly and belatedly discovers nature. The text remarks that as he ran barefoot one day in a spring storm, "that was the day when my eyes were opened and I was revealed to myself as I really am."[1] This experience brings with it, much as in Bialik's "The Pool" ("Habrekha," 1905), a new language, one more appropriate than sacred writ for the expression of youthful vitality and exuberance:[2]

> That was the moment I first came to know myself, God, and his world. All these things were revealed to me in thunder and lightning, and human intelligence came to me in the storm. That great vision is engraved on my heart and I can never forget it. In my heart—the heart of a naive child—I comprehended the vision before me, and I understood the language of nature round about. I knew the speech of the plants and the garden vegetables, the song of the running waters, and the frog's croak, as he lay up to his neck in the fetid marsh staring upward with gray eyes—all this I understood well and answered in the same voice, croaking with joy. (269)

43

Sholem Aleichem, like Mendele, Y. L. Peretz, and others, also at times lamented the early maturity imposed on Jewish children.[3] However, he went far beyond Mendele's efforts to present the child's outlook on the world. Not unlike Charles Dickens and Mark Twain, authors with whom he has often been compared, Sholem Aleichem devoted a considerable portion of his *oeuvre* to the treatment of childhood. This was so partly because, like Dickens and Twain, he composed popular fiction, suitable for family entertainment and designed to appeal to youngsters (particularly his festival stories). Partly, too, he was attracted to childhood as a theme that accented a mixture of mischief and nostalgia. His interest in child characters also coincided with and enhanced his purposes as a humorist and a satirist, for his young creations, like himself, often exhibit a lighthearted disrespect for accepted custom. His most sustained narrative of childhood, *Mottel, the Cantor's Son,* emerges out of the literary tradition that protests restrictive *heder* instruction, but the text then puts the main character to a variety of purposes that include satiric humor and, above all, an expression of hope for the continuing vigor of the Jewish people at a time of persecution and cultural upheaval.

The narrative takes as its point of departure a scene that conforms closely to many of the features in the passage just cited from *Of Bygone Days.* The tale opens with an account of a little boy's foray into the outdoors at springtime, accompanied by his favored playmate, the neighbor's calf. This initial scene combines emphasis on nature with self-expression, as Mottel avoids his school lessons, discards traditional language, and replaces it with his own. At odds with his predecessor, though, Sholem Aleichem's interests are less with nature than Mendele's, and more with human nature.[4] This passage contrasts with the lines from *Of Bygone Days* as it shifts emphasis notably from the "speech of plants" and the "song of the running waters" to the child's voice, his interpretation of the landscape, and his irreverence toward authority.

> After we climbed out into God's free and sunny world, both of us, Menie and I, out of thankfulness to nature began to display our joy [and] from my swelling breast a kind of song burst forth—much finer than those I sang with father on holidays at the altar, a song without words, without music, without melody—a kind of nature-song, a song of waterfalls, of running waves, a song of songs: "Oh papa, oh father, oh everlasting God!" (3–4)[5]

> אַרויסגעקלאפט זיך אויף גאָטס פרייע ליכטיקע וועלט, האָבן מיר ביידע,
> איך און מעני, אויס דאַנקבאַרקייט צו דער נאַטור, זיך געגומען אויסדריקן
> אונדזער צופרידנקייט. [...] און עס רייסט זיך ארויס פון מיין
> אָנגעפילטער ברוסט, אַן מיין וויסן אַ מין געזאַנג, נאָר שענער ווי

יום–טוב מיטן טאָטן טאַטן ביים עמוד, א געזאַנג אָן ווערטער, אָן נאָטן, אָן א
שום מאַטיוו, א מין נאָטור–געזאַנג פון א וואָסער–פאל, פון יאָגנדיקע
קוואַליעס, א מין שיר–השירים, א געטלעכע התפעלות, א הימלישע
באַגייסטערונג: אוי–ווייי, טאַטע! אוי–ווייי, פּאַטער! אוי–ווייי, לעבעדיקער
גאָאַאַאַט!!! (7)

Here, as Mottel gladly exchanges the chanting of *shul* for his own song, the author further emphasizes the substitution of youthful high spirits for traditional language by engaging this character in a dialogue with the calf. Menie says, "meeeeh," the boy mimics the cow, and, enormously pleased with themselves, they continue to imitate each other and converse *"in demselben nusah."* This rather ordinary phrase in Yiddish, signifying *in the same way,* recalls the sacred meaning of *nusah,* the musical formulation or version in which the prayers are chanted in the synagogue. Drained as it is of religious connotations, *"nusah"* here parallels Mottel's own effacing of traditional meaning and his substituting of his own, secular expression for the discourse of the synagogue.

The child functions throughout the narrative to undermine the old ways. To examine his role it is crucial to point out that this stance is not a narrowly personal one nor merely an instance of childish disrespect. At issue is a moment of collective transition from tradition to modernity. *Mottel* recounts the life of a small shtetl child whose society as a whole is disintegrating due to economic hardship, pogroms, and the deterioration of religious authority. There begins a mass emigration to America, and the narrative follows the boy's adventures on both sides of the ocean. Early on in the plot action the protagonist's father dies, leaving him an orphan by the reckoning of his society; soon the entire world of his parents will find itself in irreversible decline and its patriarchal order threatened. All these matters, however, are filtered through the prism of the youngster's perception, and Mottel is renowned for putting a comic twist on events. With his famous pronouncement, "Hoorah, I'm an orphan," Mottel welcomes the special indulgence that his misfortune has brought him. He revels in no longer being expected to behave himself or attend school. As a result, debates about the book have centered on the degree to which Sholem Aleichem emphasizes tragedy and how much the child's mitigating presence serves as comic rejoinder to dire circumstance.[6] Mottel's views have decisive impact, because this text does not only orient itself to a child's perspective, it also adopts Mottel himself as a narrative persona. The long-established typology of the child as suppressed voice in Jewish life thus ostensibly gives way to representation of that very voice itself. The thematic stress on the child as source of novel vision and expression coincides with exploration of the child as narratorial figure and the artistic experimentation attendant on that possibility.

As Dan Miron has pointed out in a detailed article about Mottel, this head-on confrontation with the formal complexities inherent in representing a child's voice proves highly problematic.[7] Sholem Aleichem does not sustain a childish style, but also does not refrain from it. At times the narrative avails itself of short sentences, simple speech patterns—and, it could be added, rhymes, a bandying about of nicknames, the recounting of childish jokes and verbal games. All of these properly belong in the category of mimetic impulses that indicate a young speaker. At other times, though, the narrator waxes poetic, turns to complex syntax, or indulges in sentimental abstractions entirely inappropriate to a child's speech. The opening paragraph, portions of which were quoted above, provides a case in point. (It is telling that in some early versions of the text this scene is presented in the third person, through an implied narrator, without pretense of using a child's voice.)[8] Further incongruities riddle the text as well. While Mottel sometimes fails to grasp the metaphorical nature of idioms, at other times he himself produces elaborate metaphoric language and alliteration of his own. His performance, moreover, divides itself erratically between features of oral delivery and written composition. The narrative was at times subtitled "*ksovim fun a yingl a yosm*" (writings of an orphan boy), but on any number of occasions Mottel announces that he is illiterate. The writerly qualities that do pervade the narrative reveal quite openly that this work has not been created by a child. Mottel, for instance, shares the author's concern with serialization and takes care to summarize preceding episodes at the beginning of each new chapter. Though assuming intimacy with his audience and addressing them as if in conversation, Mottel's text does not make sense as a dramatic monologue, for it is not situated in concrete dramatic circumstances that might provide the character clear motivation for speaking.

On top of all these peculiarities, Mottel very often speaks in the present tense. He does not acquire mature awareness, and he does not develop either in the narrated events or in the narration. (His age is indeterminate; Sholem Aleichem variously designated his character to be five, seven, or nine years old on different occasions. Mottel does not progress in anything resembling plausibly sequential fashion from one stage of life to another.)[9] If for no other reason than these temporal oddities, his language would remain highly inconsistent with that of any natural speaker. Miron therefore concludes that Mottel's speech abides by only one law, "the law of energy, of constant crackling, sparkling movement" (179). This quality is symptomatic of the central thematic thrust of the narrative as a whole. Mottel's effervescence and vitality, in response to the ossification of tradition and the loss of shtetl culture, turn the child into a symbol of newness and an endorsement of optimism. As he dispenses with mourning over a moribund European past, this character enthusiastically embraces the New World. The non-developing figure in this way conveys a most acute feeling for historical change and its significance, and so the author turns to advantage the vestiges of childishness in his character, even while employing them "as elements of a larger conception which is removed from any intention of the fictional creation of a child character" (145).

Miron's astute analysis should not obscure the fact that the adoption of the child's voice, problematic as it is from the standpoint of mimetic force, bears a series of additional artistic benefits. It is possible to extend critical discussion on Mottel by considering interanimations of language that result from the focus on the child's perspective. Lending itself to comedy and the celebration of vitality, this narrative persona also bears exceptional dialogic capacities, in the Bakhtinian sense that Mottel selectively appropriates, reinterprets, speculates on, and, in the process, challenges the authority and privilege of adult idiom. The ways in which the language of the child comes in contact with, transforms, or recasts adult expression reflect the instability of his setting. His words, consequently, also emphasize the dynamic shifts and upheavals of his society. In this capacity Mottel allows for variation on the polyphonic qualities that are such a fundamental part of Sholem Aleichem's art. This is a writer known for introducing into his fiction a plethora of garrulous characters intent on talking their way out of disaster or disappointment.[10] The child has a special role in this scheme of things, for his naive incomprehension affects the way he filters, apprehends, and interprets the words of others. He is instrumental in admitting adult voices to the text or excluding them from it, allowing them to articulate their views or preventing them from doing so.

For example, Mottel fulfills an important function as a narrator by overhearing and recording conversations around him. Bakhtin has drawn analytic attention to the importance of reported speech in narrative. Of recurrent interest for his literary readings are the transmission and assessment of what others say, the rebuttals and responses that one character brings to the comments of fellow characters.[11] Because Mottel is a child, incapable of understanding many things, he becomes an ideal foil for presenting what Bakhtin considers the fundamental component of novelistic art: attention to the speaking person and spoken words. Reporting much without being fully a party to it or absorbing it, the young protagonist easily allows extra voices to be heard alongside his own. Since he does not truly assimilate their words into his personal conceptual system, he remains an outsider, but at the same time he facilitates the orchestration of multiple speakers within the narrative. Benefits to plot action brought in this way are evident. The child focalizer/narrator permits Sholem Aleichem tremendous flexibility over what to disclose and what to omit. In addition, this approach can foster a panoramic view. Like the Sholem Aleichem persona itself, Mottel enjoys mobility and a highly useful capacity to engage with and disengage from a variety of scenes and verbal exchanges. He can come and go as necessary to present events in a way congruent with the comic tone set by the author.[12]

Consider, as a case in point, the scene in which he first has active contact with adults. The boy hears grown-ups arguing but only partially incorporates their words into his own thinking. The child in effect filters out the harsher aspects of their discussion, and so the naiveté of his perspective makes for a sweeter assessment of social upheaval. The exchange is reported immediately following Mottel's introductory romp with the calf, when brother Elye comes to fetch him and announces that their father is lying ill, approaching death.

> The swarthy doctor comes to see him; he's a stout man with black whiskers and laughing eyes—a jolly doctor. He calls me *Belly button* and flips my belly with his finger. Every time he comes he tells mother not to stuff me with potatoes and to give the sick man bouillon and milk, milk and bouillon. Mother listens to him silently and after he leaves hides her face in her apron and her shoulders quiver. Then she dries her eyes, calls my brother Eliahu aside and they whisper secrets. What they talk about, I don't know, but it sounds to me as if they quarrel. Mother keeps urging Eliahu to go somewhere, but he doesn't want to go. He says to her,
> "I'd rather sink through the ground than turn to them. I'd rather die this very day." (5)

עס גייט צו אונדז דער שווארצער דאָקטאָר, א גראָבער מיט שווארצע
וואָנסעס און מיט לאכנדיקע אויגן — א פרייליעכער דאָקטאָר. מיך
רופט ער ״פּופֿיק״ און שנעלט מיר מיט די פינגער אין בייכל אריין. ער
זאָגט אָן אלע מאָל דער מאַמען, מע זאָל מיך נישט שטאָפּן מיט קיין
קאַרטאָפּליעס, און דעם קראנקן זאָל מען געבן נאָר בוליאָן און מילך,
מילך און בוליאָן. די מאַמע הערט אים אויס, און אז ער גייט אוועק,
באהאַלט זי דאָס פּנים אין פארטעך און די אַקסלען טרייסלען זיך ביי
איר... נאָכדעם ווישט זי אויס די אויגן, רופט אָפּ מיין ברודער אליהו
אויף א זייט, און מע סודעט זיך שטילערהייט. וואָס זיי רעדן — ווייס
איך נישט. נאָר מיר דאכט, זיי קריגן זיך. די מאַמע שיקט אים
ערגעץ, ער וויל נישט גיין. ער זאָגט צו איר:
— איידער אָנקומען צו זיי, וועל איך דיר בעסער גיין אין דער ערד
אריין!... איך וועל בעסער שטאַרבן היינטיקן טאָג!... (9–8)

Here, as elsewhere in the novel, the reader may appreciate the bitterness of the family's travails through the grown-ups' arguments. The older figures often complain of their straitened circumstances. At the same time the child, through his lack of response, stands in opposition to the adults' grief. As the patriarch agonizes, as the house is dismantled and family possessions are sold off one by one, Mottel's glee increases. His joy does not seem grotesque, thanks to his incomprehensions. In this particular passage, that impression is brought about as the prose runs the gamut of possibilities that Brian McHale has described to classify representations of speech in fiction.[13] The variety of speech acts enables Mottel to emphasize, accentuate, and deaccentuate certain issues. These lines, for instance, include "diegetic summary," that is, the bare report that a speech event has occurred. Mother calls Eliahu aside, "and they whisper secrets." This minimal report deemphasizes or obscures the grim content of what they are saying. There follows a somewhat more specific summary, which comes closer to naming the topic of conversation: "What they talk about I don't know, but it sounds like they quarrel." Indirect content paraphrase, which disregards the style or form of the original utterance, occurs as Mottel reports, "Mother keeps urging Eliahu to go somewhere, but he doesn't want to go."

In varying degrees each of these pronouncements keeps the grown-ups' concerns secondary, not explicit or foregrounded. This approach subsequently gives way to indirect discourse as the doctor prescribes for the sick man "bouillon and milk, milk and bouillon." The upbeat prescription, the jolly, reassuring words of the physician, more nearly approach citation and so are brought closer to the surface of the text than are the upsetting words between Mother and Eliahu. Similarly, direct discourse clearly set off by quotation marks comes only with a happier exchange: the doctor's cheerful, teasing appellation of the child as *"pupik,"* that is, belly button. The final line of the paragraph, the direct quote from Eliahu, also contributes to lightheartedness as it turns the passage to a satiric, jesting focus. Eliahu makes a buffoon of himself by spouting empty threats; he would prefer to die rather than compromise his pride by asking someone for financial help. In actuality he is in no danger of death, while his father truly is. Already the older brother is taking on the traits of inflated self-importance and pride that make him a laughingstock throughout the book. Altogether, the child's role as observer accomplishes a reversal of figure and ground. In the midst of a crisis comedy becomes more prominent and genuinely scary matters recede into the distance. The grievousness of the family's situation is conveyed to the reader, yet the child essentially remains aloof from their conflicts, mourning, and hardship.

Mottel more actively appropriates adult language through his interpretations of idiomatic phrases. These he often defamiliarizes by taking them in an overly literal way. For example, after Eliahu marries the daughter of a rich man, Mother remarks that her son has fallen into a *"shmaltsgrub,"* a mine of fat. More familiarly, in English, he has hit upon a gold mine. Mottel wonders if his brother has fallen in a mine literally filled with *"schmalts,"* and the ludicrous image that emerges is an appropriate challenge to his mother's self-satisfaction. The baker/ father-in-law soon loses his money, and Eliahu, stuck now with a petulant, disagreeable wife, must return to his old poverty. As it turns out, the mine was bankrupt and Mottel, divesting the idiomatic expression of its usual richness, turns out to have forewarned the reader of this eventuality. His misreading savvily suggested that it would be dangerous to put too much stock in the assumptions of the older generation. In comparable fashion, as Mottel muses on his own wedding day he notes, "Mother caresses me and says that a lot of water will flow under the bridge until that day arrives. Meanwhile her eyes grow wet. I don't understand why so much water has to flow until I get married and why one must cry about it" (48; in Yiddish, 38). The metaphorical water, coming to be associated with and dramatized by Mother's tears, is part of the adult speech that the child dismisses. Both represent a sorrowful outlook that he rejects, even as he thwarts the referential force of the phrases Mother proffers. These literalizations, like many other examples from the text, are not merely cute, but form part and parcel of his distancing from adult understandings.[14]

Certainly, Mottel's observations may seem cloyingly sweet or overly contrived. His innocent misappropriations of sayings are often, at best, innocuous and frequently less resonant than, for example, Tevye's misquotations of scripture. That character turns intertextualities to highly ironic commentary on the shtetl life in decline. Nonetheless, it should be noted that Mottel's is a humor that sets him apart from other Sholem Aleichem characters. The success or failure of incomprehension as a narrative strategy in this text must be gauged in relation to the fact that the main character is conceived as a child. Underestimating the seriousness of things seems natural for a child, and so Mottel serves as a pretext that allows the text to embrace a carefree attitude. This point distinguishes this protagonist not only from Tevye but also from Menachem Mendel. The boy's optimism is not immediately invalidated by the satire that Menachem Mendel's antics invite; pranks, misunderstandings, and an inability to become sobered by defeat are acceptable in a very young person where they would not be in an adult, much as Mottel's substituting mooing sounds for liturgy can be read less as a boorish disregard for sanctity than as an invigorating liberation from a deteriorating world of tradition.[15]

In a move that shows Mottel refusing to be drawn into adult frames of meaning, the character also shakes words free from their usual semantic burdens. The narrative often uses the child to call attention to

language per se and to question its denotative powers. Take, for instance, the following scene in which the emigrants have arrived in
Cracow. Another little boy explains to Mottel that his family left home
because of a pogrom:

> I ask him what a pogrom is. All the emigrants keep talking about
> "pogroms" but I don't know what they are. Koppel says,
>   "Don't you know what a pogrom is? Then you're just a baby. A
> pogrom is something that's everywhere nowadays. It starts out of
> nothing and once it starts it lasts for three days."
>   I say, "What kind of thing is it? A fair?"
>   "Some fair! They break windows, they bust up furniture, rip pil-
> lows, feathers fly like snow . . ."
>   "What for?"
>   "What for? For fun! But pogroms aren't made only on houses.
> They're made on shops, too. They break them up, throw all the wares
> out into the street, scatter them about, pour kerosene on them, set fire
> to them, and they burn . . . "
>   "Go on!"
>   "What, do you think I'm kidding? Next when there's nothing left
> to break, they go from house to house with axes, irons, and sticks, and
> the police walk after them. They sing, whistle and yell, 'Hey fellows,
> let's beat up the Jews!' And they beat and kill and murder."
>   "Who?"
>   "What do you mean, who? the Jews."
>   "What for?"
>   "What a question! It's a pogrom, isn't it?"
>   "And so it's a pogrom. What's that?"
>   "Go away, you're a fool. It's like talking to a calf." (147–48)

איך פרעג אים, ווי אזוי איז דאָס א פּאָגראָם? איך הער אַלץ פון די
עמיגראַנטן, מע זאָגט: "פּאָגראָם", "פּאָגראָם", נאָר וואָס דאָס איז —
ווייס איך נישט. רופט זיך אָן צו מיר קאָפּל:
— אַ פּאָגראָם ווייסטו נישט? עה! ביזטו דאָך גאָר אַ ניונקעלע! אַ
פּאָגראָם איז אַ זאַך, וואָס איז היינט יעדנס אומעטום. הייבט זיך עס אָן
כמעט פון גאָר נישט, און אַז עס הייבט זיך אָן, ציט זיך עס אַוועק דריי
טעג...
— וואָס זשע,זאָג איך, איז דאָס? אַ יאַריד?
— וואָסער יאַריד? אַ שיינער יאַריד! מע שלאָגט פענצטער! מע
ברעכט מעבל! מע טרענט קישנס! פעדערן פליען, אַזוי ווי שניי!
— אָקעגן וואָס?
— נאַ דיר גאָר אָקעגן וואָס! אָקעגן שמערלעון! אַ פּאָגראָם איז נישט
נאָר אויף הייזער אַליין. אַ פּאָגראָם איז אויף קרעמען. מע צעשלאָגט
אַלע קרעמען און מע וואַרפט אַרויס פון דאָרטן די סחורה אויף דער גאַס,
און מע צעטראָגט, און מע צעראבעוועט, און מע צעשיט, און מע מע
באַגיסט מיט גאַז, און מע צינדט אונטער, און מע ברענט.
— גיי שוין, גיי!

—װאָס דען מיינסטו? עיך װעל דיר אויסטראַכטן? נאָכדעם, אז ס׳איז
נישטאָ שױן װאָס צו ראַבעװען, גייט מען איבער די הײזער מיט העק,
מיט אײזנס און מיט שטעקנס, און פּאַליציי גייט נאָך פון הינטן. מע
זינגט און מע פייפט און מע שרייט: "עי, רעביאַטאַ, בעי זשידאָװ!". און
מע שלאָגט, מע הרגעט, מע קױלעט, מע שטעכט מיט ספענן...
— װעמען?
— װאָס הייסט װעמען? יידן!
— פאַר װאָס?
— נאַ דיר גאָר פאַר װאָס! ס׳איז דאָך א פּאָגראָם!
— און אז א פּאָגראָם, איז װאָס?
— גיי אַװעק, דו ביזט א קעלבל! איך װיל מיט דיר נישט רעדן! (120–119)

The passage juxtaposes naiveté with horror, underscoring the
hatefulness of the anti-Semitic violence. (In this, as David Roskies has
pointed out, *Mottel* exemplifies a stance that might be designated as a
child's chronicle of destruction; allowing for play between innocence
and awareness, Sholem Aleichem provided a narrative model for other
writers, importantly Itzik Kipnis in his tale "Of Months and Days,"
1926.)[16] The grim humor, however, also defuses pathos and even makes
for a conundrum or riddle game that mocks referentiality. That is, not
having experienced a pogrom, Mottel does not share Koppel's framework of understanding. Consequently, he reacts with an apparent thick-
headedness that unsettles the usual frightful connotations of the word
"pogrom." The other boy cannot define it, because none of Koppel's
talk makes sense to Mottel. The child's incomprehension signals the
incomprehensibility of the disaster, and the entire conversation thereby
remarks on the senselessness of pogroms. Sholem Aleichem does not
make light of suffering, but he does cast the whole issue in a less
lugubrious light as the child's pliant optimism refuses to come to terms
with bereavement. The text insists on the primacy of an imagination that
cannot be co-opted into the values of a brutal world. Significantly,
Koppel calls Mottel a calf, reinscribing in the text that same image of
innocence with which the novel opened. Here, that designation has
taken on insulting intentions from Koppel's perspective, but for the
reader the word can only be apprehended in association with the context of the earlier scene. It acquires the redemptive, creative connotations of a rejuvenating new language and a new vision.

It should be remembered that the entire chapter in which this
scene appears, "Mit die emigranten," was omitted from some editions
of *Mottel*—notably, those versions aimed at young audiences. Sholem
Aleichem felt that the attention to pogroms was too grotesque and too
weighty a matter to fit in with the overall tone of Mottel's frivolity.[17]
This decision may serve as a measure of the dialogic quality afforded by
the passage just cited. The presence of different voices and mutually

unsettling outlooks made the text richer as an adult literary work but inappropriate for children's reading. Accordingly, it gave way to a more homogenized, less multivoiced prose. In lieu of the conversation with Koppel, the author later retained only Mottel's assertion, in a different chapter, that whenever he hears the word "pogrom" he runs away. As the protagonist explains, he prefers stories (*"mayses"*) to talk of calamity. Evading the issue of anti-Semitism, his narrative is transformed into a more uniform prose that deletes contrapuntal combinations of voices and thereby regains its composure and confidence at the price of complexity and layeredness.

Chapter 13, "We Steal Across the Border," merits close reading as it introduces in microcosm the intersections of voice and the recontextualizations that inform the text as a whole. Here, once again, the plot revolves about adult speech as it penetrates into the consciousness of the child, and once again the narrative emphasizes that the child figure only partly absorbs adult meanings, refusing to endorse them fully. As Mottel challenges the usual semantic force of particular words, he puts into relief the whole problem of context and referentiality, drawing attention to language per se.

The chapter opens as the family has just left home on their way to America. In the first line Mottel notes that riding on a train is heavenly, a *"gan eydn"* (Garden of Eden). This comment, recalling earlier shifting definitions of that phrase, immediately introduces into the chapter an attention to reinterpretation and reaccentuations of words. According to Mother, Father is in heaven—that is, dead; according to Mottel's uncle, *"gan eydn"* is a steambath. Mottel himself reassigns meaning to the phrase by using it to refer to his own pastime, filching apples from the neighbor's garden. The paradisiacal locomotive in chapter 13 is an extension of this last meaning. Undermining the sacred connotations of *"gan eydn,"* Mottel gaily welcomes novel experience as the Old World crumbles. By the same token, much as at the beginning he expressed his joy by singing a song without words, on the train Mottel finds himself so filled with wonder as to be speechless. He is wedged tightly into an overcrowded railroad car, but remarks,

> And me, don't you worry about me. I'm all right. I'm fine. I'm almost flattened out, but I'm standing near a window. What I see I'm sure you never have. Past me there fly houses, mileposts, streets, people, woods, fields . . . indescribable! How the train speeds! How it rumbles, squeaks, groans, whistles, squeals . . . (117)

מיר איז גוט. מיר איז אויסגעצייכנט. מע קװעטשט מיך טאקע פון
אלע זײטן. איך שטיי אָבער ביי א פענצטער. דאָס װאָס איך זע,

הָאט איר געוויס קיינמאָל נישט געזען. פאר מיינע אויגן פליען שטיבער,
וויאָרסטן,ביימער, מענטשן, פעלדער, וועלדער — ס'איז נישט צו
באשרייבן! און ווי אזוי פליט די באן! און ווי אזוי קלאפן די רעדער!
ווי אזוי טראסקאט דאס! ווי אזוי פייפט דאָס! ווי אזוי קוויטשעט דאָס! (97)

Ordinary expression is simply not commensurate with the unfamiliar marvels the boy experiences (the world is indescribable, *"nit tsu
bashraybn"*), and the onomatopoeia indicating the noise of the wheels
(*"fayft," "trasket," "kvitshet"*) recalls the opening "meeeeh" of Menie's lowing. Like that animal sound, exceeding the old vocabulary, these
sounds better convey the little boy's gladness.

Mottel's challenge to conventional language is made more explicit
when the family arrives at the border. The grown-ups have begun to
speak frequently about the frontier as a forbidding hurdle to overcome,
and they trade stories with their fellow travelers about border crossings.
The child asserts, "I thought a 'frontier' was something with horns"
(120; *"Di grenets hob ich gemeynt iz mit herner,"* 99). His literalizing,
as it comically personifies the border, making it seem strange, prefaces a
more thorough undoing of assumptions. Providing a series of circumstances that alter the impact and implications of the word *"ganvenen"*
(to steal), the text puts into question the values of the old social order.
First, Mother warns her child not to wander about the market in the
border town, for fear someone may kidnap him. Next, the agent they
engage to assist them, a piously dressed woman, ends up fleecing them
of their possessions and reneging on her promise to lead them across the
border. Once on their way, they fall into the clutches of robbers who
hold them at knifepoint. These varieties of thievery prove that appearances and traditional criteria for judging goodness, such as wearing a
wig and praying, are not trustworthy or reliable measures of virtue.

These same events also raise questions about whether or not the
immigrants themselves are engaged in transgression. In this connection
Mottel brings the semiotic issue, the question of instability in meaning,
clearly to the fore: "I don't understand what stealing the border means.
Are we thieves then?" (120; *"Ikh farshtey nisht, vos heyst dos ganvenen
di grenets. Mir zenen den ganovim?"* 99). Naturally, the author directs
the reader toward sympathy with the family's illegal border crossing.
The word *"ganvenen"* in this context is divested of its negative connotations. This turn of events stands in direct contrast to an earlier episode in
which thievery was presented as anathema. In that episode, to Mother's
horror, Eliahu angrily called Mottel a thief. The younger boy had eaten
a roll, uninvited, at the father-in-law's bakery, and the mother at that
time defended Mottel indignantly. She excused his behavior on the
grounds that he was an orphan, and she insisted haughtily on the hon-

esty and respectability of the family. By chapter 13 the valuations placed on the notion of stealing have been altered to resemble Mottel's association of *"gan eydn"* with filching apples. Illegality here is cast as mischief, relegated to the category of a carnivalesque renunciation of propriety, which turns ordinary rules topsy-turvy.[18]

Attention to the whole issue of transgression elsewhere in the chapter invests these variations on *"ganvenen"* with increased polyvalence. On the way to the train station, for instance, the family had hired a wagon whose surly driver Mottel described as a *"gazlen."* Literally meaning "like a bandit," *gazlen* here signifies that this man had a murderous temper. Playing further on the same set of nuances and the opposition of honesty and vice, the driver is presented as a virtuous man who suffers only one fault, *"eyn aveyre"* (literally a sin or transgression). He leaves the family without delivering their baggage at the proper place, and a rowdy brawl ensues. These reevaluations and colorations of the notion of transgression reinforce uncertainty about degrees of right and wrong. The driver's ill temper, which is cast in rather severe terms, does not compare to the genuine evil of the robbery later encountered. At the same time, the act construed as a small fault leads to considerable upheaval. It is against this background of definitional turmoil that Mottel asks, *"vos heyst dos ganvenen di grenets?"*

Significantly, in this quandary Mottel feels no one has an answer to his question. No one can fill him in due to the instability of his world. Patriarchal authority has broken down, and he cannot ask the women, for, the boy concludes, "what do women know?" (98). Brother Elye, for his part, cannot be consulted, since he assumes pretentious airs of authority and insists that children should not interfere with grown-ups' discussions. Elye, furthermore, is not merely inaccessible. He has also disqualified himself as a paternal figure through his misadventures at earning a living: flooding the world with ink, selling adulterated *kvass*, and starting a plague of sneezes. Therefore, for all his pomposity, he has proven himself hilariously inept at taking over Father's functions as breadwinner and head of the family. Pinney, likewise, despite his posturing as a worldly-wise adventurer, is also fundamentally ignorant about the reality of travel and of America. Together with the rest of them he faces a highly uncertain future.

The impression of defenselessness in these characters is subsequently reinforced as the group finally crosses the frontier. Shots ring out, the robbers flee, and Mother shouts, "Run, children!" To be sure, she is the matriarch, a generation older than her companions, and so has the right to call them children. Her use of the word *"kinder,"* however, also underscores that the whole group, like Mottel, finds itself in a crisis without leaders and without the support of stable custom. Mottel's

incomprehensions, then (here, most prominently, his attempt to figure
out whether or not the family has turned into thieves), become an emblem of the adults' own unknowing and naiveté. All are taking on a new
world, and the child narrative persona serves as a synecdoche of their
unpreparedness. He is the narrative agent for pointing out a vulnerability his elders are sometimes loath to admit.

Mottel's function as the outsider who records others' words also
takes on heightened importance in this connection. Consider, for example, the scene at the border, where the agent, Chaimova, gives the travelers elaborate instructions on how to escape. Sholem Aleichem has
Mottel quote her at great length, repeating her directions verbatim:

> When it's midnight, she says, we should go out behind the city. There,
> she says, there's a hill. She says we should go past the hill and turn left.
> (121)

אז ס'וועט ווערן, זאָגט זי, האַלבע נאַכט, זאָלן מיר אַרויסגײן הינטער דער
שטאָט. דאָרט איז פאַראַן, זאָגט זי, אַ בערגל. זאָלן מיר, זאָגט זי,
דאָס בערגל דורכלאָזן, און נעמען זיך לינקס, [...] (100)

This pattern of narration continues, and the phrase *"zogt zi"*
recurs ten times in the space of one paragraph.[19] Reiterated over and
over, it demonstrates insistently that Chaimova's words stand in woeful
contrast to actuality. No one, finally, waits for the family at the inn, no
one guides them to safety, and, again contrary to the account given to
them by the agent, their goods are never returned to them. Reported by
Mottel, a figure consistently oriented less to referential objects than to
someone else's speech, this passage makes clear that the whole family is
not only attentive to, but entirely dependent on, the words of others.
They rely on the agent's good will, much as they also hang on the stories
they have heard about America: about streets paved with gold and all
the rest of the myth of an easy life. They do not have the experience
necessary to judge the veracity of this discourse vital to their own survival. Such decisive imbalance in their relation to words and referential
reliability leaves ample room for deception or for gaps between dreams
and their realization. Later, by noting that initially things worked out
just as Chaimova had foretold (*"azoy vi di yidine hot nevies* [proph-
ecies] *gezogt"*), Mottel underscores the family's gullibility. To be sure,
there is a hill behind the city, and after that there are woods and an inn as
Chaimova had predicted. The crucial fact that no one awaits them there,
however, becomes all the more distressing because the party had believed so strongly at first in a false prophet. This treatment of unrealistic
expectations takes on added resonance in the context of the author's
personal life. The *Mottel* narratives were begun shortly after Sholem
Aleichem returned to Europe from New York. The pogroms of 1905

had convinced him to seek a better future in America, but, once there, he met with significant financial and professional disappointments.[20] The child character, Mottel, introduces humorous treatment of emigrants' hopes and dreams, and, as a personification of optimism, reflects the author's own hopefulness. At the same time, reflecting Sholem Aleichem's own difficulties, his chronicle also admits serious undertones and cognizance of the uncertainties faced by families fleeing the Old World.

Altogether, thanks to the superimposition of a child's voice and an adult perspective in chapter 13, the reader receives vacillating impressions of the fictional world. If, as Mottel first suspected, the border is not something that has horns, still, it did prove most dangerous. His interpretation therefore unsettles that of the grown-ups; he makes the whole episode out to be something of a lark. Subsequently, his view is also unsettled, this time by the menacing appearance of the thieves and the rifle shots. The result is a double-edged irony. The co-presence of tragedy and comedy is readily expressed and even fomented by the necessarily dual, mature/immature stance inherent in the use of the child focalizer. In short, Mottel's monologue serves propitiously as a locus of dialogue as conceived by Bakhtin.[21]

Related inversions of expectations and the upsetting of preconceptions continue once the family arrives on the other side of the border. They discover that they are safe, because they happen upon a Jew leading a goat by a rope. Costumed somewhat differently than they, speaking Yiddish with a slightly unfamiliar pronunciation, this man is nonetheless clearly one of their own and not a threat. When they ask after their whereabouts, he informs them they are nowhere near the frontier. This means that the border with its imagined horns is behind them and the goat, presumably with real horns, is not scary at all. Appropriately, after this reversal of danger, the small band of travelers bursts into *"moyredike gelekhter."* Their terror has turned to laughter, and the very word *"moyre"* (fear), which appeared a number of times earlier in the chapter (96, 97), has been drained of its threatening force. Here it indicates not terror, but rather an outcome of events that is *terribly* funny. Once again context has transformed the accentuations of the word.

The transitions of this fictional world, constantly yielding new frames of reference and new understandings, also involve the crossing of different social strata and so give rise to a host of additional dialogic encounters. Travel increasingly confronts the provincial group with different kinds of speech. Within chapter 13, for instance, the family is presented for the first time as coming in extended contact with non-Jews. (Later they pass through Cracow, Vienna, Amsterdam, and London, among other places, en route to America, and meet up with all sorts of people.) The new situations, as they arise, call attention to a variety of ethnic or national clashes and to the multilingual milieu in which the narrated events take place. Accordingly, various techniques of representing alien words begin to surface in the prose of the text. For example, in "We Steal Across the Border," an exchange with a non-Jewish porter at the train station is presented both in transliterated Russian and in Yiddish (115). This incident illustrates direct citation of foreign language.[22] By contrast, in the following passage a kind of intermittent quotation serves as a mimetic synecdoche of Pinney's utterances. Mottel remarks,

> With the stationmaster Pinney uses an altogether different vocabulary. He doesn't use such strong expressions, but he does gesticulate a lot. He uses strange words which I've never heard before: "Columbus . . . Civilization . . . Alexander von Humboldt . . . Slonimsky . . . Mathematics . . . (117)

> מיטן "נאטשאלניק" שטעלט זיך אוועק פיניע אויסטענהן שוין גאָר מיט
> אן אנדער לשון. ער בייזערט זיך שוין נישט אזוי שטארק, נאָר ער
> רעדט און מאכט מיט די הענט. ער זאָגט אים עפעס מאָדנע ווערטער,
> וואָס איך האב זיי קיינמאל נישט גאהערט: "קאָלומבוס"...
> "ציוויליזאציע"..."אלעקסאנדער פאָן הומבאָלד"... "סלאָנימסקי"...
> מאטעמאטיקע"... (96)

The conversation is recorded only in bits and pieces, for the child does not understand the Germanized Yiddish nor the abstractions Pinney invokes. The use of the child to convey overheard conversation makes this kind of procedure in representing speech seem persuasively natural and appropriate. The technique has the advantage of maintaining an element of quotational fidelity while also remaining concise. Here, recreating in very abbreviated form Pinney's attempt to regale the stationmaster with a massive shower of words, the prose suggests both his comically grandiose, idealistic notions about what it means to be an immigrant and his underestimation of the power of authority. The family and their friends want to keep all their baggage with them, but Pinney's effort on their behalf is to no practical avail; the stationmaster is unconvinced, and the passengers have to relinquish their precious bedding. In the final scenes of the chapter the text invokes another alien voice, this time through discussion in one language about another.[23] Calling attention to the oddity and newness of their surroundings, Mottel comments on the difference between his own Yiddish and the Yiddish of the man on the other side of the border, which is the same but full of broad a's, *"mit pasakhn"* (102).

Illustrative of Bakhtin's contention that language is dynamic and plural, the presentation of variegated speech communities in this chapter also combines with emphasis on distinctions of social class to show how the emigrants, in a world of flux, must deal with shifting meanings. Two incidents demonstrate how different groups color the connotations of particular words. First, when the guard at the station says to the family that they are carrying too much, he warns that they will not be allowed on the train with so many rags. In parenthesis, indicating a shift in context and expectations, Mottel expresses shock at this man's disrespect for their possessions.

> He means, apparently, the quilts. A little bit tattered and that already for him means rags! (117)

> (דאָס מיינט ער, אפנים, די קאָלדערעס: א ביסל צעריסן דער
> אונטערשלאָג, זעט זיך ארויס די וואָטע, הייסט דאָס שוין ביי אים
> שמאַטעס!) (96)

Once more, there appears the phrase *"heyst dos,"* commented on already in connection with Mottel's queries about crossing the border. This indicator of reaccentuation is mentioned frequently throughout the remaining portions of *Mottel*. Repeatedly signaling differences of views about a single event, *dos heyst* comes to function virtually as a refrain of redefinition.[24]

A subsequent incident alerts the reader to heteroglossia, that is, the collision of conflicting social forces within a specific word, and so further documents the upheavals of this world in motion. Once inside the railroad car the family is scattered, for all the seats have already been taken. Mother, afraid that her son might fall out a window, calls to him, "Mottel, Mottel" (99). A non-Jew, mimicking her to the merriment of the Christian crowd, repeats, "Mottel, Mottel" (*"Un epes eyner a poritsl mit bloye briln krimt ir iber un zogt ir nokh mitn eygenen nign, motl? motl? ale kristn lakhn,"* 99). The interethnic tensions present in the car convey themselves here neatly in the repetition of a single word that, changing in context, changes in implications. Overladen with the intentions of others, the boy's name turns from an expression of motherly concern to antagonistic mockery. Mottel himself, of course, as narrator, has the power to reinscribe that discourse within his own and so to redefine the attack not as power but as cruelty, less as superior self-confidence than as inferior hatefulness. He accomplishes this reversal by calling the Gentile a *"poritsl"*; the diminutive of the word for lord or wealthy man implies that this character, in the third-class compartment, has put on airs and deluded himself with a laughable self-importance. In this way the speakers modify one another's statements, but Mottel's perspective retains a certain privilege and claim on the reader's sympathy. To the extent that the child is a naive recorder of speech acts and does not dominate or reinterpret the words he hears, the prose does admit several refractions of one character's words in those of another. At the same time, at stake here is not fiction that radically decenters authorial point of view by exalting the thought and opinions of a spectrum of characters. Sholem Aleichem both creates multiple voices and also firmly controls his focalization, combining conflicting aspirations well within the bounds of a single consciousness, which he constructs as a child narrator.

All these passages that feature the appropriation of one individual's language by another are, aptly enough, associated in chapter 13 with the particle *iber*. It appears repeatedly in this section of narrative where the action revolves about varieties of transformation, passages to a new life, reinterpretations of the world, and contact with new views and new modes of speaking. Transport, transfer, transitions, translations, and transactions between varied social groups are pervasive concerns here. *Iber* captures the shifting of circumstance and of social stances at play. Mottel, for example, announces he will first give Eliahu's dialogue with the guard in Russian (*"ibergebn"*), and then that he will translate (*"ibersetsn"*) into Yiddish. The family tries to win a porter over to their side (*"iberbetn"*) as he passes the baggage over to its proper place (*"ibertrogn"*). In the train the family must traverse social and spatial distances in order to talk (they are scattered *"ibern gantsn vagon"*), and this sparks the mimicry of the *poritsl* (*"iberkrimn"*) that also traverses difference. Altogether, in stealing across the border, the family continually puts into relief the borders of their own discourse as it comes in contact with others. Showing the multiple stratifications of their language milieu, this chapter also shows how they have come to challenge the parameters of their own past life, at times making old, accepted definitions more fluid or more susceptible to reformulation or rejoinder.

As an uncomprehending outsider who playfully disregards society's rules, Mottel to some extent resembles that classic novelesque figure, the picaroon. Like the picaresque novel, Sholem Aleichem's narrative concerns ingenious struggles for livelihood and getting by in a world without a center. Thematically, Mottel most resembles the prototypical Lazarillo in his service to different masters: an apprenticeship to a mean-spirited cantor with a crippled daughter, a stay with a madman named Luria, his assistance in brother Elye's ill-conceived plans to get rich quick. More essentially, for discussion of the dialogic imagination in fiction, the status of the child as someone on the margins of adult activity recalls the marginality of the picaroon (who also often starts out on adventures at an early age, and whose naiveté or incomprehension helps him cast social convention in an unfamiliar light). Mottel fulfills comparable functions of undermining established values and ways of speaking. By quoting adult words and transforming them into his own, the boy allows for a highly ironic view of the foibles and moral unsoundness in his society. (Chaimova's deceptions and Pinney's impracticality are but two examples.) It should be noted, however, that the childhood angle of this narrative allows a more affectionate, less bitter satire of society than is characteristic of the picaresque novel proper. All incidents are cast finally in a lighthearted mold.

This phenomenon may be explained in accord with Ruth Wisse's assessment of Sholem Aleichem and his reaction to a discredited Haskalah. The Yiddish and Hebrew writers of the Enlightenment leveled severe criticism at Jewish society and urged self-improvement and measures of assimilation in order for the Jews to be accepted into European society. Such acceptance, of course, turned out not to be forthcoming. Sholem Aleichem, aware of Jewish shortcomings but even more aware of anti-Semitism and the hardships imposed on the Jews by others, was disinclined to view his own people too harshly. For these reasons, Wisse concludes, the only fictional characters in his work who successfully challenge tradition are children:

> The boy who would rather play with a calf than sit in the house of study, or the boy who would rather play the fiddle than adjust to the machinery of shtetl stratification, are the sole vehicles through whom the evils of shtetl life may safely be criticized. And only because they stand against all and any society, because they are more "unrealistic" than even their elders, and better still at denying the tyrannical crucible in which their tortured destiny is being forged.[25]

Mottel is just such a figure who, in rebellion against social strictures, does not abandon his community. He turns first to nature and then, in defiance of previous norms, to art (pledging to become a cartoonist). His innocence, though, takes the criminal edge off his own roguishness and mischief, even as it takes the harsh satirical bite off his portrayal of problems around him. In short, the dialogic capacities of the narrative persona in *Mottel* are used less to berate Jewish society than to register changes and uncertainties at a time of flux and mass emigrations.

Mottel does adhere to the model of the picaroon in a further way. The picaroon's recasting of the world generally entails no internal agony of consciousness, and this point distinguishes the picaresque from the Bildungsroman as a genre. Appearing as "a fixed personality who never substantially alters during the course of his varied experiences," the picaroon learns but does not change.[26] That is to say, the protagonist wises up, figures out how to play the game and to survive as a self uprooted and alone, but does not develop into a figure of complex psychological interiority. At issue is not discovery of self but thirst for experience and variety. Delighting in his adventures, such a character provides a panoramic view of changing circumstance. This lack of inwardness parallels or coincides with that of Mottel, who, more than a believable child, is a "typological amalgam" of childishness and maturity that serves the author's rhetorical purposes.[27] Certainly, he is distant even from the psychological depth explored in others of Sholem Aleichem's tales about children, such as "The Penknife" and "The Fiddle." Mottel, in his mischievousness, is detached from stable collective definitions of propriety and, refusing to be defined by the existing social system, is a figure who defines himself. His uncertain status, like that of the picaresque hero, makes him a suitable symbol for freedom from community. Associated with the artist and with individual expression, he is an ideal embodiment of the impulse to break loose from the old order. All the same, the deemphasis on depth and interiority in his characterization suggests that he is, finally, a narrative construct that gauges changing collective values, not a complex individual in his own right. Above all he consists of an intersection of discourses, and he resists being swallowed up in any one of them.

It seems only appropriate that in this narrative the artifice of imagined child language and the imagining of the child's imagination serve to depict transformations of communal circumstance more than to explore the inner dimensions of childhood. In Sholem Aleichem's text the orphan cut adrift from his father's past is not alone. The whole family and their entourage are part of a *"faryosemt"* folk, collectively orphaned in feeling cut off from the past and beset with a new beginning.[28] The novelty of the child's perspective reinforces this point clearly, as it shows adult assumptions to be unstable. Not only does Mottel confuse destruction and recovery, as Miron has argued. This narrative also dismantles the very opposition child/adult which in the traditional world decisively subordinated youngsters to their elders. Demonstrating the flux of changing circumstance and the breakdown of previous meanings, *Mottel* shows adults are childlike in their unpreparedness and vulnerability, even as childish resilience and disregard for tragedy come to signify an all-important vitality.

If, as has been argued,[29] the virtue of powerlessness, the sanctity of the insulted and the injured, constitutes the great theme of Yiddish literature, Mottel in his innocence represents a cheerful variation on the figure of the little man, long-suffering and antiheroic but able to bear up thanks to his own redeeming perceptions of the world. Moving beyond the earlier established portrayal of the child as little adult in Jewish literature, Mottel functions aptly as an example of *"dos kleyne men-tschele."* Sholem Aleichem's creation of a young narrator/protagonist makes only a very partial move toward exploring the consciousness of children in Jewish literature, but it yields an experiment that is at once innovative and an integral part of the wider concerns in this author's *oeuvre,* particularly in its treatment of Jewish accommodation to modernity.

4 HAYIM NAHMAN BIALIK— *AFTERGROWTH*

> *Could my eyes but open and, like the eyes of a child, light up,*
>
> . . . .
>
> *Once more I might stand before the world of pure wonder,*
> *a locked, sealed garden sown with riddles and marvels*
> *which no hand had touched, in which no word of mouth*
> *had ventured.*
>
> —H. N. Bialik, "One by One, When No One Sees"

*B*ialik's late essay "Gilui vekhisui balashon" ("Reveal-ment and Concealment in Language," 1915), has been read as a kind of *ars poetica* and a key to the writer's poetic *oeuvre*.[1] A concern with words as camouflage or disguise, voiced in "Gilui vekhisui," figures importantly in much of Bialik's lyric production. Many of his works echo, reinforce, or modify the essay's central contention that conventional language is but the husk of meaning. External and shallow, such language is easily dissociated from the matters of spiritual significance to which its words may refer. In this scheme of things, poetry serves to break open the bonds of conventional language and so rediscover meaning by uncovering perceptions previously masked or blocked by stale formulations. This prospect is seen by Bialik as at once beckoning and frightening, for it allows truths both beautiful and terrifying to emerge to consciousness even as it provides new access to deeper recesses of the individual's being.

The ideas articulated in "Gilui vekhisui" affirm a modernist understanding of the fundamentally nonmimetic nature of language and the consequent distrust of language that this understanding has engendered. Given Bialik's concern with the irreparable rift between world and word, the impact of modernism on this poet's thinking should not be underestimated.[2] However, while often heralded as twentieth-century inventions, these concerns also hark back to the romanticism with which Bialik's name is so firmly linked. The impenetrable subjectivity of ideas is a fundamental postulate of romantic aesthetics.[3] "The

65

sad incompetence of human speech" to which Wordsworth referred in
his "Prelude" is a concept close to Bialik's heart.[4] This is a concept, too,
that reverberates throughout Bialik's *Aftergrowth* (*Safiaḥ*), a piece of
prose fiction written in installments between 1908 and 1923. In this
narrative, strained relations between language and individual experience receive sustained thematic treatment. Indeed, the topic attains a
new intensity and crystallized focus as it coincides with Bialik's central
interest in childhood. Linguistic drama finds a natural stage in this story
of semiotic initiation as the plot follows a small Eastern European boy's
first encounters with language, his discovery of reading, and his exposure to sacred texts at the *heder*.

The gap between the sayable and the unsayable generates the
narrated events of *Aftergrowth*. It also fundamentally affects the narration itself. The various artistic approaches taken by the author in this
account of boyhood all center on a mature narrator who reminisces
about the long ago but can never recover it satisfactorily in words. In this
way the text underscores one of the most problematic aspects of retrospective self-narration. The present verbal act can never recapture the
nonverbal reality of past experience. *Aftergrowth* accentuates this problem, for it begins with a child character defined as an infant, in the
etymological sense of the word meaning "one without language." Dealing with a prelinguistic phase of life, this text delineates the radical
difficulty of inhabiting the perspective of the child, that is, of describing
in words the inner life of a creature who has not yet entered the universe
of discourse employed by the adult writer.

For these reasons the entire text is also informed by issues that
have recently gained prominence in the theoretical discussion of autobiography. The autobiographical enterprise has increasingly been
viewed as self-definition or self-invention, which entails an alienation
from self. There is a growing tendency to acknowledge writing as a
process of loss and to view language as an instrument that distances
literary expression from a lived past.[5] Yael Feldman argues that the new
models of autobiography share in common a recognition of

> a gradual historical shift from the belief in some kind of presence (be it
> physical, metaphysical, psychological, or metaphoric) which has war-
> ranted the possibility of restitution, to a contemporary awareness of
> absence (of a tangible life, an imagined self or the language to recon-
> struct it), one that may spell out the death of autobiography.[6]

Feldman continues on to say that in this debate one can recognize
the "ghost of Lacan hovering over his 'subject,'" snatching away the last

remnants of romantic belief in the "recreative and individualizing powers of language" (191). Now, if it is recognized that this spectral Lacanian force was beginning to emerge already out of romanticism, and if it is acknowledged that belief in the recreative powers of language was not unshaken even for Wordsworth, it then seems less anachronistic to consider these very qualities as prominent features of Bialik's *Aftergrowth*. The interpretation of childhood in this narrative, formulated as it is from within the framework of Bialik's later understandings of language, makes this fiction peculiarly amenable to reading in contemporary terms of loss, absence, and referential doubt.

Only partly an act of nostalgia and retrieval by a mature writer, *Aftergrowth* also serves as a forum in which to rehearse linguistic concerns and demonstrate the impossibility of recovering the past. Not abstract, these issues are grounded specifically in the profound cultural transitions the writer himself experienced. Like other writers of the Hebrew Renaissance, Bialik made an accelerated transition from the traditional Jewish world into the modern age and Western values.[7] This process involved the adoption and exploration of new languages, an education in European texts, an abandonment of the mother tongue (Yiddish), and a studied effort to overhaul Hebrew and revive it for the purposes of a new, secular Jewish culture. Thus, distrust of language and autobiographical writing, pervasive in modernist and postmodernist thinking, evolved for Bialik through a very concrete phenomenon of loss and displacement from roots.

Preoccupation with clashing cultural values and expression, arising from the author's literary historical circumstances, gains direct thematic importance in the narrative as the child views tradition and holy writ naively. Seeing "otherwise" the religious texts of Judaism, the young character stands outside the tradition and then later comes to appropriate it into his own imagination. Taking on the function deemed proper to poetry in "Gilui vekhisui," the young figure embodies a novelty of perception that ultimately breaks apart old words to discover new meaning and vitality in language. A product of the author's imagination, this character serves as an intimate stranger, a consciousness familiar with sacred language yet viewing it anew. The boy thus conveys the distances Bialik himself traversed as he moved away from an Orthodox upbringing to struggle with new, nationalist definitions of Jewishness and valorization of individual, private vision.

To understand the ramifications of these issues in *Aftergrowth*, it is worthwhile first to look at the thematization of linguistic drama at the level of narrated events, then to move to analysis of the ways in which similar concerns affect the narration itself.

Attention to words, speech, and writing functions as a crucial structuring device of the plot in *Aftergrowth* and divides the text into four clearly discernible sections.

The initial segment dwells on the protagonist's earliest days, before he has reached the age of five. Patterned after the opening passages of Sholem Aleichem's *Mottel, The Cantor's Son*, the first paragraphs present a little boy reveling in the out-of-doors.[8] This character, like Mottel, comes from a traditional family in an Eastern European milieu. And, like Sholem Aleichem, Bialik invokes a motif widely familiar in nineteenth-century Hebrew and Yiddish literature; the text celebrates the world of nature often denied the Jewish boy, who—in a pious society—was expected to attend solely to the world of sacred study. In contrast to Mottel, though, who flees to the woods in rebellion against *heder* instruction, Bialik's protagonist is not yet of school age. Later this child will resent the world of the *heder,* but in the opening portions of *Aftergrowth* Bialik extends and expands the familiar motif, the split between learning and nature, inscribing it into a wider opposition between language and being. Delighting in the loveliness of grass and sky, his character does not need language to apprehend what he calls the primal sights (*"hamar'ot harishonim"*).[9] These defy communication and are presented as both preceding and exceeding language. More profound than words, they come from "fathomless deeps of silence" and form part of a primordial archetypal universe encountered by the boy, Shmulik, when he is still so young that he does not yet know "how to ask questions or call things by their name" (40). The narrator evokes the deep sense of wonder characterizing this age by underscoring its ineffable qualities:

> There would be neither utterance nor speech; nothing but a seeing. What speech there was in all these had neither voice nor sound. A magical speech it was, that came as required. Though sound as such had been sublimated therefrom, yet it was fully existent as speech. Myself, I never heard it with my ears; it entered my soul through some other, hidden portal. In some such way the throbbing heart of a mother and her loving gaze reach the soul of the baby asleep in its cradle when she stands tremulous at his head. (42)

> אין אמר ואין דברים – זולתי מראה. גם הדבור שבהם אין קול ואין
> הברה לו. דבור פלאים הוא, בריה לשעתה, שהקול התנדף ממנו – והוא
> קָיָם. וגם אני לא בְאָזְנַי שמעתיו, כי דרך מבוא אחר, נעלם, הגיע אל
> נפשי. כן יַגִיע אל נפש עולל נרדם בערישתו המון לב אמו ורהמי
> עיניה בְעָמְדָה עליו למראשותיו נפעמת וַחֲרָדָה, (173)

As suggested by the concluding reference to mother/child relations, the meditation on language in the first portion of *Aftergrowth* takes on distinctly psychological nuances. In this connection the narrative anticipates much later accounts of interdependence between psychic and linguistic development. Jacques Lacan's theories offer a set of conceptual coordinates that are particularly useful in charting the drama of *Aftergrowth*. The protagonist progresses through events that recall Lacan's emphasis on deprivation as an unavoidable part of the child's emotional and cognitive growth.[10]

First, Shmulik's evolving experience conforms to the psychoanalytic supposition that infants, at birth, do not differentiate between the self and the outside world. Instead, the child enters into a world of distinctions, discrimination, identity, and difference only later and, in significant measure, through the acquisition of language. Initially, reality for the child means the body of the mother. Subsequently, with increasing separation from the maternal figure, a new attachment develops for substitute objects. To the child experiencing absence, these provide a feeling of wholeness, restitution, and pleasure. Trying to introject itself into such objects, the body does not yet recognize boundaries or distinguish itself from others or the world outside of it. Much of the opening portion of *Aftergrowth* could be read as a description of just this process. "My soul," the narrator recounts, "entered like some possessing spirit into the deeps of each thing, and dwelt mid trees and speechless stones, absorbing all they contained and giving nothing in return" (56). Indeed, the wholeness and sense of divine wonder the young child experiences are attributed quite explicitly to a withdrawal of parental nurturing and a substitute feeling of oneness with surrounding objects. The boy's sensations of merging or union with nature flourish precisely because he has been abandoned to his own devices: "None took me by the hand, none bore me in mind. I wandered solitary around my nest as might an orphan fledgling. My father and mother let me be; no eye yearned over me" (40).

The sense of orphanhood is associated with the birth of aesthetic sensibility.[11] Though Shmulik's parents are, in fact, still alive, abandonment is an integral part of the narrator's definitions of his origins. The first indication of the link between isolation and artistic sensitivity is the title. "*Safiaḥ*," that which is not cultivated but grows nonetheless (Leviticus 25), was assigned conventionalized meaning in nineteenth-century Hebrew literature and came to signify the lonely imagination. Y. L. Gordon identified the notion of "aftergrowth" with the figure of the poet, disregarded by society, whose work is a product of isolation. The writer in this view is both less and more than other people. Often misunderstood, the artist nonetheless is blessed with a special creative gift or appreciation for beauty.[12] Within Bialik's narrative, it is Shmulik's sense of loss that propels him toward a life of the imagination and toward self-expression as a way to restore a feeling of communion. Compensating for his loneliness, he clings to his perceptions of beauty; these are described as the "brightest and most vivid sights" of a lifetime, and they are characterized as "alms and charity of God," granted the boy because of his "tender years and helplessness" (40). These emphases of the text, together with the title, help establish a set of tensions between absence and sought-for wholeness, which will define the entire narrative. It is within this framework that the novella examines the child's relation to language.

Following the extended commentary on early childhood in chapter 1, *Aftergrowth* directs attention to these issues by shifting away from contemplative musing to a sharper focus on specific actions. The narrator introduces variations on the theme of absence by recounting a series of episodes, all concerned with weaning. He notes that as a baby he was given to a wet nurse whose milk had dried up; he also recalls sucking his thumb, and he explains, too, that he once tried to milk a wall. These incidents then culminate in a scene that accords roughly with Lacan's notion of "the mirror stage." According to this model, the child first apprehends himself or herself as a unified, coherent totality by seeing a reflection or an image (literally in a mirror, or in the reactions of those who tend to the child). Previous to that time the infant has no conception of itself as a unity distinct from the outside world. The mirror stage confers a felicitous illusion of wholeness and autonomy. This same event, though, depends on perceiving that self as other, as something exterior to the body. This image of the self is a double that externalizes and distorts as it reverses and rigidifies. An alienation is inevitable in this stage, which Lacan dubs the "imaginary order" (because it is based on an imagined unity of self). That alienation is later surpassed by an even greater one, which accompanies the next quantum leap into social existence. The transition into what is called the "symbolic order" comes about through the entrance into language and so into culturally orchestrated values. This advance necessarily entails additional distancing and division, for the child begins to conceive of himself or herself as part of a system of preexisting understandings and definitions. Even before its birth, a name was ready and waiting for the baby. The child therefore has always figured in a set of established interpersonal and collective relations. Discovering this circumstance, the young person must accept discontinuity between the earliest experiences of sensation or inner feeling and the self as it is assigned or defined from without. That is to say, painful choices attend the entry into language. Submission to the discursive practices of society is a necessary step if the child is to function as a healthy human being, but it is a step that creates division between the conscious subject, the "I" who speaks (and which can be designated as

conscious because it is able to feature in discourse) and those other parts
of the same human being—the subconscious or the preverbal, for
example—only partially represented, or unrepresentable, in discourse.

It is clearly significant that Shmulik's transition from the wondrous world of his early childhood sensibilities to the symbolic world of
texts is marked by his encounter with a mirror. Of all the furniture in the
house, Shmulik is most attracted to the looking glass. Discovering himself in it (57–59), he observes his own image with joyous delight. He
also reacts with trepidation, however, sensing that this image must be
something alien, perhaps manipulated by an imp or evil spirit hiding
behind the wall. Noting that the mirror was "the greatest riddle in the
universe," the adult narrator recalls himself alternating between fascination and fear, laughter and perplexity:

> Another Shmulik stood directly facing me so that our very noses
> touched. I drew back a little; so did he. I drew near and he did the
> same. In that case I had to make a face and poke my tongue out; he did
> the same. "Hee hee hee," I laughed. He laughed as well but without
> the hee hee hee; I felt a little afraid; but still I stared. (58)

> שמואליק שני עומד כנגדי ממש וחוטמו נוגע בחוטמי. נרתעתי קצת
> לאחורי — ואף הוא נרתע. מתקרב אני — אף הוא מתקרב. אם כן,
> הרי אני מעוה את פני ושולח לשון — ואף חוא כך. חי–חי–חי" —
> משחק אני — ואף חוא משחק, אבל בלא "חי–חי–חי", שאין קולו
> נשמע. הדבר תמוה, ואני מתירא קצת — ואף–על–פי–כן
> מסתכל... (182–83)

The passage describes a disconcerting process of self-definition, one that
in a seemingly contradictory way grants both new self-recognition and
also a feeling of being splintered, not of one piece.

This moment of divided identity ushers in another that yields an
increased sense of fragmentation: the boy pokes at the mirror, it comes
crashing down around him and shatters all the world it contains—
including the reflection of himself. *This* rupture then sets the stage (and
symbolically anticipates) the rupture yet to come: a transition of focus
to the even more discontinuous realm of the symbolic order. The narrative announces, "on the same day it was decided that I must go to
heder." Shmulik's father, who has been annoyed by the boy's daydreaming and his undisciplined behavior (such as the attempt to milk the wall),
seizes on this occasion as the time to send his son to a *melamed.* The
teacher is to make Shmulik mind by imposing on him the most respected
discourse of the symbolic order: the authoritative word of scripture. Just
as the boy's earlier attempts to merge with the natural world disappeared, acceding to the sense of self evident in the mirror scene, now his
unified image, too, is gone. Indeed, the narrator recalls that the first

contact with *heder* "drove from me all my childhood vision" (44).[13]

Bialik's narrative diverges from the Lacanian model in a number of ways. The mirror stage, for instance, is deemed to occur between 6 and 18 months. Shmulik, if he is ready for *heder,* is clearly older than that. It is also debatable whether Lacan promotes his ideas as a precise description of developmental processes, or whether he proposes a conceptual framework that allows him to excavate the layeredness of subjectivity by distinguishing different kinds of mental activity.[14] However, his ideas remain highly useful here because they make clear some key issues in evidence during Shmulik's interactions with his surroundings. During the early scenes of *Aftergrowth* the mirror is instrumental in organizing the child's first moves toward a conscious subject position as the self is constructed within culture. The coming episodes in the fiction then mark a singular intensification in the way Shmulik feels the consequences of the human condition as a life within language. Confronted with his new circumstances, the child must react against and learn to cope with the basic disunities fostered by the symbolic.

At first unwilling to accept this state of affairs, Shmulik resists his schooling. The protagonist disregards the distance between the non-linguistic realm and what he sees on the printed page. Trying to invest the alphabet with a mimetic quality, to recapture the immediacy of vision he experienced earlier, he regards letters not as signs that correspond to phonetic equivalents but as icons that conjure up his own imaginary beings. He comes to fancy the *alephs* as soldiers, "all arms swinging and legs striding" (60), and he sees the *sin* as a horned snake with three heads, while the *lamed* becomes a stork, "stretching out its neck and standing on one leg" (62). Altogether he finds in his prayerbook a "vast medley of weird creatures." Not yet ready to deal with disjunction between signifiers and signifieds, he clings to attributes of the imaginary order, taking joy in visual resemblances and images.[15]

For his failure to grasp the rift between word and world and his consequent inability to master the alphabet, the boy meets with the derision of the other children and brings upon himself the wrath and punishment of the teacher; a cruel, ill-tempered man appears here as the stereotype of the hateful *melamed.* In reaction, the child withdraws into his shell and shuns both reading and companionship. However, after this early trauma a transition does take place, signaling a major shift in the narrator's presentation of relations between language and the imagination. Eventually Shmulik discovers that the same obstacles he has met with in reading are also its rewards. While he fails to recover a mimetic, iconic link between words and his own perceptions, he begins to appreciate how language offers freedom from context. With the help

of a new and more kindly teacher the boy overcomes his initial failures.
He progresses beyond the mechanics of sounding out words, starts to
grasp stories as a whole, and realizes with enchantment that language,
because it is not identical with the world to which it refers, can convey
events that happened long ago and far away. Through language these
events take on new life in the here and now. Even in the gloomy, dilapi-
dated hovel where he studies, legendary and biblical figures approach
little Shmulik. The narrator observes with satisfaction, "Here I was,
conversing with all these ancients and participating in their life and
deeds" (91). The stories this child reads appeal to him so much that he
immerses himself in them, letting his reading become his world. An
ordinary walk home from school, therefore, is recounted in the following manner:

> On my way I had joined the caravan of the Ishmaelites or of the men of
> Dodan and I had not departed from them. Where they had gone, I
> would go; and where they lodged, there did I stay.
>
> By day we crossed the desert, a land of drouth and thirst, the
> dwelling place of serpent, basilisk and scorpion. . . .
>
> At one spot we are joined by the Gibeonites. . . . None of the
> caravan knows who they are, or what they desire, except me, Shmulik,
> since I know all their secrets and subterfuges in advance out of the
> Book of Joshua. (97–98)

> בדרך נטפלתי לאורחת ישמעאלים או לשיָרת דְנים וידי לא זזה מתוך
> ידם. באשר ילכו אלך ובאשר ילינו אליןָ...
> יומם נעבור במדבריות, בארץ צִיה וצמאון, מקום נחש, שרף ועקרב.
> באחד המקומות ילָווּ אלינו גם הגבעונים [...] איש מן השיָרה לא יַדע מי
> הם ומה בלבם, חוץ ממני שמואליק, לפי שאני – כבר נגלו לי כל
> תעלומותיהם למפרע, מתוך ספר יהושע... (208)

Past and present, secular and sacred converge in Shmulik's understanding. "The valley of the shadow," he deduces, must mean the nearby
ruin populated with evil spirits, and "in the presence of all mine enemies" alludes to the young non-Jewish urchins who torment him. By
merging his reading with his fantasy life and his daily milieu, the child
moves beyond his early grief over the dissociation of words from being.
Having acquired the basic linguistic tools he is expected to master,
having attained proficiency in the cultural codes of his social setting, he
has sacrificed unrestrained imaginative freedom for a measure of power.
Conforming to adult expectations, he masters the text to the point
where improvisation becomes possible, and so he finds a new liberty in
the power of interpretation—circumscribed within particular limits, to
be sure, but admitting of whimsy and a certain amount of creativity.[16]
This successful compromise marks the completion of the child's semio-

tic initiation and restores a measure of harmony and satisfaction to Shmulik's life.

Thus far, then, three major movements have structured the text. In the first stage the separation between the linguistic and the nonlinguistic is so absolute that the child is blissfully unaware of it. In the second stage the gap between those opposing realms is reconfirmed as the child meets the written word and attempts, unsuccessfully, to appropriate this language into his own sensibility. In the third movement the child does successfully integrate the adult discourse and his own imaginative thinking. Finding that he cannot entirely escape the dictates of the symbolic order (the discursive practices, categories of thought, and narrative patterns accepted by his culture), Shmulik can press them into the service of his own fantasy life and so reassert the worth of his private perceptions.

This thematic division corresponds closely to other recognized divisions in the text. As Gershon Shaked documents in a detailed explication of the narrative, *Aftergrowth* was written in several stages. The text consequently reflects different moments of recollection and differing attitudes toward the past.[17] This compositional history resulted in four principal sections of text, which display distinctive tones and relations between adult narrator and child character.

According to this analysis, the first segment is an essay that defines childhood as paradise and expresses romantic yearnings to recapture this lost Garden of Eden. Offering a lyrical celebration of the past and of the child's capacity for wonder, Bialik's essayistic narrative also poses ironic commentary on the impossibility of regaining paradise. The second part of *Aftergrowth* then presents anecdotes about the child's confrontation with authority and so pits imagination against social reality through dramatic plot action. The third portion constitutes a humoristic, idyllic panorama of Shmulik's natural and social surroundings. Comparisons between the elevated diction of sacred source texts and the lowly reality of the physical world described through those terms recall similar rhetorical strategies in Mendele's *Of Bygone Days*. Here, though, the tone is much less strident. Bialik's purpose is not social satire but a reliving of boyhood that takes joy in the young character's reveries and also puts those visions back in proportion. Viewing them from an adult perspective as immature and naive, the narrator's stance indicates an indulgent, affectionate acceptance of the child's limited yet creative perceptions. The fourth section of *Aftergrowth* presents a symbolic vision of childhood experience and *eros*. Altogether, Shaked concludes that these sections present separate explorations of man's relations to the roots of his existence.

A consideration of the linguistic themes of *Aftergrowth* significantly supplements this understanding of the narrative's structure. Such
a consideration recognizes that language is a crucial factor in the relation between imagination and reality at each stage of the narrated
events. The child figure's earliest struggles result from the clash between
language and a sense of well-being. Shmulik's education, moreover, is
highly textual, and his resolution of the conflict is also verbal. An opposition between social language and essentially incommunicable private perception is reflected, too, in the artistry of the text. As this narrator elects to express himself verbally, despite or because of the very
problems outlined in the plot, Bialik incorporates into his modes of
writing in the various sections of the text those very same issues the
young protagonist must face. This endeavor progresses through several
stages. The opening section sets up the problem of articulating the
preverbal wonder of the childhood world and immediately provides an
overview, a preface, and a disclaimer for the impossibility of the task the
adult narrator has assigned himself. He tries to do justice to the ineffable
by being circumspect. Emphasizing the unrecountability of wonder, the
narrator warns the reader that he is attempting something inherently
undoable. After section 1 defines the text as essentially counterfeit, a
false representation of childhood, the other sections come to function as
rejoinder and counterexample to the very assumptions set out at the
start. These portions of narrative constitute the answer of the writer, an
individual who turns to art—despite its handicaps—to confront and
transform disjunctions between past and present. This activity reaches
its greatest fulfillment in the fourth part of *Aftergrowth*.

Section 1 postulates and enacts the greatest distance between narrator and character. Supposing clearly separate realms of existence for
adult and child, the narrator devises a rhetorical strategy to emphasize
that existential chasm. To begin with, the text orients itself to the province of adult language. There are a variety of ways that imagined children characters can speak through adult narrators, ranging from techniques that directly cite the character's words, to authorial rearticulation
of a character's internal utterances, to narratorial commentary on or
assessments of the character's inner thoughts. The initial section of
Aftergrowth offers virtually no intersection of voice between the mature
storyteller and his former child self. Instead, the narrator engages in
dialogue with other grown-ups. Speaking to unidentified readers about
a fabulous, wonder-filled world, he is constantly aware that his audience
may be skeptical about tales that insist on magic and fantastic occurrences. He makes many qualifying remarks to head off such skepticism.[18] Adding to this orienting of narrative to the reader, the narrator
acknowledges openly that there is no authentic entrance into the child's

mind. He restricts himself to discussing his early inner life only from without, and he even spells out his authorial quandaries:

> I do not remember how often summer and winter went by from the time I became aware of myself in my native village till we all left it for the suburb of the neighboring town. I was still nothing more than a child playing in the dirt, not yet five full years old, it would seem; and what sense of time or sequence can an infant have? In my native village, presumably the course of Nature around me was not other than normal; season came and season went at the appointed time, and the world made its customary round. Yet that primal archetypal Universe which I brought out of the village with me, and which still lies hid in some especial nook of my heart's secret places—that strange, wondrous, singular world can never, it would seem, have known autumn or winter. (39)

> כמה תקופות קַיץ וחֹרף עברו עלי משעה שנגליתי לנפשי בכפר מולדתי
> עד אותה שעה שיצאנו משם, אני ובית אבי, לגור בפרבר של העיר
> הקרובה — איני זוכר. תינוק מוטל באשפה הייתי, עוד לא מָלְאוּ לי,
> כמדומה, חמש שנים תמימות, ומה סדר זמנים יש לתינוק? ודאי גם
> בכפר מולדתי לא נשתנו עלי סדרי בראשית: תקופה באה ותקופה
> יצאה בשעתה והעולם כמנהגו נהג. אבל אותו העולם הראשון, הקדמוני,
> שהוצאתיו עמי מן הכפר וַעֲדַיִן הוא כמוס עִמָּדִי במדור מיוחד לו בגנזי
> לבי – אותו העולם המשונה, הפלאי, היחידי – הוא, כמדומה, שלא ידע
> חֹרף וסתיו מימיו. (172)

This passage starts by presenting itself as a memory, but only in a negative sense: namely, as a failure of recall. "I do not remember," the narrator avers. This maneuver establishes a retrospective vantage point and also an emphasis on the past as something irrecoverable. Time in the primordial world was neither accountable nor, afterward, accessible, for it is not part of the world of adult discourse. It cannot be presented either in its own terms or in the narrator's mature terms, and so can be referred to only as a denial of what is familiar. Accordingly, the wonder described is defined by contrast with those things known to the readers, hence the obtrusive reference to that which is "customary" (keminhago) and "normal." (In the Hebrew, with more resonance, the phrase translated here as the "course of Nature" appears as sidrei bereshit, i.e., the order of the natural world as established in the beginning and recounted in Genesis.) Hallowed by tradition and dictated from without by an all-powerful divinity, the first days of creation stand in opposition to Shmulik's own earliness. His world, operating from a different sense of time, is "all of summer" (40), knowing neither "autumn or winter." Designating the youngster's universe as "wondrous" and "singular," the text here contrasts grown-up presuppositions with childish distortions but clearly cherishes the latter. Bialik buttresses this rhetorical stance with such expressions as "presumably" (*vadai*) and "it would seem" (*kamedumeh*). Disavowing the child's perceptions, insisting that the seasons long ago must have operated in the usual fashion, the narrator stops short of entirely endorsing the ordinary. A tentativeness remains in this formulation of matters, and that element of doubt opens a gap in the adult view, preparing the way for a subsequent plunge into description of the child's perspective. A definitive distinction has been made between *then* and *now,* but this division does not discount the value of the child's world.

Later, just as reference to the timeless paradise is achieved through an awareness of time and remembering, so the prelinguistic world is described in terms of language. The narrator defines his former existence by what it is not. Gesturing toward a world that does not assume a binary opposition between words and silence, he speaks oxymoronically of a "speech without utterance" or "speech which is seeing." The statement is at once a deconstruction, made possible by the marginal position of the child beyond the borders of usual language, and a reconfirmation that the text itself is governed by the terms of the adult discourse. Evidence of the narrator's presence emerges, too, through the generalizations he makes ("what sense of time or sequence can a child have?"). That same authorial control nonetheless repeatedly undercuts itself and honors the mysterious world of the child. The narrator creates ambivalence, for instance, by inserting into the voice of accepted truth an observation that would seem to defy his rational stance. Remembering a windstorm that carried Shmulik soaring into the air, he queries, "Who can be so simpleminded as to try to tell others of my sensations during that flight? Only in dreams at night can a man enjoy even a sixtieth part thereof" (48).

The second part of *Aftergrowth* features a new attention to the child's voice. This portion of the text diminishes the extreme distance between child character and adult narrator that was evident in the first section. Though still distinctly separate realms, the boy's world is no longer unreportable nor absolutely without language. Here, for instance, dialogues in direct speech are introduced for the first time. In the following exchange, the *melamed*'s assistant shows the child the first letter of the alphabet:

> "Can you see the yoke and pair of pails?"
> "That's true, upon my soul; a yoke and pair of pails."
> "Well, that's an *aleph,*" testified the assistant.
> "Well, that's an *aleph,*" I repeated after him.
> "What's this?" the assistant asked again.
> "A yoke and pair of pails," I replied, highly delighted that the Holy and Blest One had sent me such fine utensils.

"No. Say *aleph*," repeated the assistant and went on, "Remember: *aleph, aleph.*" (61–62)

"רואה אתה אֵסָל וזוג דליים?..."

"אמת, בחיי ראשי, אסל וזוג דליים..."

"הרי זו אל"ף", מעיד הסגן.

"הרי זו אל"ף", שונח אני אחריו.

"מה זאת?" שואל שוב הסגן.

"אסל ושני דליים", אומר אני ונהנה הנאה גדולה על שהזמין לי, הקדוש–ברוך–הוא כאן כלים נאים אלו.

"לא, אמור אל"ף!" חזר הסגן ואומר, "זכור: אל"ף, אל"ף". (185)

Though the child's words are misunderstood and unappreciated by his fictional interlocutor, the reader has direct access to this character's speech and so can appreciate much of what Shmulik intends. Still, the narrator does not entrust presentation of inner life entirely to the child's verbal competence but tries to recreate or reenact sensations as the child perceived them. For example, a new proliferation of onomatopoeic devices serves to reinforce awareness of the child's perceptions. A crackling fire is presented in the following way: *"pak," "tsss," "hmmm," "prrr"* (71).

In this second section of *Aftergrowth* a marked distance nonetheless remains between narrator and character. This is apparent particularly in the use of speculative and explanatory comments that show the authorial figure to be informed of events after the fact. He reminisces, for instance, that the other children dubbed him with the nickname "noodle." Asking, "why *loksch?*" (81), the adult recounts how Shmulik called undue attention to a noodle dribbling down his teacher's chin and so called down a series of cruel punishments on himself. The narrator also makes remarks that reveal his retrospective advantage: "In the *heder* I had meanwhile risen to the next class." Statements of this sort depend on sequence, chronological ordering of incident, and a temporal overview, all of which are unavailable to the child and which are played down in part 1 in favor of abstract commentary on the timelessness of the child's perceptions. Other indications of the adult's cognitive privilege surface when the narrator passes judgment on Shmulik the child. He applies distancing appellations to himself, for example, when he calls his former self a "simpleton" (79). At times he also makes a more compassionate appraisal of the past. Recalling that his innocent daydreaming had enraged his father, the now-mature Shmulik asks, in total sympathy with the child, "And what was the harm that I did him?" (71).

Part 3 continues to close the gap between the language of adult narration and the young character. Because Shmulik has acquired the basic set of signs valued by his culture, both he and his later self can now use the same vocabulary. Each, to be sure, endows those words with different valence. Whereas the child imagines those around him to be Gibeonites and the men of Dodan as well as a host of other biblical figures, the narrator points out what the villagers are not and shows how they suffer by comparison with glorious prototypes. The neighbors are decidedly not Zuzim or Zamzummim, neither valiant nor larger than life like the ancient warrior tribes described in the Bible.[19]

The fourth and concluding portion of the text follows up on this continuing process of approximation between adult and child. However, here there is less a synthesis of the two voices—in the form of free indirect discourse or related techniques—than a disregard for the difficulties inherent in retrospective narration. In a sense this segment tries to transcend the dichotomy wrestled with at such length in the preceding sections. The narrator once more tries to recreate the earliest days of childhood. He observes that his thoughts carry him back to that remote era, but his presentation is notably different in emphasis from the opening of Chapter 1. First, for instance, consider his celebration of silence. Shmulik and his beloved, Feigele, stroll through an idyllic landscape "singing at the top of their voices—yet without word or tune" (123). Theirs is a joy that allegedly exceeds language, much as the opening paragraphs of the narrative would have predicted. Here, though, the text posits this state of affairs without any apology or commentary on the inability of words to convey such plenitude. The prelinguistic character of the infantile world is taken for granted. Similarly, toward the end of the fourth section, there is a vision of elves singing "not with their mouths, but as from within themselves and their very souls, without a sound, as the stars sing" (128).

Complementing this emphasis of the text, Bialik directs heightened attention to the visual. If the magical speech of chapter 1 is claimed to be "without utterance," a kind of seeing, here there is renewed recognition of that quality in the intensity of graphic detail, which conveys a variety of scenes: the walk with Feigele into the blossoming trees, a vista of arid barrenness in which two bulls gore each other, and later, a raging, mystic fire. This section ends with a peculiarly visual delight. The small boy stares into four glass marbles, marveling as these simple instruments tinge the world with wondrous color. For their treatment of erotic impulse, religious revelation, and fears of death and sterility, as well as for their imaginative vision, these scenes make for the work's most compelling moments of psychological insight. Indeed, all have elicited considerable critical commentary.[20] For the purposes of my discussion, the scenes are of interest above all for their abdication of the previously central focus on language. That preoccupation has all but disappeared or is negated through the insistence on silence. This is the point at which the narrator tries to say all the things that in the earlier chapters he was at pains to characterize as unsayable.

One of the narrator's strategies for carrying out that project is to employ prose that approaches a density often associated with poetry. (Significantly, this move recalls Bialik's insistence, in "Gilui vekhisui balashon," on the power of poetry to express that which is inexpressible through other modes of discourse. The masters of prose, Bialik writes, are devoted to conventional meaning, "that which is established and consistent in language," the "accepted version of things"; the poets, by contrast, "flee all that is fixed and inert in language," introducing instead "never-ending motion, new combinations and associations" [136]). As Shaked has noted, in the final section of *Aftergrowth* Bialik's extended descriptive passages rely heavily on anaphora, alliteration, and internal rhyme.[21] These features contribute to a blurring of boundaries between words, both semantically and musically. The result is to heighten the obtrusiveness of the words themselves, as if to underscore that the language is symbolic and that it points at more than simply the natural phenomena the words denote. In the process the heavily pictorial writing becomes an expressive vehicle for the protagonist's inner spiritual states, projected onto the external world. This assessment applies, for instance, to a description of a spring morning:

> Roofs and trees drip with gold; buds and blossoms wear necklaces of pearls and weep with joy. On the trail of the hill, in the damp sand, lies a strip of glass, glittering and glittering away as though it had suddenly become great and mighty. Lord God! How many suns! How many heavens! Each dribble of water has its sun within it; every pool and puddle its own heaven for backing. Fragments of worlds upside down and sections of new skies under the water. They are infinite in number, veritably three hundred and ten worlds, as the number which is kept for every righteous man! Birds amid the branches and little chicks in the grass go crazy with joy, open their throats, spread out their wings, open their beaks and sing at the top of their voices. (122–23)

> גגות ואילנות נוטפים זהב וציצים ופרחים חורזים פנינים ובוכים מאושר. על משעול הגבעה, בחול הרטוב שם, מוטל רסיס זכוכית והוא נוצץ ונוצץ, כְּאִילוּ עלה פתאם לגדולה. אֵל אלהים! כמה שמשות! כמה רקיעים! אגם אגם ושמש בקרבו, שלולית שלולית ורקיע מתחתה. שברי עולמות הפוכים וגזרי רקיעים חדשים מתחת למים עד לאין מספר – ש"י עולמות! צִפֳּרִים מבין עָפאים ואפרוחים רכים מבין חציר משתגעים מחדוָה והם משרבבים גרון, פורשׂים גפים, פוצים פיפיות – וצֹוְחים וצֹוְחים... שיר ושבח מלמעלה, רון ופצח מלמטה. (225)

Shaked observes that the musicality of this selection derives in large part from parallelisms, the pairing of rhyming words, and repetitions (*tsitsim-perahim; potsim-pipiyot; 'agam-'agam; tsovhim-tsovhim*). These qualities of the prose work together with personification (for example, buds weep with joy), which blurs distinctions between the animate and the inanimate. In conjunction with conspicuous images of multiplicity, frequent repetitions, and an abundance of synonyms, all of these characteristics foster a suggestion of exuberance and vitality. These in turn effectually reveal the enthusiasms of a young boy as the child's imagination transforms the scene about him into a vision of radiant beauty. Sidestepping the issue of verisimilitude, Bialik gestures toward that which exceeds language; a multiplication of signs here reenacts analogically the proliferation of natural beauties.

These features are typical of other passages, too, in addition to the one Shaked points out. As Feigele walks with Shmulik, for instance, the butterflies around them are presented through a series of repeated *r* and *f* sounds that, gliding in and out of one another, suggest a rustling motion: "*haparparim rafu kanfeihem vehem merafrafim 'at 'at.*" The passage verges on onomatopoeia even as it calls attention to its own musicality. Later another passage encapsulates such techniques as Shmulik has a fiery vision that he takes to be a revelation of the deity:

> Fire! fire! all the corners of the earth and heaven are being consumed by fire. Streams of fire and mountains of fire, palaces of fire and forests of fire. Fire catches fire in the fire; and fire consumes fire. Red fire, white fire and green fire. Horsemen of fire and horses of fire are flying about, and burning lions chase in pursuit of them. And behold the dread and glorious God descending in fire. (124–25)

> אש אש! כל כנפות הארץ והשמים היו למאכולת אש. נחלי אש והררי אש. ארמנות אש ויערות אש. אש מתלקחת בתוך האש ואש אוכלה אש. אש אדומה. אש לבנה ואש ירוקה. רכב אש וסוסי אש ידודון וכפירים בוערים דולקים אחריהם. והנה זה האלהים נורא הוד יורד באש... (226)

These lines are marked by anaphoric reiteration of the word "fire" (*esh*). Suggesting abundance, this repetition has onomatopoeic effect as well. In allusion to mystical, Merkavah literature and apocalyptic writing, the conflagration is also animated, if not quite personified, as horses of fire (*susei esh*). In addition, a series of oppositions is set up (palaces and forests, rivers and mountains). Together with the range of colors mentioned, the effect is to signal an all-inclusive proliferation, to dramatize a bursting of flame everywhere, and so to indicate a sense of overwhelming awe on the part of the little boy. As it draws on the visual emphasis typical in this concluding section of *Aftergrowth*, this passage shows the author attempting to meld sound and sense, to move beyond the strictly denotative power of language and to gesture toward epiphany through a plenitude of words.

This move bears contradictory results, of course, for language here also calls attention to itself even as it purports to convey a nonverbal reality. The author, in short, is caught in the bind defined at the beginning of *Aftergrowth,* and he cannot extricate himself from the opposition between language and experience posited there. While here exists the most evidence of an attempt to recapture a mimetic link in writing, this is also the most pointedly verbal part of the work. These sentences direct attention back to language, the medium itself, and prevent words from acting as a transparent vehicle for an extralinguistic reality. The musicality, the overt intertextuality, and the defining of expanse through binary opposition all ground this passage in inherently linguistic phenomena and foreground its verbal artifice.

This development merits closer consideration, for it reintroduces into the narrative a connection between linguistic drama and the psychological issues established in the early chapters. That is, as the ending represents a renewed attempt to return to the early paradise (and fears) of childhood, it also recalls the ideas, prominent early on in the text, that lend themselves to a Lacanian understanding of the symbolic as a realm of loss.

According to Lacan's interpretation, desire comes into being due to a perpetual want for satisfaction that cannot be offered in reality. Because it harks back to the infant's wish for unity with its mother, from whom the child is in fact always separating, desire in later life is inherently unsatisfied and unsatisfiable. Linked to early, irretrievable memories, it is projected onto substitute objects (often in a way blocked from the consciousness of the adult). Lacan explores the disjunction between desire and desired object in terms of the disjunction between signifier and signified. In *Aftergrowth* signs (in the very literal sense of language, words, and legends) serve as replacements for possession of the protagonist's true object of desire. The main character leaves behind preverbal bliss for an encounter with holy texts. These have their own attractions at times, but cannot finally bring him the long-ago world he desires. In the concluding pages, precisely where the narrator tries in various ways to abandon or supersede the strictures of language, the result is a new profusion of signmaking that underscores the problem once again. The tricks of verbal artistry are clearly an attempt to restore the immediacy and sensory richness of childhood, but words here just as clearly flaunt their separateness from that world. The author is remarkably alert to the issues at stake. It is not just that Bialik brings explicit thematic attention to language throughout the narrative in sections 1, 2, and 3. In addition, at the end, after the descriptions of Shmulik's cathartic visions of beauty, Bialik has his narrator state the following: "Mother! I want to cry out aloud, but my throat is blocked and my voice chokes" (128–29).

The wish for restitution of the preverbal state is incompatible with expression and so, inevitably, results once more in subdued voice. The inspiring vision therefore leads not to wholeness but to an ensuing feeling of devastation. Indeed, the protagonist is said to walk about for days, "desolate for very wonder." Framing *Aftergrowth,* therefore, at its beginning and at its end, is a preoccupation with language as a highly equivocal phenomenon. Language is simultaneously a compensation for loss and also an agent of ever-extending distance from early happiness.

A continuous series of displacements animates Shmulik's story of semiotic initiation. The child character channels his imagination, by stages, away from nonverbal pursuits into verbal ones, and in the process comes to appropriate the holy tongue into his personal expression. In this way he may be seen as standing at an intersection of Lacan's and Bakhtin's understanding of otherness and language. While Lacan emphasizes the loss that accompanies the acquisition of language, Bakhtin privileges the promise and energy that may come from subversion of traditional discourse and the sounding of new voices. His interest lies in the multiple linguistic stratifications—the dialects, the jargons, the varying registers and idioms—that make up any cultural setting. In particular he observes ways in which one kind of language appropriates, reinterprets, or questions the assumptions of another. Exploring the impact of these matters in an intimate realm, he notes that psychic life consists of an amalgam of discourses spoken by others and selectively absorbed by the individual.[22] Shmulik clearly undergoes just such a process of growth towards independent thinking. As his beloved childhood becomes more and more remote, he accepts the alienation that (in Lacan's view) comes from entering into the discourse of the other, that is, into socially orchestrated values. Finally, however, he rejoices at entering a dialogue with his forebears. His words become the locus for a new synthesis of meaning as his stories appropriate, redefine, and revitalize forms of expression he has inherited from the traditional past. His words are "populated with the intentions of others" (in Bakhtin's formulation), yet they are also now stamped with his own individuality.

The author, of course, enacts a parallel appropriation of religious language for his own ends in imaginative writing. It should be remembered that the enabling condition of this art is Bialik's move away from his own traditional childhood, through a Haskalah education and beyond, to awareness of the Western cultural phenomena of romanticism and modernism. This background accounts for the observation formulated in "Gilui vekhisui balashon," which anticipates Bakhtin and which applies aptly both to the plot and to Bialik's own narratorial strategies in *Aftergrowth:* "The profane turns sacred and the sacred profane. Long established words are constantly being pulled out of their setting, as it were, and exchanging places with one another" (137).

Certainly, varied uses of allusion and sacred intertexts are instrumental in shaping the narrative, and so are indicative of the four primary stances toward the past and toward language assumed in the four sections of the narrative. In section 1, for example, reference to Genesis and to the natural order of the world at the time of creation ("*sidrei bereshit*") is symptomatic of the orientation toward adult perspectives in this segment of the text. To make the primordial world of childhood intelligible to the adult reader, the narrator turns to the holy tongue, which the young protagonist does not yet know. Here a message is sent that is intended strictly for a mature audience, circumventing any use of the child's voice. In the next two sections of *Aftergrowth* allusion proliferates with wild abandon as Shmulik's consciousness comes to deal with *heder* instruction and the discourse taught there. The character's mind is filled to overbrimming with Bible tales and legends, which he adapts to his own make-believe. Here, sacred language is not primarily an element of narratorial polemic, as in section 1, but an element of plot and of the character's own activities. The final section more fully integrates allusion into psychological portraiture and the narrator's depiction of the child's inner life. It is used not just to convey Shmulik's biblical fantasies or his particular, childish interpretations of scripture (e.g., "the valley of the shadow" read as a direct reference to a local landscape). Instead, references to sacred literature, that is, to a collective idiom, are put to the service of conveying his most private emotions. (The "horses of fire" borrowed from Merkavah literature refer to Shmulik's own inner landscape and development, which is marked by eroticism and is both wonder-filled and tinged with fear and guilt). The function of this language, then, is more referential than dialogic; that is, it is directed more to events it signifies and less to the anticipated reader. In a variety of ways, then, *Aftergrowth* brings about a domestication of holy writ to arrive at a stance that honors individual consciousness and private inner life.

A reflection of romanticism, this position was not easily achieved in Bialik's work. As Dan Miron has documented, the self is presented in Bialik's early poetry as an embodiment of collective, national issues. Only gradually did the poet accept the self, in its own right, as a legitimate topic for literary treatment.[23] *Aftergrowth* shows that Bialik came to explore the richness of the topic by adopting a patently autobiographic format fully geared to celebrating interiority, the private imagination, and the person who stands outside the norms of prevailing social discourse. Even here, though, Bialik's art is never dissociated from the language of tradition. The author uses allusion to inscribe the individual into the dominant code of prestige. That is, the child—generally a marginalized voice in adult literature—is brought to center stage through use of the holy tongue with its continuing collective nuances. At issue is a shifting of emphasis rather than an abandonment of tradition. The effect is to elevate the personal through the language of heroism and glory. Embracing a secularization of the sacred language, Bialik arrives at a major transformation of Jewish cultural life.

The choice of Hebrew as artistic medium contributes in another fundamental way to tensions between past experience and present narration. Though fundamentally concerned with language, the origins of self-definition, and semiotic initiation, *Aftergrowth* never addresses the fact that Yiddish, not Hebrew, is undoubtedly the mother tongue of the protagonist. The implication is clear. Once again, language serves as mask rather than revelation. Had the author meant to recreate a past, to wax nostalgic about a particular time and place and recover it through naturalistic description of milieu, then this slighting of Yiddish—and of bilingualism as a theme—would constitute a curious omission. That verisimilitude and recreative accuracy were never Bialik's chief aim or achievement is suggested, however, by the early autobiographical poems he did write in Yiddish. Though the poet noted in one of his letters that it would be more natural for him to describe childhood in Yiddish than in Hebrew,[24] pieces such as "Oyf dem hoykin barg" testify that he used this language as a way of distancing himself from, rather than drawing dangerously closer to, deeply painful memories. Miron has argued convincingly that Bialik modeled this poem after the conventions of Yiddish folk materials and the German Kindheitstraum with the result of formalizing the poetic persona; in this way the poet evaded overly revelatory comments on profoundly private issues of a psychosexual nature. Moreover, the argument goes, Bialik was unused to composing in Yiddish, and so it was in one way less natural for him to write in his mother tongue than in Hebrew.[25] At any rate, by suppressing the Yiddish voice, *Aftergrowth* deflects attention away from those facets of everyday childhood that might be captured only in that language. In this way there comes about one more displacement from the past through words.[26]

As a consequence of being written in Hebrew the narrative does present a link to the past in one important sense. It presumes to be more of a piece with the child's imaginative life shaped by, and in rebellion against, religious training. Bearing a heavy freight of collective meanings and so adapted only with effort to represent individual consciousness, this language is nonetheless a part of the life of the mind from the time of early childhood on. Serving as proof of rupture from the concrete actualities of the past—most significantly, severance from the mother and the mother tongue—the use of Hebrew does acknowledge an inner

life privileged over more mundane externals. This is a language, therefore, which in its own way is suited to valorizing interiority or a realm of
the imagination. Though the prose highlights an ineluctable break with
earliest private experience, and although the screen of collective language imposes restraint and guards against overly personal expression,
Hebrew here as a language of narration also posits an identification with
the child's thinking.

Only a comprehensive account of what Bialik omits and what he
includes—in terms of linguistic, psychological, and historical materials—
would fully establish the continuities and discontinuities with the past
and the degree of autobiographical impulse that went into *Aftergrowth*.
The outline of the problem here, however, is enough to indicate that
Bialik's linguistic choices reinscribe on a grand literary-historical scale
the same fundamental issues struggled with in the text at the level of plot
and narration. Language makes memory and retelling possible. It also
distorts, distances, and disconnects the speaker or writer from the past.
If the child's entry into language makes for painful choices, so, too, does
the collective effort at cultural rebirth, as it entails entry into a new set of
signifying practices. For Bialik, the foremost voice of the Hebrew Renaissance, the renascent literary enterprise is at once enormously productive and also, inevitably, marked by omissions and loss of his childhood
world. It is little wonder, then, that his is an art fundamentally concerned with ability of words to reveal and also conceal.

5 HENRY ROTH—
CALL IT SLEEP

Lost among secrets in a tangle
Of weeds by the stream
The newborn child is dreaming
His mother's dreams,
His eyes two rivers, seeking
Their place of birth
Back among hidden roots
In the blood of earth.
But his hands, like Moses beside the water
Reach for the light, for Pharoah's daughter.

—Tuvia Ruebner, "First Days"

No single piece of narrative in the American Jewish canon explores a child's consciousness and a child's apprehension of the world through language as fully as does Henry Roth's *Call It Sleep* (1934). Indeed, the central issue around which the entire text revolves has rightly been seen as the child's effort to find his own voice and so to create his own context of meaning in a world of displacements and homelessness.[1]

The reasons for the protagonist's perplexities and sense of dislocation are both personal and societal. Spanning the years 1907–13 and set in New York, the plot of this novel features a contemporary of Mottel's, but one who is far more serious and is endowed with a much greater degree of inwardness. Unlike Mottel, who celebrates freedom and revels in novelty, this little boy feels tormented by instability. He suffers first of all due to the exaggerated oedipal tensions of his family life. Made fearful and insecure by his father's jealousy, rejection, and violent temper, Davey at age six longs for a comforting haven to replace the tenderness his overly protective mother provided him at an earlier age. Fueling the conflict is the boy's discovery that his mother once had a love affair in Europe, before marrying and coming to America. The child sees this fact as possible corroboration for the father's conjecture that Davey is illegitimate. Among his peers the little boy also feels lost, for he is an unusually shy and impressionable child. Light years ahead of the rest of his playmates in terms of brightness and sensitivity, he is unable to keep up with the rough-and-tumble of their competition. Intimidated by their vulgarity and toughness, he is troubled, too, by their precocious sexual play. As a result of all these pressures, preoccupied with guilt and fear, he searches for some belief to ward off uncertainty, and so develops curiosity about religion and hungers for an understanding of God. His is a lonely quest, one he does not sound aloud, for he has no true allies or confidants who might understand his perspective.

That Davey lives in an immigrant milieu exacerbates his problems of belonging. His is a world in extraordinary flux, populated by people uprooted from the Old World and cast into the new one as an impoverished minority. The multilingual setting of *Call It Sleep*, which reflects the social diversity of Davey's world, magnifies and accentuates the little boy's sense of being divided and fitting in nowhere. A bewildering array of discourse characterizes this fictional world. The parents speak Yiddish and Polish, the language of the streets is English, and Hebrew, as holy tongue, is taught in *heder*. The proliferation of distinct registers and languages Davey must contend with makes his search for self-expression that much more confusing, for his world is fragmented into spheres of being alien to one another and, often, mutually unintelligible. Polish is the language of adult secrets that exclude the American-born children; the youngsters' activities frequently remain barely perceived by the parents; Yiddish sets Davey apart from the non-Jews he meets; finally, a variety of accents among English speakers—primarily Italian and Irish—add awkward moments of misunderstanding. Wandering, disoriented, beyond his familiar neighborhood, Davey knows the name of his street but becomes thoroughly lost when his pronunciation, "Boddeh," is taken variously to mean "Body," Barhdee," and "Bahday" street.

Two crucial episodes in *Call It Sleep* deserve closer critical attention as the child's search for voice crystallizes in them. These scenes, which both take place at Davey's *heder,* show that a significant part of his maturation entails an appropriation and revisioning of adult language. His case vividly illustrates what Bakhtin would deem an awakening to independent thinking through internalizing the words of others. Partial comprehension of adult talk allows this character both familiarity with and distance from accepted formulations of reality. These scenes also share an emphasis on the boy's efforts at vocal self-assertion. After renewing and reconstituting the words he takes in, this figure attempts to introject his perceptions back into the world of adult exchange and understanding around him. The *heder* incidents have additional importance because, in suggesting the impact of tradition and the Jewish milieu on the child's thinking, they dramatize his evolving choices in relation to Jewishness and religion. While the community from which he springs suffers a break with the past and feels increasing pressures toward assimilation, his life gauges those pressures, filtering and transforming them through a converse kind of assimilation: his absorption of the language and values around him. The child turns a multitude of influences into a complex amalgam of convictions stamped finally with his own individuality.

All these matters link the two *heder* episodes with the concluding portions of the novel. The earlier scenes serve as important way stations on Davey's road to culminating insight, particularly as they concern this character's increasing awareness about language. The plot insists on ways in which his thinking and his cognizance of his own thinking alter his early muteness, transforming it into a more nearly audible and insightful form of expression. Most importantly, this character arrives at a realization that languages entail dynamic fluctuations of signification. As a result, the child begins to recognize his own capabilities as well as his limitations in interpreting and defining the world.

As the novel thematizes respect for the child's word and focuses on the child's voice, which asserts its own worth, *Call It Sleep* invites special attention to ways in which the adult narrator depicts the child's voice. Roth often strives for verisimilitude in rendering a child character's verbal thoughts, his spoken words, and his speech behavior. Few pieces of fiction that deal with childhood lend themselves so readily to close analysis in terms of psycholinguistic models. However, mimetic authenticity is only part of the issue. A variety of narrative means are engaged here to speak on behalf of a character who is not yet fully equipped to speak for himself or whose ideas are too inchoate to verbalize. Part of the challenge is to represent regions of the figure's consciousness that remain opaque to other characters in the novel; part is to go further and to indicate experiences conceived as nonverbal in the first place. Inevitably, a double movement governs the text. An adult's artistic attempt to grasp a child's inner life combines here with a plot that emphasizes a youngster's attempt to grasp adult meaning. To chart the child's emergent voice, then, is necessarily to document the subtleties of narrative voice as they attest to a dialogic imagination in *Call It Sleep.* This is a novel marked obtrusively by an overlaying of discourse in both its narration and its narrated events.

The first episode presents the protagonist's initial contact with scripture, an occasion that is memorable especially as it forces him to reconcile discrepancies between formal religious training and his own private intimations of the sacred or the divine. Davey's sensitive, deeply personal perceptions are conceived as ones that exceed or resist verbal formulation, and so, while they challenge the author's mimetic capabilities, this is an occasion when the child's voice is not heard at all in the plot action.

An inveterate daydreamer, Roth's young character experiences privileged moments of insight or epiphany that border on mystical vision.[2] At the age of seven or eight, sitting by the side of a wharf, this child marvels, spellbound, at sunlight flashing brightly on the water.

> Minutes passed while he stared. The brilliance was hypnotic. He could not take his eyes away. His spirit yielded, melted into light. In the molten sheen memories and objects overlapped. Smokestacks fused to palings flickering in silence by. Pale lathes grew grey, turned dusky, contracted and in the swimming dimness, he saw sparse teeth that gnawed upon a lip and again smokestacks. Straight in air they stood a moment, only to fall on silvered cardboard corrugating brilliance. And he heard the rubbing on a washboard and the splashing suds, smelled again the acrid soap and a voice speaking words that opened like the bands of a burnished silver accordion—Brighter than day . . . Brighter . . . Sin melted into light . . .
>   Uh chugchug ug chug!
>   Cucka cucka . . . Is a chicken . . .
>   Uh chug ug chch ch—Tew weet!
>   No . . . can't be . . .
>   Ug chug, ug chug, ug—TEW WEET!
>   What! He started as if out of a dream. (247–48)[3]

This trancelike moment, a multisensual or, perhaps, suprasensual experience of breathtaking fascination, defies easy expression. Davey here is transported beyond conventional language to listen instead to a voice ("speaking words that opened like the bands of a burnished silver accordion") that conveys a mysterious tongue from another, more dreamlike world.

By contrast with this otherworldly, magical speech, his *heder* schooling and its accent on the mechanics of reading seem a diminution of richness. Davey balks at the divorce of sound and sense that characterizes his reading instruction. Thus, as his mind wanders from a lesson he grumbles inwardly:

> Why do you have to read chumish? No fun . . . First you read, Adonoi elahenoo abababa, and then you say, And Moses said you mustn't, and then you read some more abababa and then you say, mustn't eat in the traife butcher store. Don't like it anyway. Big brown bags hang down from the hooks. Ham. And all kinds of grey wurst with like marbles in 'em. Peeuh! (226)

This kind of religious training is by far inadequate to satisfy Davey's curiosity or to guide him through the rude turmoil of a confusing, poverty-ridden, and sometimes sordid environment. The narrator signals the failings of the *heder* instruction, not only through Davey's overt condemnation of it, but also by contrasting its rote repetition with the supple vitality of the boy's own language. Cited directly, these words exemplify inner speech as defined by psycholinguistics. Not speech minus sound, but a linguistic phenomenon displaying basic structures and functions of its own, inner speech tends toward abbreviation. It often omits articles, subject pronouns, prepositions, and copulas. Because certain things are apparent to the thinker, they needn't be spelled out in elaborate fashion. One word can often evoke a whole complex of ideas.[4] The rendering of Davey's thoughts in this passage depends on ellipsis or telegraphic statement ("Ham"), subjectless sentences ("Don't like it anyway"), and a tendency toward predication. Together with tag words ("with like marbles"), the preponderance of the conjunction "and" in the run-on sentence provides evidence of age-appropriate speech.[5] Altogether these stylistic points clearly indicate that the child's language is distinct from both the mystical one and that of his lessons; the explicit narrative representation of his thinking, with its attention to the details of his mental life, implies at least some endorsement of the worth of his inner voice. The juxtaposition of discourse here, within fiction that privileges the child as a center of consciousness, raises the question of whether a further encounter will come about between the protagonist's spiritual instincts and the traditional texts.

Thanks to this impulse to interpret, Davey's discovery of tradition does not end with disappointment. A pivotal reversal comes about shortly after the scene just quoted, when the rabbi briefly mentions Isaiah's vision in which an angel brings a burning coal to purify the prophet's lips. Yearning for his own sense of purification, Davey hopes to learn more about the story. Then, following the events at the wharf, he is assaulted by a gang of Gentile boys and they force him to short-circuit some nearby trolley tracks. The powerful flash of electricity released from the tracks becomes associated in Davey's mind with that captivating brilliance he witnessed at the waterfront, and the result is that he conflates both experiences into a notion of God as a being of radiant light. Sensing that some insight about these matters resides in the text of Isaiah, he rushes back to his *heder* to search for the passage about the burning coal. Wondrously, as he sounds out the words—none of which he understands per se—the scriptural text gratifyingly re-vivifies for him the spellbinding scene at the dock:

> "Beshnas mos hamelech Uziyahu vawere es adonoi yoshav al kesai rum venesaw, vshulav malaiim es hahahol. Serafim omidim memal lo shash kanowfayim, sash kanowfayim lawehhad, beshtayim yahase fanav vishtayim yahase raglov uvishtayim yaofaif."

All his senses dissolved into the sound. The lines, unknown, dimly

surmised, thundered in his heart with limitless meaning, rolled out
and flooded the last shores of his being. Unmoored in space, he saw
one walking on impalpable pavements that rose with the rising trees.
Or were they trees or telegraph-poles, each crossed and leafy, none
could say, but forms stood there with footholds in unmitigated light.
And their faces shone because the light in their midst was luminous
laughter. He read on. (255–56)

The imagery of fluidity and spatial displacement here recapitulates
that of the earlier passage describing the sunlight on the water. While the
previous text mentioned "molten sheen," "smokestacks fused to pal-
ings," and lathes that "contracted in the swimming dimness," here the
narrative offers senses that "dissolve" and lines that "roll out and flood
the shores" of Davey's being. Further establishing parallels between the
two descriptions, the ladders in the first vision correspond here to the
trees that might also be taken as telegraph poles. Both are susceptible to
interpretation in the Freudian terms frequently applied to *Call It Sleep,*
and both, because of their resemblance to crosses, may be read as part of
a Christian motif that will prove to figure prominently throughout the
novel. Whether or not they are understood as sexual symbols or as
indicators of religious exaltation, they represent for Davey an image of
elation, radiance, joy, freedom, and transcendence over the sorrow of his
daily life.

This scene, in which mysterious words reactivate earlier images,
does not simply represent a wrongheaded misconstruing of a text. Instead, it presents a creative and significant misreading that involves
intense linguistic drama and a struggle for understanding intimately
bound up with Davey's ideas about religion. According to Bakhtin, "In
the actual life of speech, every concrete act of understanding is active,"
as it assimilates the word to be understood into the conceptual system of
the listener. In each particular intellectual and emotional context, the
message is merged with consonant or dissonant—that is, receptive or
unreceptive—expectations. To some extent, then, "primacy belongs to
the response as the activating principle."[6] Davey is constructed as a
character who can use the excerpt from Isaiah, in its entirety, as a kind of
verbal reallocation of perceptions. No single word in his vocabulary can
sufficiently express the stunning vision he has had, and so his recitation
of unknown words becomes an act of naming, a way of invoking something that otherwise would not be easy to define.[7] In this way the passage becomes internally persuasive, fully within Davey's possession and
of meaning to him. His act of cognitive retrieval is less an interpretation
than a personalized act of synthesis that uses Jewish symbols but imbues
them with his own significance.

The introduction of a written text in this scene significantly affects this process. Since this writing is relatively detached from a speech-act situation, the words are not clearly grounded in a dramatic context that might delimit or control audience response. Davey, unrestrained by schooling, lets his imagination go and reads his own ecstasy into the text. The foreignness of the words also leaves them more malleable and flexible. However, the power of the character's inner conviction is based in part on and benefits from the force of the authoritative word, the Isaiah story, whose impressive, magisterial quality derives from its status as holy writ. That this is a prior discourse, connected with a past felt to be more sublime, is clear from its presentation as language demarcated from Davey's own. The special status of these words is conveyed through quotation marks that put into relief the transliteration. That is to say, the scriptural text demands allegiance; it cannot allow for entirely free appropriation. Davey respects the power of this text as an elevated, awe-inspiring voice of authority, even as he also introduces into it a double voicing, a very personal renewing of it through his own ignorance.

This scene in *Call It Sleep* is important in part because it suggests the excitement of a little boy who synthesizes diverse ideas to arrive at his personally felt conception of God. In this scene, reading also brings Davey a discovery of discovery. Here he begins to realize his own potential to uncover and produce meaning from individual experience. This episode takes on importance, too, as it exemplifies what will become Davey's principal strategy for threading his way through a hostile world. Getting what he can in this instance from the Hebrew Bible, he later similarly adopts Christian symbols (the rosary and the sacred heart painting that belong to his friend Leo) as talismans able to ward off evil. These he combines with personal memories of intense serenity or anguish and with ideas culled from his mother's tales: the legends and superstitions she remembers from her girlhood in Poland. Together, all these factors contribute to the boy's notion of a transcendent power. It is the heterogeneous cultural environment of immigrant America which, providing him with scattered sources of inspiration, allows him to arrive at a childish but sincere spiritual eclecticism. Lacking strong religious guidance (both in the *heder* and in his largely secular and troubled home), Davey relies on his own explorations of the complex world about him to fend off insecurity.

Thus, the narrative asks the reader to view his reading sympathetically and to respect it on its own terms. While the boy's notion of religion as protective magic is immature and limited, it represents a sincere and serious desire for understanding of powerful issues. The worth of Davey's inner struggle is conveyed through the powerful lyric formulations and the elevated diction that report his reading of Isaiah and his vision by the water. Here is where the adult narrator's voice makes itself most palpably present, as the text struggles in a number of ways against the representational limitations of language and stretches the expressive capacities of words beyond simple denotation. Hermetic, written in a Joycean manner, the narrator's descriptions gain some of their force from the use of verbal metaphor. This stylistic device infuses intensity into the prose, implying the extraordinary impact of Davey's reaction to his reading: "the lines *flooded* the last shores of his being." In a related strategy the text links nouns with verbs or predicates usually considered inappropriate for them. The result is to create a synesthetic effect, confusing various cognitive categories. Hearing, during the scene at the dock, overlaps with visual perception and the intangible with the tangible: "*words . . . opened*" like an accordion; "*light* in their midst was luminous *laughter*"; "*sin melted.*" Roth at times also omits verbs or presents an elliptical kind of sentence with enigmatic effect: "And he heard the rubbing on a washboard and the splashing suds, smelled again the acrid soap and a voice speaking words that opened like the bands of a burnished silver accordion—Brighter than day . . . Brighter . . . "

In these lines no specific subject governs the predicate, and so it is hard to know exactly what is becoming brighter: the sunlight on the water? Davey's memories of lights? a supernatural force that he alone envisions? Similarly, no particular verb governs the object phrase "a voice speaking words." The absence of a verb suggests that the voice is something ultimately mysterious, operating as a disembodied presence, and not to be perceived through the usual sensory channels. Finally, no specific reference defines which rubbing or which acrid soap the narrator has in mind. The definite articles in these phrases endow the statement with an imposing self-evidence, as if these were events of elemental importance, and yet the reader is left unsure what events the narrator intends to recall. There is a notable coincidence between these stylistic elements and the features of inner speech operative in the previous passage on reading *chumish*. The use of ellipsis and subjectless predication, here as there, signals the incommunicable quality of inner life. In a comparable manner, the onomatopoeia at the end of the passage about the dock ("Ug chugchug ug chug!" and so on) represents a further expansion of lexicon beyond ordinary reference. Dramatizing the approach of the tugboat that startles Davey out of his reverie, these words attempt to recapture a mimetic link between signifier and signified, affording an immediacy not available to standard vocabulary. This move again suggests that the boy's mind, recovering now from his hypnotic trance, has assumed a state not to be expressed through more denotative means. The alliterative qualities of the prose and the repetitions also heighten the register of these passages and imply moments of heightened sensibility: pale lathes *grew grey*, and contracted in *swimming dimness*;

pavements *rose* with the *rising* trees; light becomes *luminous laughter;* as Davey's spirit *melted into light,* so also sin *melted into light.*

Contrasting with this carefully crafted version of the afternoon's events, Davey's own account is lame, almost inarticulate. An unbridgeable gap remains between his inner perceptions and his capacity for conversational exchange. The boy's idiosyncratic reading of scripture therefore inevitably meets with misunderstanding and contempt, for he lacks the means by which to translate his unique feelings into a discourse persuasive to others. When the *melamed* happens upon him, surprising him at his recitation of Isaiah, Davey stumbles over an explanation for his presence in the *heder:*

> "I went and I saw a coal like—like Isaiah."
> "What kind of a coal, where?"
> "Where the car-tracks run I saw it. On Tenth Street."
> "Car tracks? You saw a coal?" The rabbi shut his eyes like one completely befuddled.
> "Yes. It gave a big light in the middle, between the crack!" (257)

After hearing this weak rendition of Davey's epiphany, the rabbi proceeds to mock and rebuke the boy severely for confusing God with a flash of electricity. Reb Yidel Pankower, under the best of circumstances, might not have been a sympathetic listener, but his reaction here is exacerbated by the child's poor performance at communicating his thoughts. While the *melamed* bewails the ignorance of the young, a generation which he views as insensitive ruffians unable and unworthy to uphold the traditions, he himself is insensitive to Davey's genuine curiosity about Isaiah. Without the support of mutual understanding, Davey's feeling of breakthrough and insight remains but a momentary attainment. Alone he cannot long sustain the intensity of his sublime discoveries, and under the strain of fending off the rabbi's anger, Davey's solemnity begins to break down. As he recites some additional passages in Hebrew, the words begin to dissolve back into nonsense syllables and Davey dissolves into giddy laughter. Once again merely sounds, empty of meaning, words revert from being the most meaningful of things back to being the most arbitrary and senseless: "Ma tovu oholeha yaakov meshkanoseha Yisroel. He poured the sounds out in a breathless chaotic stream . . . they were growing funny! Adonoi awhavti maon baseha umkom mishcan kvodhaw. It was hard for him now to keep his face straight" (258). Davey's voice at this point remains the province of narratorial comment. The child's voice itself has failed, explicitly, to have an impact within the plot action, and his inner life, portrayed as developing in profound ways, gains expression only through the adult vocabulary of the author.

An episode parallel to this first one, again centered in the *heder,* takes place toward the end of *Call It Sleep.* Here, too, the child absorbs adult words, assessing them within his own framework of interpretation and endowing them with new meaning. The difference is that in this episode the narrator registers greater awareness on Davey's part that words are effective as social tools when they fit into a preestablished set of understandings. Davey, as he gains an audience and takes a step closer to communicating his feelings, also achieves a partial catharsis and discharges some of his overwhelming emotional burdens.

Leading up to the scene is Davey's acquaintanceship with a Polish Catholic boy, Leo. Davey's senior by several years, Leo is interested in girls. In exchange for the older boy's rosary, which Davey believes to have magical powers, the younger one agrees to engineer a rendezvous with Aunt Bertha's two twelve-year-old daughters. Leo takes one of them into a cellar for some sexual play only vaguely imagined by Davey. Afterward all hell breaks loose. The girl is upset and ashamed; her sister threatens to tell their parents. Leo barrages them with anti-Semitic taunts and jeers, and Davey, not fully understanding what has happened but aware of his complicity, flees in terror. Running back to the *heder* for his Hebrew lesson, he tries frantically to block the events out of his memory. The teacher then calls on him to read, once again, from Isaiah, and this event triggers a proliferation of colliding discourses. At first Davey is elated, and his spirit begins to soar. However, when the rabbi expresses his approval by showering him with traditional praises—"a true Yiddish child," "cherished seedling of Judah," "Blessed is your mother"—the word *mother* intrudes itself into the little boy's thoughts, and mixes with the biblical passage: "(-*Mother!*) 'Kadosh, Kadosh, Kadosh adonoi tsevawos.' The words blurred. A howl of terror beat down all majesty. (-*Mother!*) 'Mlo hol haeretz h-vo-do—' He stumbled. (-*Mother!*)" (367).

Converging at this moment of crisis are Davey's inner speech (indicated by parentheses), his outer pronunciation of scripture (represented by direct citation), and the child's nonverbal awareness (appearing as psychonarration), all of which then yield a new level of language: a vocal outburst from the little boy. He breaks into tears and, when questioned, he hesitantly, yet compulsively and without knowing why, offers a patent fabrication: his mother is dead. In addition, he continues, the woman who has brought him to school is not his mother but his aunt, and she has just recently revealed this truth to him; his real father was a Christian back in Europe.

Davey has now finally expressed what was building up inside of him all along. Most immediately he transmits a version of the overheard conversation his mother and Aunt Bertha held earlier (in chapter 2,

"The Picture"), concerning Genya's secret romance from long ago. Davey transforms the story as he retells it, presenting as fact what others have only surmised, namely, that he himself is illegitimate. Into this plot line he incorporates an additional elaboration: his mother's supposed demise. The effectiveness of the fiction he concocts is its overdetermined nature, which allows him to synthesize the fierce and fiercely competing emotions he has been harboring. These stem from the pressures of his strained relationship with his parents, his ambivalent attraction to and fear of Gentiles, and his curiosity about religion.

First, through the story he announces his alienation. The lie permits him to disavow Albert, the angry, violent father, and claim to be someone else's son. Furthermore, Davey identifies here with the alien but alluring Christian culture, about which Leo has told him and which he perceives to be so powerful. Second, to say that his mother is dead allows him to mourn for her. He takes in the elevated, respectful reference to motherhood that the rabbis introduce into the scene, and he acknowledges his own earlier reverence for his mother, indirectly, by refuting it. The idealized maternal image he adored has been lost. In part the reason is simply that he is growing up and, no longer tied to her apron strings, he cannot hold onto the same intense tenderness for which he longs. In addition the motherly figure he once cherished has been sullied because of Genya's contacts with the vulgar world around her. The son, for example, suspects her of responding to sexual advances by the family's boarder. On another occasion some boys have caught a glimpse of her in the bath, and Davey takes their merriment about this incident as a personal affront. Consequently, at the same time that the child grieves, he also vents his rage and accuses his mother of betrayal on several levels. As the allegedly deceased mother she is blamed for having an illicit affair. Designated as the aunt, she also stands condemned for cruelty and falsity, for having hidden the truth and then abruptly and unfeelingly having told a young child of his mother's death and involvement in scandal. Since in reality Genya is both "mother" and "aunt," she stands doubly charged.

Aunt Bertha, too, is included in this accusation. At this particular moment, when Davey presents his account to the rabbis, he is preoccupied with the fear that Bertha will learn what went on in the cellar with Leo. He therefore transmutes his anxiety into a portrait of adult evil that justifies himself as innocent victim. The object of his fear, the aunt, he transfigures into a loathsome person, making the boy himself look wronged and blameless. Albert, for his part, is implicated in the story, since Davey recounts that his "aunt" revealed the truth to him on a day when he didn't do well at school. In fact that particular instance of poor performance resulted from a frightening incident when his father got into a brawl. Albert, not Bertha, therefore has exposed the youngster to the harsher, seamy side of life. In short, the boy condenses, displaces, and synthesizes in a way that constitutes a lie for the other characters in the narrated events, but which in the narration clearly and persuasively expresses to the reader something of the little boy's genuine inner dilemmas.

As was the case with the explanation about the train tracks offered earlier to Reb Pankower, Davey's unskilled narration here contrasts markedly with the complexity and wealth of emotion that constitutes his inner world. When, for instance, the *melamed* asks the whereabouts of the boy's father, the conversation plays itself out this way:

> "I—I don't know!"
> "Hmpph! Did she say anything about him?"
> "She s-said he was a—a—"
> "What?"
> "I forgot! I forgot how to say it!" He wept.
> "Then think! Think. What was he, a tailor, a butcher, a peddler, what?"
> "No. He was—He was—He played—"
> "Played? A musician? Played what?"
> "A—A—Like a piano. A—A organ!" He blurted out.
> "An organ? An organ! Reb Schulim, do you see land?"
> "I think I see what is seen first, Reb Yidel. The spire."
> "Mmm! Why aren't you with him?" His voice was cautious.
> "Because—because he's in Eu-Europe."
> "And?"
> "And he plays in—in a—She says he plays in a ch-church. A church!"
> "Woe me!" (369)

The youngster's responses are lame and broken, much as they were in the previous exchange with the *melamed*. This time, though, Davey's words are more deliberately deceptive and significantly more effective, because they are appropriated into a framework of interpretation familiar to the grown-ups.[8] The second rabbi, a guest of Reb Pankower's, expects to hear that the father is Christian. His use of the word "spire" signals this interpretive predisposition, and Davey's forthcoming confession then reconfirms Reb Schulim's expectations. Subsequently both men concur, "there's truth in an old adage," that is, that a bastard is wise. Just as Albert has suspected Davey's illegitimacy, these characters are willing, even eager, to believe in the mother's transgression. (Additional evidence in the course of the novel suggests, to the contrary, that Davey *is* Albert's son.) The rabbis, moreover, adopt the boy's story with such alacrity because the child bases his report on the speech of others more authoritative than himself. That is to say, he inscribes his own discourse within a legitimized context (what grown-ups say), rather than attempting, as he had done earlier, to translate his experience directly into his own words. By contrast with the description of the track, here the child transmits and assesses the speech of the "aunt" ("She s-said he was a—a—"; "She says he plays in a ch-church"). By quoting and summarizing her—however uncognizant of his purposes— the boy plays into the prejudices of his listeners. Horrified that this woman would disclose such secrets to a child, the men do not doubt the veracity of Davey's account.

Davey himself is aware that words may deceive and that their power often relies more on intentions and audiences than on referential force. He even clues the rabbis in to this insight through his accusation that the "aunt" lies; she "just says" that she is his mother. The adults fail to pick up on the hint, though, even as they ignore other clues to the boy's true emotional plight. By contrast, these are easily decoded by the reader who is now familiar with highly articulate accounts of the child's inner life. The adult narration has shown convincingly that Davey's escapade with Leo does not represent ill-willed perversity so much as naiveté inadvertently misdirected into shameful consequences. Coming at the moment of most intense adult approval (the successful reading at *heder*), which is also the moment of his worst sexual and religious transgressions (his complicity with Leo and the desire to win the rosary), Davey's outburst is an attempt to integrate the conflicting pulls on his feelings. His telling of the story represents a bid to reconcile the contradictions within by reclaiming the safety of the familiar Jewish world and proclaiming his own innocence, while also acknowledging connections with the unknown, non-Jewish world, with mischief, and with sexuality.

This moment is a transitional one. It stands between the first scene, when, true to his own perceptions, Davey tried unsuccessfully to persuade, and the ending of the novel. Here the character gains sympathy, but his voice remains significantly misapprehended by his immediate audience. In the final pages Davey reaches a new equilibrium between inner thought and outer expression. More importantly, he reaches greater understanding of the difficulty of communication and the vagaries of referentiality.

To approach the concluding scene and its emphasis on linguistic self-consciousness, it is important to note that Davey's awareness of language does not materialize suddenly as an isolated occurrence. On the contrary, it accumulates steadily in the course of the novel. Throughout *Call It Sleep* differentiations of speech bring the child to an awareness of ethnic and age divisions in society and so to an appreciation of language as social tool and arbiter of belonging and exclusion. It is, for instance, an easily recognized badge of identification in Davey's world. When the boys at the track gang up on Davey, he tries, unsuccessfully, to deny his Jewishness by regaling his attackers with a mock Hungarian ("Abashishishababbyo tomamama wawa," 250). On another occasion, developing an ear for accent, he perceives two birds this way: "A parrot and a canary. 'Awk! Awk!' the first cried. 'Ee-tee-tee-tweet.' The other. A smooth and rusty pulley. He wondered if they understood each other. Maybe it was like Yiddish and English, or Yiddish and Polish, the way his mother and aunt sometimes spoke. Secrets" (174).

Davey hopes to avail himself of language differences in similar fashion. In order to avenge himself for exclusion from his mother's secrets, he plots to deny the grown-ups access to his own thoughts by learning to talk "the way girls talked in the street—alligay walligay" (198).[9] In short, awareness of language forms, of diction appropriate to different situations, of speech communities—these the little boy learns about at an early age, and they clue him in to problems of referentiality. Davey is often skeptical about words, which change meaning in changing contexts. Lost, looking for the elusive Boddeh Street, he recalls a painful moment when he had unwittingly accepted an invitation to a sexual game from a little girl named Annie: "Never believe. Never play. Never believe. Not anything. Everything shifted. Everything changed. Even words. Words, you said. Wanna, you said. I wanna. Yea I wanna. What? You know what. They were something else, something horrible!" (102).

Davey's insight—that meaning depends on the existence of a speech community and that reference is not a static bond between signifier and signified—is one that often eludes children at early ages. It develops only later, in a process accelerated by the presence of many languages. In a monolingual milieu it also comes about as the child recognizes the plurality of speech, that is, realizes that distinctive registers and modes of expression are associated with occupation, gender, formality of setting, and other factors.[10] Various features of children's language themselves emerge in response to the need to define the young as a group unto themselves. Oral rituals, nonsense rhymes, slang, pig Latin or vulgarity, name calling, dares, and nicknames—these bind youngsters together in a common lingo inaccessible to or disapproved of by grown-ups, and so children adopt them readily as an assertion of incipient independence from adult authority. From the first example of children's conversation in *Call It Sleep* ("I god a calenduh." "Puh, who ain' god a calenduh," 26), Henry Roth depicts with remarkable sensitivity what George Steiner has called the "ceremonies of insult and kinship" typical of child speech behavior.[11] These details add to the novel's portrayal of verbal behavior as territorial imperative and as a marker of social divisions. As such they also contribute to the protagonist's increasing self-consciousness about language. The scenes at *heder* are significant landmarks in the plot, as they clearly illustrate a shift that takes place in Davey's outlook. There he redirects his energy away from referentiality to an attempt at integrating his expression within an accepted code of understanding. This turnabout develops when, just as Bakhtin would postulate, the collision of discourses leads him to an assessment of the words of others. Linguistic self-consciousness is notable in (1) his recollection and redeployment of meaning from the biblical passage and from remarks made earlier by parents or relatives, (2) in his awareness of his struggle to find his own words ("I forgot how to say it"), and (3) in his skepticism about intentions and his realization that words may lie.

Davey's developing sophistication about language culminates in the last paragraphs of the text, after the little boy's outburst to the rabbis precipitates further crisis. Reb Pankower goes to see Davey's family to investigate his home situation, and then, as the grown-ups discover the lie Davey has told, Albert flies into a rage. The boy flees, heads for the trolley tracks, and knowingly short-circuits them, searching presumably for the dazzling light and immense power of the electricity he once associated with divine revelation. This time, however, he is badly injured by the shock, with the effect that for one moment Davey is not caught between groups but becomes the center of attention for his parents, for the other children on the street, and for a large crowd of bystanders. In this converging attention and care Davey finds a moment of tempered victory. He has made his feelings known far and wide, but he has achieved this success in only a most ambivalent way that almost obliterates his voice forever. It is upon returning safely home and reflecting on this incident that he reaches his greatest equilibrium with regard to self-expression. The issue of how to articulate his experience becomes paramount as his mother asks, "Are you sleepy?"

> He might as well call it sleep. It was only toward sleep that every wink of the eyelids could strike a spark into the cloudy tinder of the dark, kindle out of shadowy corners of the bedroom such myriad and such vivid jets of images—of the glint on tilted beards, of the uneven shine on roller skates, of the dry light on grey stone stoops, of the tapering glitter of rails, of the oily sheen on the night-smooth rivers, of the glow on thin blonde hair, red faces, of the glow on the outstretched, open palms of legions upon legions of hands hurtling toward him. He might as well call it sleep. It was only toward sleep that ears had power to cull again and reassemble the shrill cry, the hoarse voice, the scream of

fear, the bells, the thick-breathing, the roar of crowds and all sounds
that lay fermenting in the vats of silence and the past. It was only
toward sleep one knew himself still lying on the cobbles, felt the
cobbles under him, and over him and scudding ever toward him like a
black foam, the perpetual blur of shod and running feet, the broken
shoes, new shoes, stubby, pointed, caked, polished, buniony, pavement-
beveled, lumpish, under skirts, under trousers, shoes, over one and
through one, and feel them all and feel, not pain, not terror, but
strangest triumph, strangest acquiescence. One might as well call it
sleep. He shut his eyes. (441)

Familiar though it is, this passage merits citing in its entirety to illustrate
how the ending of the novel recapitulates and resolves major aspects of
Davey's linguistic dramas present from preceding episodes.

First, there is that which the character cannot put into words and
which the narrator must present through psychonarration. The long,
sonorous description of the child's sensory perceptions, elevated by
anaphora ("of the glint," "of the uneven shine," "of the dry light," "of
the oily sheen," "of the tapering glitter," and more), features high diction and unusual poetic locutions far beyond the vocabulary of the child
himself ("myriad," "night-smooth," "vats of silence and the past,"
among others). All of these qualities transform the scene of powerlessness, injury, and even abasement into one of reassuring beauty. Though
the boy had been lying helpless beneath a multitude of feet, he recreates
the incident in his own mind as a series of spellbinding images and an
appreciation of energies directed toward himself. The people are presented synecdochically as shoes—stubby, pointed, caked, polished,
pavement-beveled, etc.—or as hands, hair, and beards. Together with
the fluidity of light, the majestic repetition, and the long sentences, these
details do not so much describe individuals as create a multiform but
unified and resonant vision synthesized by the child and dictated by his
own need for feelings of wholeness.

Second, the passage highlights the child's struggle to become articulate, particularly through the threefold repetition of the phrase "call it
sleep." Because this text has revolved about the whole problem of narratability and of gaps between the sayable and the unsayable, the vague
referential force of the pronoun "it" gains unmistakable prominence.
The word cannot be defined precisely.[12] The narrative may be gesturing
here toward Davey's current state of mind, the power of his imagination,
memory enriched by the entire set of events experienced in the course of
the novel, or his acquiescence to and acceptance of his circumstances.
What does become clear is that others do not share this character's
frame of reference. Like the mystical moment by the dock, that aspect of
Davey's inner life designated here as "it" does not have an exact label. To

make that phenomenon accessible to other people, the boy would have to make his peace with conventional language, words others can comprehend that would be but an approximation of his inner world. Here Davey opts for just such a compromise, settling for the laconic, ordinary word "sleep." If the entire narrative has been concerned with semiotic initiation, with the child's discovery of different value systems and ways of encoding or decoding the world, this final scene constitutes a genuine climax: a kind of recognition by the character of the process he has undergone. The phrase "he might as well call it sleep," presented as narrated monologue, not only signals the narrator's judgment, but serves, too, to indicate that Davey himself has arrived at this conclusion. Whether in so many words or not, he acknowledges that he must convert his experience into a familiar vocabulary and inscribe it into a wider cultural code, if he is to be understood.

This depiction of semiotic initiation also neatly illustrates important aspects of cognitive and linguistic growth typical in children. Prime differences that distinguish adult speech from that of children include, first, an ability to take account of variations in shared knowledge; second, a freedom from the here and now; and, finally, a self-consciousness about language that allows for reflection on linguistic forms.[13] Like most children, Davey at a young age fails to realize sufficiently that he has privileged access to his own thoughts. He does not understand that others cannot read his mind. In the scenes at the *heder,* though, in accordance with the first principle mentioned, he is learning that he must share knowledge about his past, his memories, and his ideas more explicitly. Illustrating Davey's maturation in regard to the second point, the boy's conclusion, "he might as well call it sleep" represents a detaching of words from immediate context. Language imparts memory and allows him to refashion the past, to rework events so that he may approach them without terror. It is significant that the phrase "he might as well" appears as a conditional, that is, an acceptance that language is not bound to concrete circumstance but may be used also to invent or suppose. Future tense and hypothetical propositions are notoriously difficult language constructions for children to acquire. The child protagonist of Roth's novel, prepared now for such speculative activity, also arrives at a rudimentary but profound conception of language as fiction. In his newfound ability to think *about* words, he does not take the medium itself for granted as many children do. As part of his newly acquired self-consciousness about language, in accordance with the third principle, he recognizes that the word "sleep" is distinct from the experience to which "it" refers, whatever that may be.

Every language act is an act of reinterpretation, of recreation, and not a perfect, verifiable act of communication. As George Steiner notes,

due to changes in tone, valuation, intention, and the private connotations each individual brings to words, "a human being performs an act
of translation, in the full sense of the word, when receiving a speech
message from any other human being."[14] Intimacy, in this scheme of
things, is simply more "self-confident translation" than most. This principle is what Davey has begun to discover in *Call It Sleep*. At the beginning of the novel Davey shared an intimacy with his mother, which he
felt transcended words. When he spoke with her once about death (the
topic of greatest terror for him) he did not understand her explanations,
but the narrator notes that what he "failed to grasp as thought, her last
gesture, the last supple huskiness of her voice conveyed" (68). At the end
of the novel, in contrast, his relationship with his mother, though loving,
is presented quite differently. Now the character believes that they are
individuals who each harbor fundamentally incommunicable experiences and can speak with each other only in approximations. Paradoxically, this scene comes closer than any other to resolving, at the level of
plot, differences between the boy's inner world and outer expression. It
is precisely because this child character has recognized the limitations of
words that he now acquires new mastery over them. In this sense he
makes them more completely his own.

To the extent that *Call It Sleep* is autobiographical (Roth himself
grew up in an immigrant milieu not perfectly coincident with Davey's
but close in many ways), the novel as a whole may be read as an attempt
to elicit belated understanding and sympathy for the misunderstood
child its author once was. In other words, the text itself takes a further
step in the progression evident from the *heder* scenes and the close of the
novel; it is another, and artistically definitive, move toward sounding the
voice of the child.

Certainly, *Call It Sleep* may be read at least partially as an account
of its own genesis. The cultural transitions taking place within the plot
are very similar to the ones that fostered the text in the first place. Roth's
own successful education and his adaptation to America, which meant a
break with the traditional past, made possible his portrayal of a child
moving beyond a Jewish milieu and fighting for the primacy of his
individual sensitivities. It should be remembered that the novel was
written from within a refined literary milieu and a highly assimilated
stance. At the time Roth was a young man who had attended Columbia
University and was then living with his non-Jewish lover and benefactress. In addition, Davey's forays into the Christian world—so frightening and scandalous to his parents—are conveyed by a Roth who freely
and deliberately uses Christian motifs as part of his cultural idiom. The
imagery of crosses, the descriptions of the rosary's radiance, the self-
sacrifice of the denouement (the electrical shock), which is meant to

compensate for the sins of the parents and elicits compassion in them—
these are among the artistic tools of a Jewish writer who has traversed
the cultural divide that both lures and intimidates his character.[15] The
older generation in the novel retreats or recoils from non-Jews (specifically, in the case of Genya's romance), and Davey, the younger generation, opens wider the possibility for contact. He blurs the once firmly
demarcated boundary lines through his spiritual eclecticism, but it
should be noted that this ability of his to undo past assumptions is
constructed through and validated by the efforts and values of the author, at the time of writing the novel.

Similarly, Roth's English represents a highly accomplished transition into the majority culture, a move away from his native Yiddish,
which would be inconceivable for the adult characters of *Call It Sleep*
and a dream that has barely begun to be dreamed for Davey. That
character's ambitions for linguistic mastery are simply to speak, as the
girls do in the street, "alligay, walligay," and so exceed his parents' grasp
of English. The author, in contrast, makes the child's limited horizons
available precisely because he relies on sophisticated experiment in the
conventions of modernism: particularly, in the representation of consciousness, which avails itself of a knowledge of Joyce and Freud.

The result is an exalted revisioning of an impoverished, frequently
ugly long ago. Roth, having achieved his transitions of language and
cultural perspective, directs those accomplishments back to his past to
celebrate a childhood and a world that was. The sensitivity with which
the author depicts a multilingual setting, and for which he has justly
been acclaimed, takes on special importance in this regard. While the
child's innermost feelings are conveyed through the powerful, lyric
prose associated with the moments of insight and epiphany, the text
presents Yiddish through translation into what is also a lofty, poetic
English. This is the language Reb Pankower and Reb Schulim, among
others, speak to each other. Roth expresses respect and admiration for it
by presenting it as an expressive idiom filled with graphic imagery and
folk wisdom ("Do you see land?"; "there's truth in an old adage"). The
transliterations of written Hebrew indicate a language of respect and
holiness. Remaining, then, is the interesting case of the broken English
which the immigrants speak and which is conveyed through unor-
thodox spelling. Though it creates a sharp counterpoint to the other
kinds of diction displayed in the text, and though it shows the awkward-
ness of the immigrants in their new tongue, even this English takes a
place of pride in the novel simply by virtue of its prominence. It is cited
directly, neither shuffled away nor referred to only from a distance within the idiom and values of another social context. Roth's is a position of
sympathy that invokes the era of childhood, even in its harshness, as a

significant and formative experience. Altogether, the author uses English as an artistic medium that acknowledges difference. The clever rendering of many-layered discourse accords complexity and prominence to the diverse voices that surround Davey, and so it underscores the difficulties of the choices he must make in responding to his environment.

As it emphasizes these difficulties, *Call It Sleep* commands more than nostalgia. It does not present a simplistic or counterfeit idyll. Indeed, the beauty achieved is a compromise between the sordid and the sublime. By way of stylistic heterogeneity, mixing lowest slang and highest diction, the text enacts a singularly modernist merging of opposites; it combines the text of Isaiah with the mechanical imagery of the short-circuited rail to suggest visionary intensity. And, in this way, out of the painful, rude circumstances of the setting the narrative devises an affirmative story. It bears saying, too, that much of the uplifting impetus of *Call It Sleep,* as well as much of its subtlety, is linked to the sensitivity and the transformative power of the child's imagination, which dismantles accepted notions of high and low, sacred and profane. Joining forces with the narrator's manufacture of extremely variegated prose, that capacity for revisioning fashions a fictional world of flux, transformation, and inversions of an older order. Davey, with his inchoate voice and understandings, is keenly challenged by the polyglot situation. The fluidity of the world makes it hard for him to set firm judgments and firm boundaries. At the same time, his being a child, his quality of being not yet fully formed, proves artistically beneficial. Telling about immigrant America through his eyes helps convey the openness, the potential for change, and the lack of rigid definition that characterize that world. Put another way, this protagonist's story poses the questions, in a pluralistic setting, where does authenticity lie? Will a cultural synthesis emerge, and, in the turmoil, how much understanding will the individual heart attain? Fiction, of course, is the natural ally of that lonely heart, for in the silent register of writing, the unspoken, inexpressible realm of the imagination may reign.

THE HOLOCAUST AND AFTERWARD

6 JERZY KOSINSKI— THE PAINTED BIRD

The stone is not heavy.
The bread is like the bird,
I watch as it flies.
Blood is on my cheeks.
My teeth
seek a less empty mouth
in the earth or in the water,
in the fire.
The world is red.
All the iron bars are spears.
Dead horsemen always gallop
in my sleep and in my eyes.

—Edmond Jabès, "Song of the Last Jewish Child"

Remarking on the relentless and gruesomely violent incidents recounted in *The Painted Bird,* Jerzy Kosinski has likened this narrative to a fairy tale that happens to a child, instead of being told to him.[1] Implied in this assessment is a marked ambivalence. The text, on the one hand, depends on a defamiliarizing perspective; Kosinski makes the world strange by viewing it through the conventions of a literary genre congruent with a child's imagination. On the other hand, the suffering and horror are not to be dismissed as a figment of the imagination, a purely interpretive response, or simply a fantasy, but rather something palpable that imposes itself intractably from the material world onto the child's life. Following the misadventures and torments of a young boy who wanders through the Eastern European countryside at the time of the Holocaust, *The Painted Bird* is filled with larger-than-life cruelties, frightening forests, witchlike figures, and magic weapons. Enchantment and primitive emotions come to the fore as undeniable concrete actualities. Blending naturalistic detail with surreal terrors of gargantuan proportions, the writer turns unremitting brutality to self-evident norm. The result is a dismantling of clear oppositions between the plausible and the implausible; the psyche is no longer the sole or primary province of nightmare.

To analyze Kosinski's artistic approach more closely in both its formal mechanisms and their thematic implications, it is helpful to examine the treatment of the child and how the young protagonist, as focalizer, enables this aesthetics of horror. In general, the bestiality of the crimes committed is intensified by contrast with the child's youth and powerlessness. At the same time, the young boy takes savagery for granted; he has little experience or memory beyond the terrors of the moment, and so horror comes to seem ordinary to him. The upshot of combining these opposing tendencies in the text is the novel's insistence, over and over, that people are quite capable of astonishing cruelty. Unbelievable atrocity is not to be disbelieved or dismissed as an unlikely aberration. It is to be seen as an integral part of human nature, and so *The Painted Bird* posits a naturalization of evil.

To achieve this effect, Kosinski cultivates the child more as a narrative device than as a psychological portrait. There is little detailed exploration of mind or inner life, so emphasis is maintained on external events and not on introspection. However, modifying the general lack of inwardness in characterization, Kosinski does give some play to the Boy's imagination, and this move adds measurably to the impression of an equivocal reality in *The Painted Bird*. The child's inability to distinguish between the real and the unreal serves the author's purpose of combining the horrific with the quotidian. For instance, this character's unusual optic ability endows the fictional world with extraordinary or supernatural elements, recalling the celebrated magic realism of Latin American literature. In part the Boy's imaginings embellish the hideousness of events. In part they also attempt to invent another dimension of being removed from immediate pain, and so they postulate some escape from horror. In either case the vision and outlook of the child contribute to the peculiarity of Kosinski's world. Creating wild, fantastic possibilities, they establish a framework within which even the weirdest and most grotesque violence seems possible.

Finally, important as the childlike imagination is for this art, a counterpressure also exerts itself against the Boy's perceptions. The child, demonized as a Jew or a Gypsy by the peasants around him, finds himself in continual flight from their savagery. Hostile forces launch constant attacks against individual consciousness and so put his subjective responses in danger. Eventually, as the exhaustion of his inner life and spiritual resources leaves him unable to feel and express, the Boy loses his voice. In this incapacitation he puts into relief the problems of narration faced by the author. The character's speechlessness in the face of horror reminds the reader that the text as a whole attempts to cast into words an extreme of frightful violence that borders on the inexpressible and defies aesthetic purpose. These matters, as they raise questions about the limitations of language, also bring into sharp focus questions about the Jewishness of Kosinski's text. The narrative relies on the child both to enhance its preoccupations with the Jewish experience of persecution and also to deflect attention from the distinctiveness of anti-Semitism, as the novel insists on the general inhumanity of human beings.

The child character's perception, as it affects the selection and treatment of many incidents in *The Painted Bird,* helps account for some of the distinctive qualities of this text. Chief among these attributes is the air of timelessness and placelessness that pervades the novel. Actions are recounted in a series of seemingly disjointed episodes or vignettes, and this evocation of milieu locates the characters less in a particular moment than in an eerily nonspecific, mythic realm of being. Furthermore, there is little mention of known historical incident, and the omission of verifiable detail adds to the impression that the text offers "selected close-ups but no panoramas."[2] Both effects may be ascribed to the myopia of a child who is concerned solely with matters directly at hand. As Kosinski asserts in his *Notes on the Painted Bird,* "events to the child are immediate: discoveries are one dimensional. This kills, that maims, this one cuffs, that one curses" (15). The Boy, conceived as being very young, quite naturally does not bring to his plight an understanding of broad sociopolitical context. The consequence of narrating in this manner is that the child figure allows at once for the setting to be taken as a recognizable, identifiable one, yet also one that is oneiric and illusive. To be sure, this generalization requires some qualification; the concluding portions of the novel introduce a shift in emphasis and allow an awareness of history by making explicit mention of Stalin and the liberation of Poland. However, these comments occur when the child has changed from a naive six-year-old to a premature, fiercely cynical and knowing adult of twelve. In the opening chapters such specificity is absent. Much of the riveting impact of the text in those sections stems from the emphasis on dislocation, which transforms a familiar countryside into something akin to the typically atemporal site of fairy tales.

There are a number of other ways in which the lack of gestalt in the Boy's apprehension of chaos accommodates a heightened sense of anomaly and simultaneously justifies that strangeness as a norm. To begin with, the protagonist's perspective admits a proliferation of incident and sharpness of detail that have helped earn Kosinski comparison with Breughel and Bosch. That is, because of his status as an apprentice and his vulnerability as a newcomer, the Boy must be an ardent observer. In each new circumstance, each new village or home where he is taken in, he must watch carefully and learn all he can about those around him, without expressing his own wishes. For this reason he functions as a witness. He becomes a conduit through which the narrator can register monstrous events: all manner of slayings, beatings, rapes, and more esoteric horrors as well. Rats devour a human being the Boy has pushed into their pit; the child is suspended from a wall as a vicious dog lunges at his feet; folk medicine proves more frightening than the ailments it is designed to combat. Linen, for instance, soaked in hot wax and set afire inside the head is prescribed to treat an earache. Many of these individual occurrences cannot be discounted as implausible. Nonetheless, as one critic has suggested, the "obsessive regularity" of cruel moments adds up to a realm of madness.[3] Denotative richness particularizes and vivifies the Boy's environment, but enumeration in excess derealizes. At the same time, it should be noted, as madness predominates, even preposterous exaggeration is not discredited as make-believe. In large part the reason is that the Boy's reactions are very much muted. Adult reportage restricts itself most often to recording sequential instances of silent perception and does not admit explorations of feelings. This manner of narrating makes even the most prodigiously awful acts seem matter-of-fact.

Now, because the surfeit of appalling detail is made accessible through the child's attentiveness, the text as a whole comes to rely on an alliance of cross-purposes. Featuring a personal angle on brutality, the novel also recounts a brutal crushing of inner life, for the child's exposure to calamity numbs his emotional and intellectual responses. The attempt to inhabit the otherness of the child in this fantastically sinister world therefore yields a space at once intense and narrow. While the child's spirit is reduced and spent, his perceptions are keenly heightened. What his vision lacks in depth and inwardness it retains in vitality. In this way the textual representation of his consciousness is marked equally by minimalism and overstatement. Spare description of cognitive complexity and a disregard for interiority are matched by an overload of sensory detail, allowing for hallucinatory intensity in the text without diminishing the Boy's experience by presenting it simply as a hallucination.

Much as this aspect of Kosinski's artistry fluctuates between the naturalistic and the nonnaturalistic, so, too, does the protagonist's anonymity. Uncertainty about the Boy's biography can be understood as reflecting his own youthful incomprehension of his situation: what has forced him to live on the run, why his parents have abandoned him, what his life was like before the war. This point justifies deemphasis on his specificity as an individual. However, Kosinski also cultivates the namelessness quite self-consciously for the purposes of patent artifice. These factors turn *The Painted Bird* into a disquieting mixture of genres, somewhere between a reliable account of a specific historical moment and a purely fictive parable of evil. Commenting on the emblematic quality of the Boy, Kosinski describes his character as a "concretization of a feeling" rather than a believably complex individual. The author also acknowledges a debt in his thinking to Jungian notions of the child as a symbol for self-preservation, and so Kosinski sees his fictional figure as an archetype "equally felt and equally intangible."[4] Finally, though, the picture is more complex than any of these qualities might suggest. A series of subtle modulations between inner perception and outward event make for much of the interest the text commands. Without turning this novel into a penetrating study of the cognitive or emotional workings of a child's mind, these moments do prevent the text from becoming simply a pornography of violence, for they raise important questions about the ability of the imagination to grapple with horror.

Attention to the Boy's imagination is generally achieved through a careful merging of perspectives, which constrains both adult narratorial prerogatives and the child's voice. The result is to allow the misperceptions of the young to leach into the portrait of his surroundings and so to increase the impression of oddity in this fictional world. Consider, for instance, what happens when his first stepmother dies suddenly one night. The youngster understands little of death and so cannot fathom at first why Marta doesn't move. Then, accidentally setting the house on fire, the Boy inadvertently lights a huge funeral pyre for the old woman. As the flames quickly approach her and she does not respond, the child's amazement endows the scene with supernatural force:

> I marveled at Marta. Was she really so indifferent to all this? Had her charms and incantations granted her immunity against a fire that turned everything else about her into ashes? . . . In the clouds of smoke rising to the sky I thought I detected a strange oblong she. What was it? Could it be Marta's soul making its escape to the heavens? Or was it Marta herself, revived by the fire, relieved of her old crusty skin, leaving this earth on a fiery broomstick, like the witch in the story my mother told me? (11)[5]

The multiple questions here turn fantasy to strangely plausible possibility. Perception, reiterated, becomes inseparable from the factual aspects of the account, and so Kosinski merges imaginative interpretation with documentable event.

The passage achieves this effect particularly as it offers a clear case of self-narrated monologue, Dorrit Cohn's term for a first-person variant on narrated monologue.[6] The mature authorial figure, recalling his youth, sounds the thoughts he harbored long ago. However, there is no child's language clearly demarcated from the words of the adult author. No quotations set aside the Boy's articulation of the situation, and the text employs no descriptive phrases (such as *I said, I asked myself,* or *I wondered*) that would attribute the comments in this passage specifically to the Boy. Furthermore, the account of his thoughts does not rely on some superior knowledge that might underscore the gap between adult self, reminiscing, and child figure, still in the midst of the experience. There ensues, then, a peculiar consonance between narrator and character. The grown-up's empathy and his apparent inability to move beyond past bewilderments, fascinations, and uncertainties suggest that this man still identifies with the past. Such a narrative approach gains importance, Cohn remarks, "when a highly self-centered narrator relates an existential crisis that has remained unresolved. Unable to cast a retrospective light on past experience, he can only relive his dark confusions" (168). By limiting himself to the child's unknowing stance, and by not undertaking analytical retrospection, the narrator does not try to explain away the incongruous mixture of dread and wonder that he felt as a child. On the contrary: giving special prominence to the child's views, the text also credits those past thoughts with a certain legitimacy. Though there is evidently some ironic distance between mature and immature perspectives (the child's interpretation is necessarily apprehended by the reader as fanciful), Kosinski's is a subdued irony. Presented within the lucid, well-organized prose of the adult, the Boy's ideas are not to be discounted offhandedly as foolishness. The text thereby preserves the spookiness of a first encounter with death. In the process, the novel also deploys a technique that will serve frequently to indicate that the prime qualities of this world—its extremes of filth, deprivation, and viciousness—do not admit rational explanation. Instead, they can be expressed more appropriately through unusually intense perceptions and incomprehensions ascribable to a child.

Self-narrated monologue is also operative later, with a slight modification of emphasis, in one of the most chilling scenes in *The Painted Bird*. The child has been taken into another foster family where, In a moment of jealous rage, the husband gouges out the eyes of a young man he suspects (baselessly) of cuckolding him. Like the whimsical questions that shaped Marta's death into a magical flight, the Boy's reactions in this passage likewise conjure a hypothetical scenario. The proximity of narrator to character again helps present an odd combination of hope and horror as if they were a persuasive possibility. Here is how the Boy describes the discarded eyes:

> I watched them with fascination. . . . Surely they could still see. I would keep them in my pocket and take them out when needed, placing them over my own. Then I would see twice as much, maybe

even more. Perhaps I could attach them to the back of my head and they would tell me, though I was not quite certain how, what went on behind me. Better still, I could leave the eyes somewhere and they would tell me later what happened during my absence.

Maybe the eyes had no intention of serving anyone. They could easily escape from the cats and roll out of the door. They could wander over the fields, lakes, and woods viewing everything about them, free as birds released from a trap. They would no longer die, since they were free, and being small they could easily hide in various places and watch people in secret. Excited, I decided to close the door quietly and capture the eyes. (38)

As before, the narrator voices the child's thoughts to grant them a special validity, if not credence. However, while the passage about Marta turns the child's vision to artistic advantage, conveying the feel of phantasmagoria in the fictional world, this description of the eyes evinces a somewhat different relationship between imagination and horror.

It has been argued that this portion of the text, more than any other, celebrates individual, interpretive consciousness much as does romanticism. Because of the episode with the eyes the Boy determines to remember everything, lest he ever lose his own sight, and so this moment marks the origins of artistic sensibility. At this time "memory enters the service of a self bent on vision." Along these lines the narrative has been read as a Kunstlerroman that is unusual mainly in the magnitude of horror it depicts.[7] The argument is sound, up to a point. The Boy does seek out a redemptive insight or hindsight. It bears notice, though, that in this scene the workings of the imagination do not stand in binary opposition to violence. They also amplify horror, highlighting the grotesquerie and senselessness of the incident. After all, the Boy's musings belabor attention to the mutilated eyes. They therefore intensify the graphically hair-raising descriptions that have made this incident so objectionable to many readers. On the one hand Kosinski's child expresses hopeful sentiments, deeming the damage to be reparable, and so the passage makes of the eyes a heartwarming metaphor. On the other hand, as it refers to specific actions in a concrete setting—a little boy stooping to pick up a pair of eyes and put them into his pocket—the scene repels. The passage, then, provides evidence that the imagination, immersed in a world of horrors, cannot easily dissociate itself from the horrific. This point, of importance to the plot action and the thematic emphasis of the text, raises questions as well about Kosinski's art as a whole. Does his artistic revisioning of a long-ago horror transform that memory into something better: a moral vision, a warning for the future, a tribute to the imagination just for surviving hellish torment? Does it simply add up, instead, to a literature that exploits lurid fascination with death and degradation? There is no easy way to distinguish between these possibilities, and *The Painted Bird* oscillates between them.

Related issues arise in another scene where an empathic fusing of child and adult, in slightly altered fashion, similarly imbues the fictional world with magical qualities. The following is recounted after the Boy has been buried in the earth up to his neck for several days. Prescribed to cure a fever, this torture proves almost fatal as ravens peck fiercely at his head: "I gave up. I was myself now a bird. I was trying to free my chilled wings from the earth. Stretching my limbs, I joined the flock of ravens. Borne abruptly up on a gust of fresh, reviving wind, I soared straight into a ray of sunshine that lay taut on the horizon like a drawn bow-string, and my joyous cawing was mimicked by my winged compan-ions" (24).

Once more, Kosinski relies on a narrow intersection of perspec-tives. These lines make clear that, while the author aims to convey the Boy's impressions and thoughts, he does not readily sound the child's voice. Lacking in introspection or indications of inner speech, this is a highly monovocal text that effaces childish vocabulary. And yet the adult narration, too, is severely limited. Though the passage may be con-sidered psychonarration, it occludes inside views of the protagonist rather than illuminating them the way a clear authorial presence often can. Observations are effectively restricted to the child's perceptions, and the narrator neither details the Boy's inner world omnisciently nor takes advantage of the cognitive privilege usually available to a mature storyteller in command of a retrospective vantage point. Evident is a distanced, almost detached narrator, but not one able to foretell events nor one able to evaluate the past through self-exegesis. What this nar-row amalgam of child and adult perspectives accomplishes is to engage an elevated if simple prose, which makes for uplifting transformation of the character's grisly circumstances. Such turns of phrase as "my joyous cawing was mimicked by my winged companions" bear little re-semblance to the way actual children speak, but the lyricism suggests the sensibility of the child in his most intense misery. The same can be said of the use of metaphor (e.g., the reference to sunshine that lies "taut on the horizon like a bowstring"). In both cases inner life is externalized, crys-tallized, and projected onto outer events in a way that recalls expression-ism. The adult prose style thereby attributes dignity and a kind of stark beauty to the Boy's suffering.

In sum, the narrator relates to the child not primarily with disso-nance (shock, condescension, humor, or pity), and so he invites the reader to accept the hallucinations as a valid, poetic, even exalted expla-nation of events. By respecting the child's outlook and the primacy of the

individual imagination, but without engaging in psychological portraiture, the text creates a laconic description of near psychosis. In the
process it demonstrates the circumscribed, nearly extinguished space
within which a sensitive mind, under severe assault, still manages to
function. To be sure, the result is not entirely positive. First, the victim
has found some ecstatic release from his travails, but only by way of
dementia. In addition, the metaphor does not lift him out of the world of
painful torment so much as it magically projects him into a different
aspect of that setting. Troublingly, the child identifies with the aggressor.
He remains well within the realm of a ruthlessly brutal world. Imagined
beauty here does not transcend horror. It serves to protect the Boy by
allowing him to flee, desperately, from his own humanity.

The Boy is not the only figure whose imagination infuses this
world with magical possibilities. His consciousness is the most closely
monitored and most instrumental in the narration of the story, but part
of its importance is that it illustrates a general point about the characters
who populate *The Painted Bird.* Their thinking, too, is governed by
ignorance and superstition, so what may seem at first to be childish
fantasies, appropriate for the young character, are in effect paradigmatic
of the larger milieu in which the protagonist lives. Indeed, there is not
always a clear line between his thoughts and theirs. His psychic life is an
amalgam of folk wisdom and the primitive religious beliefs he has heard
from those around him. These he welds together with his knowledge of
fairy tales, one of the few things he remembers from his home before the
war. In particular, this blend of influences affects his perception of Marta's death. She shows her young charge how to cast spells, she mutters
enchantments, and she speaks of snakes discarding their skins as a kind
of magic. Assimilating and internalizing this way of referring to the
world, the Boy comes to think in such terms as well. Consequently, it is
no surprise that when the old woman dies, he interprets her demise as a
supernatural occurrence.

The following passage indicates how forceful and dynamic a role.
the superstitious imagination plays in *The Painted Bird.* This scene takes
place early on in the journey. The Boy has sought refuge with some
villagers who are convinced that his hair, because it is dark, will attract
lightning.

> Often at dusk when the meager flames of candles and kerosene lamps
> began to flicker in the huts, the skies *would* become veiled by heavy
> sagging clouds that sailed obliquely over the thatched roofs. The
> villagers *would* grow silent, fearfully looking out from behind the
> windows, listening to the growing rumble. Old women squatting on
> cracked tile ovens ceased their prayers and deliberated as to who
> *would* be rewarded this time by the Almighty or who *would* be pun-

ished by ubiquitous Satan, on whom fire and destruction, death or a crippling malady *would* fall. The groans of creaking doors, the sighing of trees bent by the storm, and the whistle of the wind *would* sound to the villagers like the curses of long-dead sinners, tormented by the uncertainty of limbo or slowly roasting in the never-ending fires of hell. (57, emphasis added)

Here, language clearly establishes perceived realities. The women's deliberations about Satan and their interpretations of ordinary sounds impose spooky meaning onto everyday events. Kosinski's presentation reinforces this mentality. His text validates or legitimizes legend and folk belief as it absorbs and reproduces them in the adult author's rhetoric. That is to say, the deflection of attention away from introspection or carefully nuanced representations of consciousness and verbal activity of mind in large measure erases distinctions between words and nonverbal experience. The narrator's simple, unifying vision attributes equal significance to all that it records; statements therefore come to weigh as heavily as actions. In this way the prose conveys the seriousness with which the child himself must have taken the threatening rumors: quite rightly, too, for they whip up the fury of the villagers, whose anger then directs itself against him. The frequent use of "would" plays a special role in this connection. This word signifies both conjecture and repetition. It serves sometimes as an indicator of familiar routine and sometimes signals conditions contrary to fact. Placing two meanings in tandem, the homonym conjoins the usual round of activity with obsessive superstition. The result is to increase a sense of foreboding. In general the rhythm of the novel is determined by a multitude of cruelties that crescendo into an explosive climax.[8] In this passage, in particular, repetition of the iterative past enforces the impression that eventual catastrophe is inevitable. When lightning does strike, the primitive apprehensions of the people and the incremental build-up of tension come to a head. The plot action literally bursts into flames, and the Boy flees in terror of being blamed.

As is clear from the example, the narrator plays a special part in bringing about the fusion of folk belief and action, speech and deed in *The Painted Bird*. If, before, the author combined child character and adult narrator into a narrowly dialogic relation, conflating one with the other but without giving rein to either, here the narrator melds the villagers' reported speech acts into his own vocabulary. This move has significant impact, as it disallows any easy distinction between the authoritative authorial omniscience and the expressions of superstition. Interpenetrating voices here assure that the peasants' outlook will gain credibility, allied as it is with the narrator's authority. The effect is enhanced by the fact that no direct citation in this passage grants the characters personalities or linguistic registers of their own. The same held true also for the Boy's reports of Marta's speech. Of her he remarks, for instance, "She ordered me to spit quickly three times," or, "She forbade me to look directly into her eyes" (6, 18); when dough turns sour he notes, "She blamed me for casting a spell" (18). Nowhere does he actually reproduce her words. Part of the effectiveness of Kosinski's prose is precisely that, as it reports the speech of others, it shies away from direct discourse, detailed paraphrase, or other attempts at mimesis of the spoken word.[9] Though the world referred to is a highly polylingual one where dialect and differences of pronunciation have immediate and severe consequences (the Boy's city accent marks him dangerously as an outsider), those differences are assiduously homogenized within the author's own English. Absorbed into the author's voice, they are robbed of particularity, become part and parcel of his outlook, and so reduce reference to a material world that exists beyond the text. The resulting uniform narrative surface helps make this fictional world more fully a creation of the author's imagination, responsive to its own laws.

The point takes on special resonance because this stylistic feature forms part of a broader phenomenon in Kosinski's novel. The prose—precise, sharp, and detailed—is nonetheless not of the moment nor indicative of a specific milieu. As such, it reinforces the atemporality of the narrative and helps create the impression of an extraordinarily hostile world unmoored in time. By manufacturing a very detailed, concrete, but free-floating horror, Kosinski produces an additional frisson of alienation. The fact that Kosinski uses an adopted language in his writing contributes to this aspect of his art.[10] English provides the author a special distance from his thematic material. Learned in his twenties, shortly after he defected from Poland to the United States, this language affords him the *mot juste,* the power of naming, while also repressing colloquialism. The author thereby retains greater freedom to refashion memories of his own boyhood during the Shoah and to create a fictional realm in which anything can happen but in which even the most grotesque events must be taken seriously.

A number of the salient stylistic traits of *The Painted Bird* converge in the following paragraph. As the protagonist/narrator discusses his first preoccupations with death and ways of dying, child vista and adult narration combine to create magical animation and to collapse inner perception and outer events.

> I recalled well the time, in the first days of the war when a bomb hit a house across the street from my parents' home. Our windows were blown out. We were assaulted by falling walls, the tremor of the shaken earth, the screams of unknown dying people. I saw the brown

surfaces of doors, ceilings, walls, with the pictures still clinging desperately to them, all falling into the void. Like an avalanche rushing to
the street came majestic grand pianos opening and closing their lids in
flight, obese, clumsy armchairs, skittering stools and hassocks. They
were chased by chandeliers that were falling apart with shrill cries, by
polished kitchen pots, kettles, and sparkling aluminum chamber pots.
Pages torn out of gutted books fell down, flapping like flocks of scared
birds. Bathtubs tore themselves away slowly and deliberately from
their pipes, entwining themselves magically in the knots and scrolls of
banisters and railings and rain gutters. (75)

The one-dimensionality Kosinski has ascribed to the child's perspective in his *Notes on the Painted Bird* is apparent here as the Boy sees
each of the objects in motion, one by one, scattered by the blast. The
close-up is effected through attention to specifics, a listing of the numerous components of the scene: armchairs, pianos, stools, hassocks, pots,
pages, bathtubs. Even as the enumeration vivifies, it also disorients,
appropriately reenacting the fragmentation described. At the same time,
many objects are personified and so magically animated (pictures cling,
armchairs are clumsy and obese, chandeliers chase). Explicit mention of
magic intrudes into the last sentence of the paragraph, suggesting that
this is a vision of exceptional power(s). Altogether, while the metonymic
emphasis of this listing retains reference to the here and now, to material
objects contiguous to one another, there is a metaphoric tendency that
indicates how the child's individual view imparts another level of value
to things. Pianos are glimpsed in flight, pages flap like scared birds. The
metaphor, indicating that the household furnishings soar aloft, also lifts
them out of the immediate denotative context and valorizes them as
living creatures seeking escape. Naturally, the child's view here, as elsewhere, accommodates and is accomplished through the author's retrospective convictions. These Kosinski has articulated in a theory of art as
a loosening of boundaries between the possible and the improbable. His
is a search for ways to circumvent the "routine or banal expression."
The chief element of the writing process, in this model, is to stand back
from experience and "enter a fluid and less rigidly limited dimension"
that exists only in the author's consciousness. "Within it the elements of
reality no longer obey the earth-bound laws of gravitation."[11] Much as
this artistic credo professes a desire to defy gravity, this scene, too,
depicts falling items that resist the pull of the earth below.

Here, too, is the amalgamation of destruction and yearning for
release already familiar from those earlier passages that likewise called
attention to flight. Marta is said to fly off like a witch on a broomstick.
The Boy buried in the earth perceives himself as joining the flock of
ravens; the plucked-out eyes of the plowboy are deemed to be "free as

birds"; by the same token, when the protagonist loses his voice, he imagines it "flying alone" under the vaulted roof of the church, "knocking against the walls and panes." The child's imaginings try over and over to liberate individual consciousness from sordid surroundings. There is, however, no categorical escape from torment. Dismemberment, death, and insanity underlie all the possibilities of liberty. Implied in each of these images is a curious mix of freedom and suffering. Escape, born out of pain, remains inseparable from it. As such the imagery recalls the Boy's entire existential situation. His is a journey of survival, a free-roving life that oscillates always between new escapes and new enslavements. The painted bird of the title presents a particularly condensed example of both pain and flight, and so becomes most emblematic of the protagonist. This is a bird that other members of the flock attack, because its feathers have been colored differently with paint. Marked as Other, its outspread wings advertising its hated nonconformity, this bird is beaten to death even as it flies.

Filled with images that simultaneously express a desire for escape and also reinforce or reinscribe horror, Kosinski's novel resembles Edmond Jabès' "Song of the Last Jewish Child." Both Jabès' poem and *The Painted Bird* feature transformations enacted by metaphor. Endowed with hallucinatory intensity, these images turn the earthy, the elemental, and the brutal into a picture of stark beauty. For Jabès, flying signifies escape, freedom, and defiance of gravity, but only by way of death. In a world of weightless phantasmagoria, sustenance disappears and is replaced by pain: "The stone is not heavy / the bread is like the bird / I watch as it flies. / Blood is on my cheeks."[12] Hope in this spiritual climate implies defeat. The child seeks to be at one with earth, water, or fire, much as his parents are said to hang "from a star" and to "flow with the river." Such visions of liberation can take only a macabre interpretation: namely, that the young speaker, who has already been orphaned, also yearns for death. The poem continues by referring yet again to movements that combine comfort with horror: "Dead horsemen always gallop / in my sleep and in my eyes" and ends, "Death's horsemen bear me away. / I am born to love them." That which is most intimate is also most threatening, that which is most alive in this world is death. Freedom, marked by ambivalence, manifests itself as a simultaneously beckoning and sinister dislocation or lack. In *The Painted Bird*, similarly, suffering and victimization are inevitable. For all the author's efforts to view the world via a childlike innocence, the transformative capacities of the imagination finally make the cruelties witnessed more sickening and not less. Horror proves inescapable.

Eventually, the child's perceptions in *The Painted Bird* are no longer able to effect an aestheticization of horror. Because of prolonged torment, the child's consciousness simply cannot sustain its interpretive capacities, and, as abuse becomes unbearably extreme, the Boy loses his voice. His muteness is reminiscent of the silencing suffered by Elie Wiesel's young character in *Gates of the Forest* (1964) and later by David Grossman's Momik in *See Under: Love* (1986). In each case deprivation has reached such extremes, or violence has reached such mass proportions, that they leave no room for individual mind and expression. In Kosinski's novel there ensues an abdication of interpretation. If the first part of the novel focuses on artful attempts to inhabit the unusual perspective of the child, to find a narrative strategy suitable for giving voice to the child, the second half is more concerned with the child's apprehension of adult language as a hollow and inadequate tool of understanding. This change in orientation corresponds to another basic one. In the initial portions of *The Painted Bird* the Boy seeks out love and acceptance, only to be rejected time and again. In the second half, having despaired of that earlier ideal, he attempts to gain as much power as he can simply to survive in a malevolent world.[13]

The pivotal crisis is precipitated by a mob scene in which angry churchgoers throw the Boy into a manure pit. His crime: he has accidentally dropped a tray and missal during mass. No longer expecting decency, the protagonist begins to close out, one by one, the codes by which he might try to live.[14] First he rejects religion, the Christianity that he has learned from the villagers and that he had believed would ward off harm. He quickly abandons the discourse of Catholicism, after he discovers that all of his prayers do not prevent the pious crowd from pitching him into the ditch of excrement. Following this disillusionment the Boy embraces evil, assuming that to be as powerful as possible is the only escape from hurt. Later, when he has been picked up by the Russian army, he discards this philosophy and welcomes instead the cant and propagandistic exhortations of his communist benefactors. None of these cultural idioms proves to be a match for the savagery of the world, which always exceeds any explanations or world views the Boy may articulate. As all these creeds fail to become internally persuasive for him, they heighten this character's role as an alien voice that puts into doubt the assumptions of preexisting discourse. Just as Bakhtin would posit, his incomprehension serves a polemical purpose, one expressed most notably in passages filled with his questions. Mulling over the perplexities of religion, for instance, the child wonders why,

> if God could make sinners into pillars of salt so easily, salt was so expensive. And why didn't He turn some sinners into meat or sugar. The villagers certainly needed these as much as salt. . . . But if God really decided what was to happen, why did the peasants worry about their faith, the churches, and the clergy? . . . Even the most over-

worked God could not overlook such a menace [the Red Army] to his
people. But then would not that mean that the Germans, who also
demolished churches and murdered people, would prove the winners?
From God's point of view it seemed to make more sense if everyone
lost the war, since everyone was committing murder. (183)

Proffered once or twice, this kind of questioning effectively makes
the conventional explanations of religion the Boy has heard strange.
Repeated numerous times, this stance of disappointment and perplexity
suggests he has lost all frame of reference. This character knows only
disorientation, a constant process of emptying out of meaning and values.[15]

This portion of the book, as it demonstrates the Boy's progressing
cynicism, may well be less interesting than the first. All the same, it
merits attention for putting into relief the problems of narration the
author faced. Kosinski highlights the artistic dilemma of so much fiction
that has dealt with the Holocaust: how to find a language commensurate with catastrophe, especially the sheer ghastliness and suffering of
the Nazi era. The protagonist's explicit critique of language may alert
the reader to the struggle against silence in the early chapters and to the
artistic benefits provided by the overlap of perspectives in the first half of
the book. There, the adult wrestled with the difficulty of adopting a
child's perspective—necessarily a contrived, bifocal narration—in order to offer a less discursive, more immediate confrontation with horror.

A special moment of hope does present itself to the protagonist
when the Russians teach the Boy to read. The narrator notes that books
were fascinating to him, for they offered a new intensity of perception.
As an opening into the inner life of others, they seemed to signal the
potential plenitude of language: "From their simple printed pages one
could conjure up a world as real as that grasped by the senses. Furthermore, the world of books, like meat in cans, was somehow richer and
more flavorful than the everyday variety. In ordinary life, for example,
one saw many people without really knowing them, while in books one
even knew what people were thinking and planning" (196).

The charm of reading does not last long, however, and the protagonist is attracted more and more to vengeance rather than to empathy or attempts to understand human beings. In the final chapter of the
novel the Boy conclusively rebuffs intimacy. His parents have found him
after the war, but he resents and evades them. Justifying this response, he
notes that he has cast aside all desire to respond to, absorb, echo, or
interpret the voices of others: "It mattered little if one was mute; people
did not understand one another anyway. They collided with or charmed
one another, hugged or trampled one another, but everyone knew only
himself. His emotions, memory, and senses divided him from others as

effectively as thick reeds screen the mainstream from the muddy bank" (249).

Ambivalence about the efficacy of language continues even after this point, and tensions about communication do not ever resolve themselves. The final scene, which presents the Boy's sudden recovery of speech, has been interpreted variously as validating or invalidating language as a tool of understanding. Three separate versions of the ending suggest that the author himself had vacillating convictions about how much to endorse a celebration of words or the imagination.[16] Some wordings emphasize the wonder of reborn contact with humankind and the protagonist's newly built bridge to another voice (a nameless one, at the end of a telephone wire). Two versions, though, include details that make for highly visible reminders of repellent horror and signal the potential for danger, which is always bred anew out of renewed contact with people.

This thematic indecision is congruent with and can even serve as a metanarrative commentary on aspects of Kosinski's own approach to narration. The fundamental issue spelled out in the Boy's reaction to reading is the same one raised by the very writing of a childhood narrative: the possibility of inhabiting another's consciousness. The special province of fiction, overcoming otherness through imagining someone else's perceptions, proves problematic in the case of the young characters who are spoken for through an adult. Significantly, the first book the protagonist reads is Gorky's famous memoirs of his early years, *Childhood*. Even this account of a child's travails, which speaks so directly to the Boy's concerns, is ultimately rejected by him. This means that Kosinski's character denies the vicarious intimacy of literature even as the author, too, refuses to endorse portrayals of inner life. Though his novel is devoted to inhabiting the otherness of the child, he enters that realm only with utmost caution and restraint.

The treatment of childhood in *The Painted Bird* has served, then, most importantly to contribute to the dreamlike, phantasmagoric quality of the narrative. This conclusion is supported by Kosinski's own early remarks on the novel in *Notes of the Author:* "why was this book written about childhood? Why did the author choose this particular motif? C. G. Jung, in his essay *The Psychology of the Child Archetype,* provides enlightening viewpoints. Jung regards the child motif as representative of the preconscious state" (13).

Through the dreamlike recounting of the journey, Kosinski observes, he arrives at "a vision, not an examination, or a revisitation" of his own past. Closer examination of narrative voice has supplemented this observation by showing that the narrow intersection of child perspective and adult storytelling demonstrates thematic ambivalence about the imagination. Minimizing introspection, this novel demonstrates the devalued role of the imagination in a destructive, hate-filled setting, while it also signals the struggle of the individual imagination to stay alive and bring a dimension of hope or inner richness to that world so as to combat its hatefulness.

Contributing, too, to the impact of imagined childhood in *The Painted Bird* are elements of the picaresque, a genre that developed early in the history of the novel and typically revolved about a young character who grew out of childish innocence into disillusionment. Staples of that brand of narrative include the wandering of a protagonist who, more pragmatic than ethical, tries to adapt to a series of unnerving situations in a chaotic world. In the process this figure becomes a rascal or rogue.[17] Also familiar from the picaresque is first-person narration that does not so much reveal the main character's inner life as it permits him to observe others. These qualities in Kosinski's novel make the Boy's reactions a peculiarly apt vehicle for reinforcing both sensationalism and monotony. As such, this construction of childhood signals a repetitive violence that comes to seem inevitable in the fictional world. Here, too, as was true for the prototypical Lazarillo, the character's stance as an outsider allows him to undercut the discourse of those around him and expose its flaws. Sholem Aleichem's Mottel is his counterpart in a much less macabre and grotesque chronicle of destruction recounted from a child's vantage point. While Mottel unsettles adult words, inverts their intents, or drains them of sacred connotations, the Boy of Kosinski's novel is engaged in a constant shedding of adult meaning. This narrative offers a series of discarding motions that put into question the very value of language. And, if Mottel casts all incidents in a lighthearted mold, converting even the most daunting crises into child's play, the Boy's tale all but concedes the primacy of atrocity. The child's imagination, which at first transforms horror into a possibility of escape, comes to insist that the human penchant for violence will put a quick end to childish wonder. And, immersed in a world where everyone victimizes others, the Boy becomes an *enfant terrible* who also commits heinous acts in order to get by.

The child's status as a marginal figure makes this art possible in another way as well. It motivates the plot action in a very fundamental sense. Having less of an established identity than would an adult, the Boy is a more likely candidate for a story about wandering. This individual is easier to hide, it is more natural that the peasants take him in, and it is more likely, too, that he will survive. His presence evokes hatred, but for many he is useful as an apprentice, or he is sheltered because he does not seem overly threatening. Consequently, he is a figure of ambivalence: despised, but not entirely so. As a result, the hatred directed against him does not in the end prove fatal. In a world that annihilates the alien, the Jews and the Gypsies, he is the other of the Other, neither accepted by the peasants as one of their own nor, finally, murdered as one of their enemies. The thematic implications are considerable. The child is spared the worst and remains on the margins of destruction. As bad as things are, the Boy's suffering suggests that much more appalling, unutterably horrible things have taken place elsewhere, within the concentration camps and the death trains he watches from a distance. It is ultimately because the Boy's voice is muted, but not obliterated, that the book can come to be, and his presence therefore insists once more that the ferocity he experiences, bizarre as it is, is not to be disbelieved. As the author himself acknowledged, even the most outlandish episodes in his novel are considerably less terrible and incredible than many events that took place in the Shoah.[18]

It should be remembered that, as other to the Other, this figure is conceived as a doubly alienated individual. His chances for survival increase, but even as he is an outcast from the majority, his ties to the minority community have been severed. Presented as too young to carry a store of cultural information within him, this character has no knowledge of the past. One result, naturally, is that, knowing so little, he perceives Jewishness purely as vulnerability to persecution. This ignorance then enhances the adult narrator's approach to the Holocaust, which is to turn it into a universal myth of evil.[19] The narrative shies away from awarding the Jews any substance of their own. They have no distinctive history here, and Kosinski offers no exploration of Jewish values or symbols to convey how Jewish culture or individuals have defined themselves. The child's limited inner life gives no pause for thought about such things, and so it is a natural aid to the adult author's generalizations in undermining the distinctiveness of the Jews.

This stance, evident throughout the novel, becomes even more striking when considered against the background of Kosinski's life. From a Polish Jewish family, having spent much of his formative years in wandering, the author draws on his childhood experience but insists at regular intervals in his narrative that the Boy might be a Jew or a Gypsy.[20] The two are supposed as virtually interchangeable possibilities, essentially equalized because each is the target of seething hatred. Further prevaricating on the issue of Jewishness, the author announces that the Boy is not necessarily either one. Instead, he is simply perceived as a Jew or a Gypsy because his coloring differs from that of his neighbors. The reader is told definitively only that the child's parents hid their son out of fear that their own prewar political activities might put him in danger of internment. If the depiction of the child is tenuous, a device rather than a psychologically penetrating portrayal of a young mind, there is even more limited entrance into the consciousness of the political Other. With its inner life reduced in the extreme, the minority is seen solely in terms of the reactions it evokes in the majority.

This approach cannot but prompt debate about whether it makes sense to label *The Painted Bird* a Jewish text. Drawing little on Jewish contexts, presenting a minimalist definition of Jewishness as inescapable curse, the novel presents a limited case thematically and formally. However, the preoccupation of the novel with Jewishness can be read as a response to the Holocaust, one that attempts to deny anti-Semitic assumptions of Jewish difference. If there is no meaningful distinction between Jews and Gypsies, then the peasants' ideology is stripped bare and exposed as a raw pleasure in violence. The conjoining of the child's incomprehension with the adult author's inclination to universalize brings a special subversive power to the text; reinforcing each other, these two aspects of the narrative undo the beliefs prevalent in the world where the Boy must live.

A striking moment in the text brings out how collusion between child view and adult narration challenges the fictional world created in *The Painted Bird,* dislodging the certainties that inflame its hostilities. In this passage the author both highlights the primacy of hate in the novel's setting and discredits its claims. This is one of the first and very few instances of direct discourse in a text that suppresses the spoken address of its characters. That means that the mentality of the villagers is made exceptionally explicit here, but Kosinski does not leave them or their odious brutality the final word. The scene takes place when death trains pass on the way to the extermination camps. The peasants, watching, react with bloodthirsty self-righteousness, persuaded that the Jews are receiving just punishment for killing Christ. The text reads: "The villagers now gave me even darker looks. 'You Gypsy-Jew,' they yelled. 'You'll burn yet, bastard, you will' " (100).

The Gentiles, described earlier as people of few words and "slow deliberate speech" (85), speak loud and clear in this scene. First, they set themselves apart from the Other. Calling the Boy "you" three times in a short sentence, they set up an opposition between first and second person; by affirming a clearly demarcated "you," they imply a totally separate "we." Furthermore, overtly threatening the child and addressing him in hostile tones, they call him a bastard and suggest that his orphanhood, his abandonment and lack of parentage, means delegitimation. Accordingly, they can label him in a way that entirely disregards any possibility of his own self-definition. They conflate the terms "Gypsy" and "Jew" into a kind of oxymoronic amalgam that, more than defining him, expresses their own hatred.

In contradistinction to the peasants' straightforward statement, their message, which is not to be mistaken, the narrator offers instead a layered, subtly polyvalent and equivocal comment. As the Boy wonders why only people dusky in hue must suffer God's wrath, the narrator notes that "they gave me even darker looks." Now, *looks* may refer to the glowers and threatening glances of the villagers. Certainly, this is the understanding that can be ascribed to the child as he sees loathing and resentment filling the faces of his persecutors. In that case an irony not apparent to the Boy is evident to the reader. By the standard the villagers have set up, *dark looks* signify sin. Here they are ones whose looks are dark. The ironies multiply, however, because the deep structure of this sentence is not clear. The same word, *looks,* may also refer to the Boy's appearance. That is, the darkness of his skin is not a simple matter of pigmentation but a matter of how the Gentiles see him. They determine his status in the fictional world, and in their minds he has just become darker. In either interpretation, from the perspective of adult narrator and reader, it is clear that the behavior of the villagers makes them loathsome. Subtly shifting the blame off the Boy and onto them, the narrator quietly protests against their bigotry.

In the process the text also blurs distinctions between self and other, discrediting the notions of good and evil that the villagers espouse. In this light they are villains who perfectly illustrate the human tendency toward malicious stereotyping. People often project onto others what is unacceptably frightening within the self. Trying to make a rigid distinction between good and bad, the villagers define the person who is ethnically or racially different as something strictly apart from themselves and, ascribing wickedness externally to this person, insist on their own innocence.[21] Tellingly, the same people who commit iniquities without end in *The Painted Bird* define the Boy as one who is capable of causing violence, attracting lightning, giving them the evil eye, or killing Christ. The intersection of meanings in the word "looks" brings such matters to the fore in this short passage. Kosinski merges adult perspective with child's view, not in a way that is flamboyantly polysemous, but in a subdued and controlled form consistent with the subtle interanimations of discourse found throughout the novel. Such narrative tactics amount to an artistry that can at once emphasize an intensely poisonous prejudice and violence, yet make of the novel more than merely a catalogue of horrors. The voice that ultimately prevails is not the cry of murderous rage but a textured literary construction, a statement that, invested with multiple meanings, reserves a valued role for the interpreting mind and holds out the possibility that language can effectively register a recoil from violence.

7 AHRON APPELFELD—
THE AGE OF WONDERS

The heaviest wheel rolls across our foreheads
To bury itself deep somewhere inside our memories.

—Mif, "Terezín"

But now I am no more a child
For I have learned to hate.
I am a grown-up person now,
I have known fear.

Bloody words and a dead day then,
That's something different than bogie men!

But anyway, I still believe I only sleep today,
That I'll wake up, a child again, and start to laugh and
play.

—Hanuš Hachenburg, "Terezín," *I Never Saw Another*
Butterfly: Children's Drawings and Poems from
Terezín Concentration Camp, 1942–1944

*I*n his essays Ahron Appelfeld has commented directly on some of the dilemmas that artists face as they attempt to speak, in retrospect, of unspeakable horror. He formulates his ideas in the same vocabulary and concepts that Bialik provided half a century before and which figured so importantly in that author's own narrative of childhood, *Aftergrowth*. Acknowledging his debt to Bialik as a predecessor in the chronicles of catastrophe and absurd suffering, Appelfeld notes that revealment and concealment, *gilui vekhisui*, are the essence of all expression, but for those who experienced the Shoah, this phenomenon takes on heightened importance.[1] Contradictory impulses toward articulation and silence constitute the very soul of the survivor, who wavers ever about the thin line between saying and not saying. During the war, the author remarks, one powerful motive for remaining alive was the hope of bearing witness. The desire to tell about the ordeal later was an impetus that often gave people the strength to go on. Afterward, ironically, many were silent. Some wanted to distance themselves as much as possible from the horror; for others, words seemed totally inadequate for the purposes of testimony. Furthermore, to recount a story it is crucial to have an audience with shared understandings. The events of the Nazi era seemed unbelievable even for those who had lived them personally. Literature, in Appelfeld's conception, presents particular difficulties in this regard, for it is not content with public language or generalizations. While much discourse about the Shoah tends toward the pathos of high-toned abstractions, literature's very substance and *raison d'être* is personal expression and engagement with detail. For these reasons literary art is that much more painful for the survivor to confront or create.

In the aftermath of the war there was eventually a return to speech and art, and in this connection Appelfeld quite explicitly identifies children as a major source for expressive response. His explanation is that adults were incapable of renewed vision. Their entire understanding of the world had been shattered by the conflagration, and they sought to forget. Children, on the other hand, absorbed the suffering into their bodies. Part of their being, "like arms and legs," it was patterned into their every movement. As a result, for the very young the unforgettable nightmare served as a field of the unconscious, binding past and present. Together with their blindness and innocence, it provided them the resources for a poetics of suffering.

According to this view, the first manifestations of the child's impact on art took place in refugee camps on the beaches of Italy after the war. Troops of children led about by impresarios sang cabaret songs, old Jewish melodies, and monastery organ tunes learned in hiding, or they offered imitations of birds and animals perfected during wanderings in the forests. Appelfeld sees in these plaintive performances an affirmation of life and a kind of grotesque but genuine religious impulse. Later, in Appelfeld's own work, childhood becomes a source of creativity because the author's memories afford him an ability to restore particularity and revive secrets of the self. While the mass destruction of the war irremediably damaged individuality, the literary option can help uncover and mine the richness of the past. Suspicious of abstract, metaphysical theory, Appelfeld avers that introspective art, while not replacing religion, can rescue both his own soul and that of his people from oblivion, in a process of rediscovery marked by wonder.

Appelfeld, then, in effect articulates a principle that has been demonstrated in other narratives of childhood. Here, too, earliness otherwise irrecoverable can achieve voice only in a fictional realm. It is the silent register of writing that provides the opportunity to bring the child's inner world to expression. And, as was true elsewhere, a discourse of childhood fulfills the function of combining especially sensitive perceptions or powers of observation with naiveté. The result is new interpretations of reality or a fresh look at the world. In Appelfeld's case, however, while the dynamics are similar to those in, for example, Bialik's *Aftergrowth,* the circumstances are immeasurably grimmer. The child's vision is particularly valuable, not only because it allows for a revivifying vitality, but because it simultaneously borders on silence. Shaped by ignorance, the child's view reveals a blindness that shields the character from trying to understand too much. Consequently this fiction may cast the world of devastation in a light that makes recollection of the past more bearable for author and reader.

As Alan Mintz has documented in *Ḥurban: Responses to Catastrophe in Hebrew Literature,* the notion of maintaining childhood sensibility within adult writing significantly informs Appelfeld's artistic vision and the workings of his fiction as a whole. It emerges with particular force in the story "Hagerush." That tale, which features a young orphan as protagonist and narrator, shows the child's mind to be uncluttered by acquired knowledge, unpracticed in interpretation and so able to observe or record in "non-interpretive amazement."[2] This is a figure, consequently, who stands for the possibility of fictional discourse that registers rather than construes. Such hallmarks of Appelfeld's fiction as his attempts to neutralize judgment and his refusal to demonize or sentimentalize stem from just this stance and express the author's desire to be a faithful witness. To be sure, in his work there are always evident the voice of an adult and the prevailing control of a mature mind. The artist has carefully reworked material from a former time. Yet the author's conceit is that "the writerly second stage of creativity carries over something of the photographic innocence of the child's outlook."[3]

This is a poetics that finds its most sustained realization in *The Age of Wonders* (1978), a narrative divided into two parts so distinct that they may function more as two novellas in one volume than as a single text.[4] The first section, the title piece, and the second, "Many Years Later When Everything Was Over," deal respectively with life in Austria before the war and after. Part 1, as it cultivates the perspective of a child protagonist, conveys the unbelievability of the impending disaster. Because the little boy is unprepared to foresee the cruel events that follow, his limited understanding makes an apt vehicle for conveying the disbelief of his family and friends as well. Living in a world that has not yet known the full extent of Nazi brutality, they cannot grasp the magnitude of the coming destruction. The Final Solution is doubly unanticipated by the characters of this fiction, members of a highly assimilated Jewish family, because they consider themselves wholly integrated into European society. Indeed, the bulk of the narrative is devoted to detailing a spectrum of reactions within the Jewish community as the varied characters act out their inability to truly fathom the seriousness of the deteriorating situation. The father, a celebrated writer who denies his Jewishness, directs his violent anger first against his own people (especially the *Ostjuden*) and then against himself. Eventually he abandons the family in pursuit of a phantom solution; he supposes that by joining a literary salon, under the patronage of a Gentile benefactress, he will escape the common fate of the Jews. The mother reacts by throwing herself into a surfeit of futile charitable works. An aunt of the child, succumbing to mental illness, also converts to Catholicism. Jewish intellectuals blame Jewish merchants, and Jewish merchants blame Jewish intellectuals, for the contempt with which non-Jews treat their people. Finally, these patterns of denial or attempted escape are put into sharp relief by the exception to the rule: the half-Jew Stark, increasingly cognizant of his Jewishness, chooses to undergo circumcision and unequivocally declares his solidarity with the Jews.

This initial segment of the narrative ends with the onset of atrocity, as the family awaits deportation. The period of most intense horror is both effaced and evoked by a hiatus in the narration. The absence of text suggests that some degrees of suffering can be expressed only as a gap in the writing. Subsequently, the story resumes as the protagonist comes from his postwar home in Jerusalem to visit the town of his childhood. Pursuing the theme of homecoming, familiar from many works of Hebrew fiction on the topic of the Shoah—for instance, Amihai's *Lo me'akhshav velo mik'an* (1963) (*Not of This Time, Not of This Place*) or Dan Ben Amotz's *Lizkor velishkoah* (1968) (*To Remember, to Forget*), this second portion of the narrative yields a project of somewhat different aims and methods than the treatment of the childhood perspective. By dramatizing the adult's return "many years later," his reassessment of the past, and his responses to contemporary Austria, this section contrasts with the recapturing of the child's inner life and the imaginative reconstitution of the prewar scene featured in part 1.[5] Part 2 differs from, but helps put into relief, the significance and function of that more daring narrative strategy and its accomplishments in the opening segment of the text.

In part 1 the implementation of Appelfeld's poetics of noninterpretive amazement depends on an allegedly autobiographical stance. A grown-up narrator reminisces about his earlier life, roughly between ages ten and twelve, recounting events in the two years preceding the family's removal to a concentration camp. The unusual retrospective power of this view is its insistence on consonant narration. In *The Age of Wonders* the narrating figure is emphatically not a dissonant narrator who, as a sovereignly cognizant speaking self, can look back and explain the confusions of his youth. Instead, the narrating figure is one who identifies with his earlier self and to a significant degree renounces cognitive privilege. Here, for instance, there is virtually no mention of specific historical events. Exposition of collective circumstances remains at a minimum and so reveals no broad picture or panoramic view of the crisis facing European Jewry. Only one date, 1938, appears in the text, but this happens almost inadvertently, late in the narrative, and does not serve as introductory orientation for the reader. Thus, when crowds of people converge on the family's estate, having been turned out of their own homes, the narrator remarks simply, "These people were panicked Jewish businessmen seeking momentary refuge in their flight" (117). No specific account is offered about what catastrophe they flee. There is a marked absence of detail about both the abuse these refugees have suffered and what will become of them later. Consequently, it is by and large the child's perceptions that prevail, and not the views of an older and wiser, more informed authorial figure. Outcomes are not revealed, and emphasis is placed on the limited understanding of the protagonist.

The adult view does intervene in a modest way. It is restricted primarily to constant reminders that this text constitutes a memory, that something has happened since. As the narration in this way cuts down on suspense, indicating that doom is always lurking, it serves as a counterpoint to the ignorance of the times and simultaneously makes that ignorance so much more glaring. Adult narration is also felt in the development of broad patterns of motifs, most importantly through the mention of trains. This motif establishes a narrow set of variables by which to trace the deterioration of the family. First the mother and son return from a resort in a well-appointed carriage. Later, taking Aunt Theresa on a train to a sanatorium, the family members are subjected to increasing suspicion and revilement by non-Jewish passengers. To arrive at Theresa's funeral they ride in a freight car, for no other transportation is available. Finally, in the last sentence, there is ominous mention of cattle cars hurtling south, and the reader can surmise the culmination of the progressive pattern of breakdown already charted. While this structuring of the narrative creates a framework that helps make the individual, fragmented events more intelligible, there is still a notable lack of retrospective, informed commentary and narratorial self-exegesis. The major hindsight offered—namely, the fundamental fact that destruction awaits the family—provides the story some objective coherence, but of singular interest is the much more obtrusive withdrawal from discursive explanation.

This general stance coincides nicely with and enhances various well-recognized features of Appelfeld's stylistics. The writer is known for his indirectness in referring to the Holocaust and for his deflection of attention away from atrocity. Often, accomplishing this effect entails putting emphasis on cyclical time rather than specific occasion. In *The*

Age of Wonders much the same pattern obtains and can be understood as the child's propensity to notice passing seasons rather than to pinpoint historical dates or political developments. Similarly, the lack of causal links between events may be ascribed to the protagonist's immature grasp of the situation. Appelfeld's typical characterization, that of joining multiple figures together as a collective entity, makes sense if it is viewed as a child's vague awareness of comings and goings and as a youngster's circumscribed ability to engage in prolonged or sophisticated analysis of character traits. In short, the presence of the child figure endows the deemphasizing of plot, the rescinding of in-depth characterization, and the vague reference to time and place with a new-found verisimilitude.

These same qualities of narrative indirection, apparent throughout Appelfeld's *oeuvre,* have been viewed as an expression of repression and as elements that constitute both the strength and weakness of this author's fiction. The writer's minimalizing focus, in contrast to the enormity of events evoked, creates an eerie, unsettling tension and so reminds the reader of the gap between what can be said and what cannot. Appelfeld's is an understatement that tries to avoid numbing the audience or repelling it through an account of overwhelmingly horrifying detail. At times, though, the concentration on small things eclipses the central phenomenon, the Shoah, such that the vital tension loses its impact.[6] Focus on a child mitigates this problem. The young character provides a perfect foil, for understatement is built into the dramatic speech situation as a matter of course. Due to the child's limited understanding, it is easy to naturalize the pervasive compression of information in the text. Indeed, this mimetically favorable narrative framework may account for some of the positive reception accorded *The Age of Wonders.* In 1979, shortly after its publication, Dan Miron saw this novella as a kind of summa of Appelfeld's works that reengages his established techniques and reworks familiar thematic material with renewed force and concentrated appeal. As do previous texts, this one features attention to a limited period of time, a unified situation leading to slow dissolution, and an emphasis on failure of communication. Here, however, Miron finds better-realized individuals and argues that this is in some ways the most dramatic of Appelfeld's writings.[7] The child, as astute but naive observer, allows for both more particularity and more deflection of attention away from horror and historical detail.

The child, then, is not a simplistic emblem of incomprehension but a locus for tensions between a capability to observe and restricted observational powers. This figure struggles to understand and also fails to understand. As such, he embodies an ambiguity fundamental to Appelfeld's aim of creating an art that both reveals and conceals. Add to this the double-voicedness, the dual perspective inherent in texts where adults depict children's experience, and it becomes clear how engagement with a child character in *The Age of Wonders* may foment a central thematic concern with knowledge. Such a move allows the text to bring to the fore a preoccupation with epistemological and expressive possibilities in writing about the Holocaust. For example, this fiction often conflates adult and child levels, blurring boundaries between afterthought and anticipation. From this there emerges a series of subtle modulations between authorial voice and experiencing character, uncovering a continuing and pervasive oscillation between purportedly interpretive and noninterpretive domains. In addition, the child figure himself flickers back and forth between feeling at a loss and entertaining prescient intimations of what the future holds. To be sure, his moments of certainty—"Suddenly I sensed with a kind of childish clarity" (85), "Now I knew" (51), "One thing I knew" (46)—are less frequent than and subordinate to a general stance of incomprehension. Both, however, are finally part of a larger gestalt that privileges and problematizes questions of knowing and not knowing. The result is undecidability that at times gives the impression of uniformity, but that finally represents less an abdication of interpretation than a stance of constant vacilation. The poetics of noninterpretation consists in effect of multiple layers of hesitation.

That the child's primary attitude is one of amazement is firmly established in the text through frequent assertions that things have become strange. The word *muzar* (odd) recurs like a refrain and often stands independently as a complete thought. Devoid of explication, this one word serves as a sentence unto itself. (In English the syntactic structure is modified; "strange" appears as a parenthetical aside, introducing another sentence.)

> Strange, Father was not angry with the friends who had abandoned him, the many societies that had stopped inviting him to their meetings. He was angry with the Jewish petite bourgeoisie. (103–4)

> Strange, not one of [the refugees] knew how to explain what had happened, how they had arrived in our town, at our house and where they intended to go next. (117)

> Strange, no one interrupted our conversation. (84)

> "Strange," said Amalia, "I thought there were Jews here." (37)

At other times the words *meshune* and *muzar* (odd) punctuate the prose as adjectives or predicates. Mother devotes herself to charity with a "strange, self-denying piety"; Father, surrounded by members of the Jewish burial society, "looked strange" (67); the narrator remarks, "my sleep that night was strange" (38). Numerous other examples attest to this emphasis.[8] Similarly related words appear, too, in overt reference to the perplexity the child or other members of the family experience. At various times they are amazed, bewildered, or shocked, and the roots *h.l.m.*, *d.h.m.*, and *t.m.h.* are scattered throughout the text.[9]

While sometimes the pervasive perceptions of oddness are explicitly ascribed to the child, at other times comments of a purportedly objective, expositional nature bolster the impression that the bizarre is not solely a figment of the child's imagination. Rather, it is endemic to the entire circumstance. Testifying to a mood of grotesque festivity, the narrator describes the atmosphere of the town as "gay, drugged despair" (103). When the end approaches, the narrative reinforces this picture of disagreeable jocularity: "As in every place exuding the stench of disaster, here too people occupied themselves with barter, the exchange of rumors and bitter jokes" (117). Another example occurs when a young girl, unmarried, pregnant, and without means, seeks asylum with the family. Her tragedy likewise fosters "gay despair" and "strange celebration" (74). Apparently, the father is overjoyed to have contact with someone from his native village. Currying acceptance by a Gentile, even a helpless unfortunate, makes him feel less powerless and cut off from his Austrian identity. Consequently, her misfortune becomes an occasion for him to host a round of raucous, financially ruinous parties. This episode, then, like the previous ones, contributes to a dynamic familiar from Appelfeld's novel *Badenheim 1939*. Life, even at the brink of disaster, goes on, but in a distorted and falsely festive way. In light of these matters the title, *Tor hapela'ot*, takes on special resonance. The appellation "age of wonders" may refer to the general strangeness of the era even as it draws, too, on an understanding pervasive in Western literary tradition: that of the child as a creature who perceives the world in magical terms and possesses a special capacity for wonder. In this text the two notions converge in an inverse, sinister way. At issue is not joyous wonder nor even comic misinterpretations of the world and ironic revisions of traditional wisdom. Here, instead, the child experiences amazement as the world astounds in acutely cruel and troubling ways. In the process the protagonist becomes an indicator of Zeitgeist and an expressive vehicle for collective historical experience.

The treatment of the child's ability to know and understand moves beyond this fundamental point of departure most decisively through thematic attention to language. Above all there is an awareness that words are instrumental as a way of clarifying experience, but one that most often fails to provide order and meaning. These matters work themselves out in three major patterns. First, the narrative obtrusively emphasizes that many verbal exchanges are beyond the young boy. Second, it becomes clear that a certain amount of information is available to the protagonist. There exists a shared public framework of discussion, but it is one on which he can hang only partial understanding. Finally, the text alludes to a subverbal realm of experience or a point at which words become entirely inadequate yet still affect the character's perceptions.

In the first pattern the narrator frequently spells out that the boy doesn't comprehend.

> Words I did not understand flew through the air like flaming torches. (32)

> Mother kept trying to pacify Theresa with all kinds of words whose meaning I could not understand. (52)

> When Mother said "I don't understand," it meant that something had happened. But whatever it was was beyond my comprehension. (63)

The double avowal of incomprehension in the last example brings to the fore that the child's perplexity is often matched or paralleled by that of the grown-ups. This kind of sentence alerts the reader to the overall strategy of the text; the child puts into relief a widespread phenomenon of bewilderment in the face of crisis. When Cousin Charlotte, formerly a celebrated actress, loses her job, the uncle responds, "I can't understand it. I can't understand it." An acquaintance of the family echoes, "This is incomprehensible" (30–31). With similar effect the phrase "for some reason" (*mishum mah*) surfaces frequently in the narrative and turns the child's wonderment into an index of adult confusion: "Mother asked for some reason if Theresa needed a coat" (55). As constructed here, the words "for some reason" may constitute the boy's admission that he fails to understand. Alternatively, they may also indicate that grown-up actions are disjointed and unclearly motivated. The adults themselves do not always have a good reason for their behavior. Subsequently, as the narrative progresses, it becomes increasingly clear that the adults understand as little as, perhaps less than, the boy and are incapable of dealing with their plight. Explicitly exploiting his retrospective advantage, the narrator puts this phenomenon most acutely into relief by drawing attention to the culminating instance of incomprehension. In the final scenes, as the Jews are compelled by Nazi authorities to register en masse in the synagogue, they ask in astonished tones what they are doing there. Some have to be dragged in and refuse to believe they are part of the community of the condemned. Still unwilling to face up to the situation, their reaction is to attack the rabbi and blame him for their predicament.

Throughout the novel, as overt statements of incomprehension testify that the little boy does not fully understand events about him, these same comments also bear a certain ambivalence. At issue is not total blindness to and disregard of surrounding conditions but an instance of a character who knows that he doesn't know. The result is to imply that knowledge is problematic in *The Age of Wonders*. Further traces of this ambivalence mark the effort to provide information by reproducing lengthy quotations and conversations beyond the boy's comprehension. Much informative talk is reported as the child overhears it, even as he does not appreciate the force of the arguments whirling about him. This narrative strategy entails a shift to direct address that obviates any need to mediate speech acts with the boy's interpretation. It should be noted, though, that the character must be present, as a device to register and record the overheard words. Furthermore, his attention to these words belies his sensitivity, his partial awareness that something significant is occurring. Such scenes furnish the purest instances of a child character as witness, and by performing this function the protagonist keeps the audience apprised of collective events while still demonstrating his own cognitive limitations.

Early on, for example, as the family plans a gathering to celebrate their son's birthday, the atmosphere is decidedly unjoyous. The narrative reports only external signs of gloom because the boy has no clue as to the source of the unhappiness: "The colors of light faded. . . . I sensed that something was coming to a head in the silence . . . whispered remarks were exchanged that I failed to understand" (26). Belatedly, the reader becomes privy to adult exchange: "Haven't you heard that they've fired Charlotte from the National Theater?" (30). It turns out that anti-Jewish measures under the Nazi regime are beginning to affect the life of the affluent family and have cast a pall over the party. The reader can grasp the context just in bits and snatches as childish reportage would allow, and much as a child would, by overhearing.

The approach conveys, in several senses, a double message. First, character and reader experience the conversations differently. The comments signify differently in the two separate frames of presupposition: that of the immature individual who, before the worst has happened, can only surmise approaching evil, and that of the adult equipped with historical hindsight. Second, Appelfeld underscores that the child both knows and doesn't know. The youngster's apprehension of events depends on what is articulated for him by his elders, but their statements and explanations are insufficient.

The partial occlusion of events through incomplete apprehension of them puts into prominence that words are not always accessible or meaningful. A more intense expression of this same ambivalence is evident in the conversations reported indirectly, rather than directly. The child is highly aware of words and silences, if not always of their content. This technique grants words a kind of concreteness and animates them as a palpable influential factor in his surroundings. All the same they are unforthcoming, unable to disclose meaning. This is a contradictory portrayal of language as something both crucial and unavailable, inadequate but ever felt as a presence. Examples are numerous.

> Inside silence seeped through the rooms like a liquid about to jell. (32)

> A few shallow words still hung in the air together with the last notes of the band.
> Although no one spoke, it seemed to me that everything we did was governed by the jangling rhythm of Charlotte's words. (33)

> The next day my parents returned from the provincial capital bringing with them a breath of alien tumult, words and phrases they had picked up in the law courts. (44)

In a variety of other circumstances language assumes a similar quality of fundamental yet evasive importance. Although many times the inaccessibility of particular statements could be justified by factors not associated directly with a childlike perspective, these examples are noteworthy because in them words continue to function more as an ominous presence than as a medium to reference or understanding. For example, when the doctors treat Aunt Augusta on her deathbed the protagonist remarks, "The whispered words reaching our ears were faint and unintelligible, as if they came from another world" (66). Certainly, physicians are often reluctant to convey bad news to a patient's family, but here the secrecy dovetails with and underscores the general impression of language as something uncommunicative and remote. Similarly, the reader is informed that in the hospital where Stark's circumcision takes place, men "sat drinking coffee out of little cups, baiting each other in a babble of unintelligible words that sounded like curses" (98). On one level the words seem distant simply because the men speak Yiddish, a foreign language as far as the protagonist's family is concerned. On another level the scene contributes to the overall sense that the province of the partially overheard is emblematic of a general elusiveness of understanding and an ever-widening gap between words and explanation. In this way there is reenacted, on the level of the individual incident, the dilemmas of *The Age of Wonders* as a whole and, indeed, of Appelfeld's entire *oeuvre.* Here, as elsewhere, the central issue is one of coming to terms with saying and not saying, language as at once crucial and ineffective when speaking about the unspeakable. Thanks to this kind of inchoate dialogue and to abortive attempts to internalize the words of others, apprehension of meaning throughout the text recovers both senses of the word *apprehension*. Cognition is synonymous or coterminous with incipient fear. The arrival at knowledge proceeds with trepidation.

On other occasions the child protagonist relaxes his attempt to penetrate the world with words, and it becomes clear that there is much reality above or beyond verbal effort. This happens, for example, when Mother tells bedtime tales, and the narrator, remembering how grateful he felt at those times, explains, "Mother would take my hand in hers and this was as enjoyable as the story itself. Even then the evenings were clearer than the mornings. Perhaps because words spoken at night, before sleep comes, partake of the nature of sleep and fall like seeds into the receptive earth" (71). This scene suggests that the way in which words are said—the tone, context, and gesture that accompany them—are as important, or more important, than content.

The realm of nonverbal experience that bears its own legitimacy and dominates the character's inner life is conveyed largely through simile and metaphor. These are infused into the thoughts of the character and become so abundant as to constitute a veritable method of rendering consciousness. Dorrit Cohn's conception of "psychoanalogy" offers a useful description of this technique.[10] The term refers to situations in which a narrator distrusts a character's idiom but wants to capture that figure's sensitivity or perceptions. Such distancing of narratorial voice from protagonist's parlance is a model that accommodates itself easily to *The Age of Wonders,* for the prose in general has been far removed from childish diction. Virtually no indicators of the boy's verbal activity of mind (neither quoted monologue nor self-narrated monologue) are featured by the work. The entire text, while maintaining at least partially the perspective of the child, is rendered in the adult narrator's voice. The analogies and similes, moreover, are particularly unchildlike in their formulation. They recall a child's propensity for creative metaphor and the ability to see things in an unconventional way, but the comparisons are articulated here in a sophisticated and studied manner.

Uses of this pattern are legion and fulfill a variety of purposes. Often they serve to grant actions immediacy and to suggest concrete, vivid presence as those occurrences would gain graphic impact, filtered through a child's imagination. A feeling of doom, for instance, goes through the protagonist "like a thick liquid" (9), in Hebrew "*kenozel samikh*" (9, emphasis added). Theresa enclosed in a room studying is "like a prisoner" (34), "*ke'asir*" (30). The outline of Theresa's face seeps into the child "like a sweet soft touch" (34), "*ke'ehad harehafim hametukim"* (30). Of particular significance are the comparisons that associate Jewish characters with animals. In their own town the family lives "like animals on display, mocked and abused" (103), *"hayinu bah kebetokh kluv, mutsagim lera'avah, mevuzim, umesuragim 'eyvah"* (90). Father paces the rooms "like a caged animal" (94), *"kebesoger"* (82). The Jewish passengers who get off the train for an inspection by the authorities looked "like little insects wrinkling the straw with their feet" (11), *"harakim ze'irim hamekamtim 'et hakash bedarkam"* (10), and as Father berates the rabbi responsible for Stark's conversion, skinny men come rushing out at him "like a swarm of angry wasps" (100), *"ke-nahil"* (87). This kind of portrayal of the Jews, familiar from others of Appelfeld's works and brought out pointedly in the English translation even more than in the Hebrew original, clearly echoes the Nazi ideology of Jewish racial inferiority. The narrator and/or the child character (it is difficult to distinguish exactly where the idea originates) incorporate this negativity into their own views, like the father who explicitly assays that the Jews runs about "like rats" (102), *"mitrotsetsim ke'akhbarim"* (89), infesting all of Austria with their poisonous presence. The difficulty of differentiating between narratorial and figural view encapsulates the essence of Appelfeld's poetics. His art depends on overlap between maturity and youth, a child's perceptions retained and exploited in adult creation. Many things expressed here could not be said without adult vocabulary, but they are predicated on a child's mode of thinking and show to what extent self-hatred has affected not just the father but the son as well.

Another kind of analogy further develops the function of these techniques. Presenting conditions contrary to fact, one brand of trope points up the behavior of self-deception, which dominates the Jewish community. The Jews stubbornly persist in believing that things will turn out all right, and the word *kemo* appears several times to show that this is a mistaken assumption. Consider, for instance, the scene in which Theresa dies. The nuns at the convent take over all responsibility for funeral arrangements, leaving the family feeling useless. The narrator reports: "'We must go,' said father, as if we had another pressing engagement somewhere else" (89), *"kemo tsipa lanu 'inyan aher bemaqom 'aher"* (77). Later the father insists on going to visit a friend of his youth, a powerful nobleman whose support he craves. Servants turn the family away ignominiously when the master refuses to see them, and Father's response is similar to the one in the convent: "'We're getting out of here on the first train,' he said, as if we had any other choice" (113), *"kemo 'amdah lifanav 'od brera"* (98). In each of these instances this figure fools himself into believing he can still exercise his own will and authority.

A host of similar but somewhat distinct cases also hint at discrepancy between the characters' behavior and their situation. Here, how-ever, the feeling of dissociation cannot be ascribed only to the action at the level of narrated events. It stems as well from the interpretive role of the narratorial voice. For example:

> Theresa was now brisk, polite and hospitable like a woman returning to her own home and familiar furnishings. (56)

> קומתה של תרזה אמרה עתה מעשיות אדיבה, כאדם החוזר למקומו ואל חפציו הקרובים; (50)

> Father was stunned. He said, "I don't understand," and turned his head away, looking into the gloom as if he hoped to meet the eyes of the guilty there. (95)

> אבא נדהם ומרוב תדהמה אמר: אינני מבין, והסב את ראשו אל החלל האפל כמתכוון לפגוש שם את מבטיהם של האשמים. (83)

> Mother approached the coffin, her head slightly bent, as if she was looking into a baby's cradle. (88)

> אמא קרבה אל הארון, ראשה מוטה קמעה, כפי שמתבוננים בעריסה של תינוק. (77)

> "We're here. What now?" called the coachman, as if he were dealing not with people but with ghosts. (53)

> "הגענו. מה רצונכם?" קרא הרכב כמו לא היה לו עסק באנשים אלא ברוחות. (47–48)

As before, in these passages, too, there is clear evidence that the characters deny the reality of their plight. In the first example Theresa has objected to being returned to the convent sanatorium but then embraces that return wholeheartedly. She sees the Catholic environment as home, when in effect she is mentally ill and in flight from herself. After Theresa dies, the mother stands over her coffin as if it were a cradle, confusing death with birth. Father looks for someone to blame for his friend's adoption of Judaism, when in actuality no one is guilty of coercing Stark. The half-Jew, of his own volition, has actively sought out Jewish identity, and his name ("strong" in German) implies that he is a figure of strength. The last example expresses the coach driver's attitude toward the Jews. The Gentile simply sees through them as if they weren't there, denying their existence. These comparisons, then, indicate that the characters are never entirely consonant with themselves in their own actions or in the eyes of the non-Jews. The narrator's constant search for analogy suggests in addition that the characters are not fully themselves within *his* estimation either. They are always paradigmatic of something else, never described simply in terms of one context. This circumstance creates the impression of a pressure toward interpretation. The narrator is ever trying to pin things down, never definitively able to identify or refer to phenomena directly, and so always tentatively explaining them in terms of another context. He is unwilling to assert with authority, and the overload of imagery suggests an assaying of meaning at once urgent but hesitant. Implications emerge in several directions. The narrative indicates the unreality of the times themselves, as an era suffused with duplicities. Furthermore, the use of simile and analogy indicates that the narrator at once interprets and renounces responsibility for imposing meaning onto events.

The use of the present tense reinforces this reading as it contributes to the complexity of the psychoanalogies.[11] In the examples given, the words *kefi she* and *ke* introduce a gnomic present suitable for expressing generalizations or cultivating an essayistic quality. This is a move that leads the text away from a specific temporal account and the progression of narrative sequence. Creating an antinarrative component or an element of timelessness, the procedure calls attention to the perceiving mind, which casts actions from one context into another. Consequently, the passages convey a sense that events are constantly mediated by consciousness. External actions and phenomena demand interpretation. They are too strange or estranged to be taken for granted as self-explanatory, yet the interpreting mind grasps constantly after an elusive objective correlative. The use of the present tense has a further related effect as well, which is to collapse the child and adult levels of the narration. In these passages it is impossible to know exactly who perceives. The synchronization of narrated time and the moment of narration conflates the narrative voice with the experiencing self. The temporal indicators suggest that past has become present and that the narrator relives the time about which he tells. (This effect is reinforced by the occasional but extended use of the evocative present in *The Age of Wonders*. Whole paragraphs of the narrative at times feature this "peculiar grammatical make believe"[12] that shifts the prose into the present tense as if the events were taking place at the very moment of writing about them. The grown-up remembers the past vividly. It has not left the child survivor, who is now an adult. The artist still embodies his suffering "like an arm or a leg" and relives those experiences in all their immediacy.)[13]

As a result, then, yet another displacement has been put into operation, and the unreality of the epoch has infused itself into the narration as well as into the narrated events. The characters react to the strangeness of their circumstance with willed dissociation and are never totally present in their actualities. The narrator, too, is divided, never entirely at home in the present because always captive, in his thoughts, to the past.

Further contributing to the sense of displacement or dissociation from an immediate dramatic situation is the narrator's unusual use of *kemo* and *ke*. In colloquial contemporary parlance *kemo* introduces similes, and *ke'ilu* introduces conditions contrary to fact. Appelfeld, by contrast, most often employs *ke* only for similes and *kemo* for conditions contrary to fact. While such formulations are acceptable in mishnaic Hebrew, they sound a note of incongruity in modern Hebrew prose. The author, invoking a language not of today, presents in his narrative a world of introspection, a cautious probing of an inner realm that exists only in memory and imagination, not in the present of idiomatic, spoken exchange. Overt artifice of language here connotes a tentative formulation of a realm neither here nor there, past nor present, and so creates an evidently fictional register in which to convey the extraordinary reality of this age of wonders.

These formal features contribute to a confusion of remembering self and experiencing self that proves the child to be more a device of authorial voice than a portrait with pretensions to psychological verisimilitude. Attempted here is not the mimetic capturing of child discourse or cognitive development, nor a reasoned assessment of childhood through memory. Appelfeld's protagonist is singularly without individuality. He acts more as a conduit for narratorial perceptions and testimony than anything else, yet this is an artifice that claims to convey kinds of truth otherwise inexpressible. In its artifice, though its purposes are different and the mood more somber, *The Age of Wonders* more closely resembles Sholem Aleichem's *Mottel* than the other texts covered in this study. In *Mottel* an artificially perpetual presence testified to an attitude of optimism, a willingness to embrace the future by greeting each new moment with laughter through tears. Here a lingering of the past in the present and a present enslaved to the past also create a temporal never never, but preoccupation with early trauma yields only the grotesquerie of exultant despair and precludes true joy. Altogether, Appelfeld's effect is one of merging and fusing narrative levels. The impact is quite different from that of, say, Uri Orlev, whose novel *The Lead Soldiers* operates on much the same fundamental premises as *The Age of Wonders*.[14] It, too, exploits a child character's incomprehension in order to allow an adult writer to speak of incomprehensible disaster. However, Orlev's effectiveness depends on maximizing the gap between young character and older narrator. A closer look at that narrative is in order so as to put into relief the singularity of Appelfeld's writing.

In *The Lead Soldiers* the protagonist's matter-of-fact acceptance of gruesome suffering is designed to shock. War is what the little boy has known for most of his life, and so he takes it for granted. Later, the terrors he has lived and witnessed will affect his entire way of thinking, but in the midst of events he continues to play childish games. His toy soldiers are more significant to him than the grown-ups' war. The author keeps narratorial comment and child's perspective clearly separate, and the narrator, chameleon-like, steps in and out of narrated events to referee and transmit the child's thoughts to the reader. For example, in a scene from an infirmary, a girl whose feet have been amputated crawls over to the little boy's bed to bring him a sheaf of papers. Laying bare the essentials of Orlev's narrative strategy, the narrator cautions his audience, "Don't read your emotions into him. He wasn't at all upset. He was sure that this was how it was supposed to be" (101). Another more dramatically effective technique used to reveal much the same idea is the presentation of dialogue. The narrator remains aloof, permitting the children's own discourse to prevail and to demonstrate of its own accord how different their outlook is from the expected reaction of horror.

By way of illustration, consider an occasion when two boys in the ghetto first play at teasing a toddler and later go off to their school lessons. In the course of these ordinary activities, a brief, intervening exchange takes place. One child asks the other if he would like to see a horse, and the exposition that follows puts their discussion into an interpretive context that the adult reader can understand.

> They crossed the trolley tracks and headed for the last row of houses in the neighborhood.
> "Over there," Tadek pointed.
> They came to the edge of a pit.
> "It's a hole," Yurik said.
> "It must have been some bomb."
> "Is it a horse?" asked Yurik.
> "The head looks like a horse's," said Tadek. "Everyone says it's a horse." He picked up a stone and threw it at the carcass. Yurik found more stones and threw them too. (45)

> ״זה כאן, ״ הראה טאדק.
> נעצרו על שפתו של בור.
> ״בור, ״ ציין יורק.
> ״כן. זה מפצצה הגונה. ״
> ״זה של סוס?״ שאל יורק.
> ״הראש כמו של סוס, ״ אמר טאדק. ״כולם אומרים שזה של סוס. ״
> טאדק הרים אבן וידה אותה בשלד. יורק אסף כמה אבנים ועשה כמותו. (44)

This is prose that clearly invites reader-response criticism, as it only belatedly makes apparent that the horse the children go to see is a dead one. The impact and surprise, largely dissipated in a second reading, derive from the obscure referentiality indicated in English translation through the repeated use of "it" and in Hebrew, though distributed somewhat differently, through the use of *"zeh."* A carcass as a plaything is a horrifying phenomenon, but the reader recognizes the facts of the situation only gradually. The boys, by contrast, find the situation self-evident and so remark on it in words that neatly illustrate Bernstein's distinction between restricted and elaborated codes.[15] That is to say, they needn't explicate in detailed vocabulary or syntax because they know to what they are referring. The clearly shared frame of reference obviates the need to articulate their interpretation, and so they can use simple deictics— *"zeh,"* *"k'an,"* and *"mi"*—without further explanation. These are words (demonstratives, adverbs of time or place, and personal pronouns) whose signification depends on the situation in which they are uttered. Here they have clear meaning for the boys, who take their environment for granted. Above all, there is a disinclination to translate visual impressions into words or value judgments, because there is no preexisting framework of interpretation within which those things register as being remarkable. Child and adult views couldn't be farther apart.

Appelfeld, by contrast with Orlev, arrives at a smoother integration of child and adult levels of the text. His approach is particularly noteworthy because it subverts one of the common characteristics of autobiographical novels. In this genre the time of intense reflection is more often the present than the past. Some of the most memorable of fictional minds, as Dorrit Cohn observes, belong to narrating rather than experiencing selves. Tristram Shandy, Moll Flanders, and Beckett's Molloy all illustrate this point. Consonant presentation of a past consciousness is dependent on self-effacement of the narratorial voice, and few authors of autobiographical fiction have been willing to silence this voice completely. Appelfeld's peculiar accomplishment is to achieve a kind of consonance that doesn't call attention away unduly from narrated events to the consciousness of the narrator. The depiction of the child figure's thinking infuses the time of narration with immediacy and access to stupefying events, yet the author never endows that character with its own words or grants it importance as a speaker. Appelfeld's is a technique that detracts from or diminishes the prominence of both experiencing self and narrating figure, but synthesizes the two and thereby enriches both.

Indicative of the resonance the text gains from its idiosyncratic confusing of child and adult realms is the difference between parts 1 and 2. The second segment is narrated in the third person and so forms a neat contrast with the preceding account. Whether the "I" of the first part and "Bruno" of the second are the same protagonist is a question raised by the abrupt structural discontinuity of the text. Not only is there formal divorce between the two books. There is, in addition, overt commentary on how much has changed when the man goes back to the town of his birth. Everything is altered. Bruno meets Louise, the servant for whom he felt such affection in his youth and who had enjoyed close ties with the family. She had even been the lover of a number of relatives and family friends. The belated reunion, however, yields a sad conclusion: "Now he knew for sure: of Louise nothing remained and all that sat before him was an old Austrian woman" (172). Another former acquaintance, Brum, refuses to recognize Bruno, and the main point of the entire episode is put into relief when a homesick Japanese student residing in Austria insistently belabors conversations about reincarnation. The implication emerges that, if Bruno is still himself, it is only as a kind of reincarnation estranged from his former self. In this world, where everything has changed, the protagonist develops a dissonant retrospective glance at his childhood; and the text, likewise, proffers dissonant narration that sets "Many Years Later" distinctly apart from *The Age of Wonders.* Part 2, for example, provides extended, discursive explanations of Bruno's feelings about Louise in which magic is not so much recaptured as explicated. The intimacy of living the past, childhood experience is available much more through the curious autobiographical stance of part 1 than it is in the concluding section.

Part 2, moreover, functions as a kind of commentary on the significance of part 1. The ending section demonstrates how the effects of time (and deliberate attempts on the part of some to erase the past) invalidate the protagonist's memories. Doing so, "Many Years Later" underscores the uniqueness of part 1. It insists on the value of preserving Jewish memories and on the indispensable importance of art, which alone can recover the feel of the Holocaust era. This observation accords with Harold Fisch's reading of *The Age of Wonders.* Fisch has assessed the disjunction between the two sections of narration as a move that negates the conventions of the Bildungsroman.[16] The initial segment presents an apprentice novel about growing up and sketches an inner drama of awakening consciousness. Subsequently, the expected moment of epiphany or traditional realization of vocation fails to take place, must fail to take place, because the deportations start. The plot therefore does not follow the evolution of youth into maturity, but rather depicts an aftermath, a maturity that demonstrates how very distant the protagonist's early reality has become.

The division of the book into two separate sections is artistically felicitous, as it incorporates into the overall narrative organization that same radical disjunction of circumstance which, in separate ways, also motivates parts 1 and 2. The discontinuity, which expresses itself initially as consonant narration in the cultivation of the childhood perspective, manifests itself later as dissonant narration, and it results, too, in the very split that structures the volume into two disconnected sections. The question of discontinuity and its impact on Appelfeld's art also raises yet another set of issues crucial to *The Age of Wonders*. Intertexts and interpretive frameworks, as thematic and stylistic components of the text, are complicated by the dislocations that shape this fiction.

Commenting on the displacements in his own life, the author has spoken movingly of his reliance on Kafka as a literary precursor.[17] For a considerable period after the trauma of the war years, Appelfeld shied away from literature, throwing himself instead into other activities and into the demands of adjusting to life in Israel. When he did turn to writing, modern Hebrew literature was not much of a help in developing an art about the Holocaust. Hebrew was a language entirely new to Appelfeld and therefore, in his estimation, not suitable for a deeply personal mode of writing. It served instead as a public idiom, a surface or mask behind which to hide.[18] Kafka, by contrast, provided a model after which Appelfeld could pattern his own fiction and so break his silence about the Shoah.

Appelfeld's work is reminiscent of Kafka's in its combination of understatement with horrific event and in its focus on the disorientation of individuals who are dwarfed by monstrous powers, monstrously larger than themselves.[19] Without doubt there are also very significant differences between the two writers. Among other things, Kafka often features the quick but futile intelligence that attempts to deal unsuccessfully with inexplicable events. His writing, too, offers detailed descriptions of excruciating cruelty or horrifying acts. (The execution carried out in the Penal Colony and Gregor Samsa's metamorphosis into a cockroach are but two examples.) In *The Age of Wonders,* by contrast, there is much more approximately an abdication of reason, just as there is a shying away from brutality. However, the factors that do bear a resemblance to Kafka allow the author to develop his own brand of childhood discourse. The adult writer can never transcribe the child's voice or experience with absolute authenticity, but Kafka's portrayals of defenselessness provide a parallel to the child's sense of smallness, and the matter-of-fact acceptance of the bizarre as a given offers parallels to the child's noninterpretive wonderment and acquiescence to surrounding events.[20]

Significantly, Kafka is mentioned at length in *The Age of Wonders,* and this fact helps insinuate thematic attention to literary models into the plot actions. The father is a writer friendly with eminent lights of Austrian letters. Above all he is an ardent admirer of Kafka. In the course of events he inevitably falls from grace with the authorities, his readers, and the literary establishment because he is a Jew. The point is of interest, for, in acknowledging his own debt to Kafka, Appelfeld emphasizes that Jewishness is the basis of his feelings of affinity with that predecessor and *his* concern with persecution, alienation, and estrangement. In *The Age of Wonders* the father does not recognize any such reason for his admiration of Kafka, and the painful irony emerges that this man clings to his identity as an Austrian to the point that he spurns his fellow Jews and, finally, all Jewish writers. Losing his grip on a paradigm that might help him see his own plight in more perceptive terms, he loses his awareness of absurdity. Acceding to the interpretive dictates of the time, he tries to justify Aryan notions of Jewish inferiority. In this way the mention of Kafka in *The Age of Wonders* does more than contribute to the negative characterization of the father. It also underscores, within the narrated events, the need for models of interpretation. This is a matter that came up before, when the text pointed out how the child's awareness depends in part on what is articulated by his parents. Because he overhears puzzling conversations, this child is a step ahead of Orlev's Tadek and Yurik; they don't even know there is something remarkable occurring on which they might comment. However, Appelfeld's novel does share with *The Lead Soldiers* an insistence that meaning is not inherent in the protagonist's experience. Both narratives, then, pose two questions: to what extent do events lead to expression, and to what extent do preexisting assumptions determine the child's ability to perceive?

Responses to catastrophe in literary works are profoundly modulated by the paradigms of meaning with which the author approaches the subject, and Appelfeld turns this issue of presupposition to a principal focus of the novel as he thematizes the question of interpretation. In turn, the child's various encounters with language, together with the father's dwelling on Kafka, heighten the reader's awareness of the narrator's own dependence on narrative conventions: in particular, his liberation from silence thanks to Kafka. In sum, the same preoccupations underlie the author's struggle with expression in his own life and define the fundamental problems explored at the level of narrated events (the child's dealings with language as revealment and concealment). These tensions translate themselves at the level of narration into oscillations between narratorial voice and experiencing self.

The Age of Wonders in all these different guises emphasizes the problematic nature of knowledge and language in an art that attempts to speak of the unspeakable and recover an irrecoverable past. The artistic voice that at first reading seems uniform, understated, a stance of noninterpretation, finally reveals a highly complex set of tensions. A closer look at a single passage may demonstrate how these subtleties adumbrate the deceptively simple prose. Perhaps nowhere are so many of the salient concerns of the entire narrative brought together more richly and concisely than in the following passage. This scene is recounted after the departure of Yetti, the unwed mother whose presence served as a pretext for immoderate partying and so brought the family to the brink of destitution.

> The nights were long, brightly lit, and empty. A sick bitterness pinched Father's lips. He became more and more entangled in his lawsuits until there seemed no way out. At night the fleeting memories of Yetti took on menacing substantiality. She still seemed to be sitting there in the corner with her shadows.
>
> In vain Mother tried to give our meals their old serenity. Intimations of orphanhood had fallen on everything, even the drapes. Charged, unspoken words floated in the air like hidden accusations. Mother's face too was infected with the same sick bitterness. One evening Father said, "What more do you want? You chased her away, didn't you?" Mother wept and Father did not try to comfort her. I knew: everything I had once known, my childhood, too, was over. (77)

הלילות היו ארוכים, מוארים וריקים. על שפתיו של אבא הלכה ונקמצה
איזו מרירות חולה. המשפטים שנסתבך בהם הלכו ונסתבכו ולא נראה
כל מוצא. זכרה החולף של יטי לבש בלילות מין מוחשיות מאיימת.
כאילו עדיין יושבת בפינה עם צלליה.
לשוא ניסתה אמא לשוות לארוחות את הנוסח הישן. דמדום של יתמות
היה בכל, גם בוילאות. מלים טעונות, אילמות, שוטטו בחלל כהאשמות
מוצנעות. גם בפניה של אמא דבקה אותה מרירות חולה. באחד
הערבים אמר אבא: מה את רוצה, הרי גירשת אותה. אמא בכתה
ואבא לא ניגש לנחמה. ידעתי: כל שהיה לא ישוב עוד, גם ילדותי. (68)

The actions of the characters, symptomatic of their no-exit situation, are similar to those that typify their behavior throughout the novel. Father, unable to cope with his loss of prestige, is entrenched in useless court battles hoping to make the press rescind libelous reviews of his writing. Mother, for her part, deliberately tries to perpetuate illusions of normal routine. Furthermore, language here is conceived as something elusive and problematic. It is only through unspoken words and snatches of conversation that the child recognizes the seriousness of the situation and the substance of the parents' psychological denial. The impression arises that silence communicates more than speech acts. Most powerful is that which is not articulated. Then, words explicitly designated as mute take on concrete presence (*"milim 'ilemmot shotetu baḥallal"*) and highlight the eeriness of the circumstances. In this they resemble the memory of Yetti, a figure whose absence takes on substance and remains present. (Once again the condition contrary to fact dominates: Yetti is sensed by the family *"ke'ilu 'adayin yoshevet bapinah"*). The illusions of the parents and the substantive impact of that which is lacking dramatize that this is a time not consonant with itself. This is a world haunted by ghosts, in which appearances deceive. Such a dynamic carries over into the entire narrative of *The Age of Wonders*, whose adult narrator continues to be haunted by events of that earlier age.

Out of this mixture of deception, feigned normality, and miscommunication comes the child character's incomprehension or noninterpretation. His perceptions yield a deadpan, matter-of-fact recording of developments, along with a contradictory knowledge. The child knows that he doesn't know. The ambivalence of this knowledge, moreover, yields a paradoxical insight that the very patterns of understanding, the interpretive frameworks that once were operative, no longer are. The English translation felicitously brings out this concept more than the Hebrew. While the original reads, "everything that was, even my childhood, would not return" (*"kol shehaya lo yashuv 'od, 'afilu yalduti"*), the English doubles the verb *to know* in the main clause and in a relative clause, thereby juxtaposing the old, familiar knowledge and the new, unsettling kind: "I knew: everything I had once known, my childhood too, was over." This move is not an unjustifiable liberty taken in translation. The concern with models of interpretation is implicit in the Hebrew, explicitly brought out not in the exact words of this sentence but in the opening of the paragraph. There the mother tries to establish not "serenity" but *"hanusah hayashan"*—that is, the old formula, the previous tradition. In Judaism the word *nusah* refers to modes of prayer, and here it is significant that the expression is divested of, though not entirely divorced from, its religious connotations. The implication emerges that if former times for the boy bore a kind of sanctity, a serenity and wonder akin to prayer (especially in the early chapters, which describe peaceful summer holidays), now that quality is extinguished, as is the very meaning of *nusah* in a spiritual sense.

The narrator's suffering, his loss of childhood, does not remain singular here. It is generalized. Orphanhood is not his alone, but everyone's. The child becomes the emblem of collective sorrow as orphanhood signifies a burden of massive proportions, a communal loss of support and social moorings. The word *"yatmut"* in itself bears interesting polyvalence. Orphanhood is at once proper to children (since adults whose parents die are not designated as orphans) but also leaves children bereft of the innocence associated with childhood. Leaving them facing the painful reality of death, it often forces them to grow up that much more quickly. The protagonist's entire world here is characterized, then, in terms of childhood simultaneously maintained and

threatened. Bereavement, pain, helplessness, and incomprehension pre-
dominate. The same ambivalence obtains in the novel as a whole. Appelfeld's artistry throughout is based on a discourse of childhood suffused with the knowledge that there has already been an end to
innocence.

8

DAVID GROSSMAN—
SEE UNDER: LOVE

She turns the pages. Naked men
running, naked and so thin.
Women, too, with their tushies out.
And people in pyjamas, like in the theater,
wearing stars of cloth.
They are all so ugly and thin
with great big eyes, like birds.

It's so terribly strange and gray. Ilana has lots of
*   pencils:*
red, blue, green, yellow, pink.
So she goes to her room
and brings all the pretty colors
and gladly draws
spectacles and funny faces.
Especially for the thin, bald boy
she makes a giant red moustache,
and on the very tip, a lark.

—Meir Wieseltier, "Mother and Father Went to the
    Movies and Ilana Sits Alone in the Armchair,
    Looking at a Book"

*L*ike Ahron Appelfeld's *The Age of Wonders,* Uri Or-
lev's *The Lead Soldiers,* and Jerzy Kosinski's *The Painted Bird,* David
Grossman's *See Under: Love* cultivates a depiction of childhood to
speak of unspeakable horror. Here, too, focus on a child's partial understanding helps alleviate the adult narrator's struggle with language and
artistic expression, for the young character's incomprehension serves to
indicate the incomprehensibility of the catastrophe. Unlike those other
writers, however, who concentrate on suffering during the Nazi era and
who often draw on their own tormented memories from that time,
Grossman creates a child protagonist born, like himself, after World
War II. This is a child who attempts to fathom what Nazism was. The
boy's parents are survivors of Hitler's camps and reluctant to speak of
their experience. Consequently, the son must combat incomprehension
at two levels. First he must contend with the family silence; then he must

try to grapple emotionally and intellectually with the sheer ghastliness of what he learns.

Featured in the first of four segments that constitute the novel, this protagonist is a nine-year-old boy named Momik, who lives with his parents in Jerusalem. The events of the story take place in 1959, and they begin to unfold with the arrival of an ambulance. Without previous notice it brings the family an elderly relative, emotionally and mentally crippled from abuse at the hands of the Nazis. The invalid, Anshel Wasserman, is unable to communicate with those around him and mumbles continually to himself, condemned to an inner world of horror from which he cannot escape. Since his arrival in Israel he had been living in a nursing home, unidentified, and it is only now that the authorities at long last have succeeded in locating his surviving relatives. Though Momik's parents agree to take the old man in, they are determined to shield their little boy and to try not to upset him with the truth of his adoptive grandfather's past. These circumstances arouse the child's curiosity, and he feels driven to discover all he can about the new member of the household and the secret world the grown-ups share.

Upon its appearance in 1986, *See Under: Love* caused a sensation on the Israeli literary scene. Each of its four sections, in complex and highly diverse ways, attempts an innovative treatment of Holocaust themes. Chapter 1, in particular, received wide critical acclaim. Part of the significance of this text was that it dealt with the second generation after the Holocaust, a topic not yet developed in Hebrew fiction and one only beginning to emerge in other Jewish literatures. This portion of the novel, which can be read effectively as a self-contained unit of narrative, is also remarkable for its engagement with a child's inner life. This combination of focus on childhood and the Shoah allows for a double exploration of otherness. As Grossman gives expression to the child protagonist, this character's naiveté serves to undo the limitations and to expose the blind spots of grown-up discourse in the fictional world. The child disregards the constraints of his milieu and sees marginalized figures in his own way, with the result that this narrative draws closer to one of the most important Others of Israeli society: the Holocaust survivor in the early years of the Jewish state.

The intractable alterity of the refugees is in part a function of the horrific experiences they underwent, but in the Israel of the fifties the survivors are further estranged from those around them because they live in a culture committed to creating a heroic ideal. For a prolonged period of time following World War II, Israeli culture resisted identification with the Diaspora Jew, who was considered the antithesis of the new strong, self-reliant sabra. Furthest from this celebrated image were those victimized by the Nazis, especially the masses seen as having gone to their deaths like sheep to the slaughter. Accordingly, the Israelis understood their role vis-à-vis the survivors as one of rescue and rehabilitation, not of similarity.[1] The boy, Momik, whose outlook on the world is informed by an opposition between heroism and victimhood, nonetheless unsettles the boundaries dividing the two. In the process he also brings the text to speak to another issue, the relationship of strength to brutality. Written in 1986, *See Under: Love* must be read as a response to widespread malaise and pervasive discussion in Israeli society over the uses of military force.

For all these reasons the "Momik" section of *See Under: Love* deserves careful analysis. A consideration of complementary formal and thematic tensions in the initial narrative segment is in order, too, as chapter 1 serves an important function in prefacing or setting the stage for subsequent chapters of the novel.

To chart the process of discovery that the child character undergoes in this fiction, the representation of Momik's consciousness relies on combinations of psychonarration and narrated monologue. These are the terms Dorrit Cohn uses to classify, first of all, accounts of a character's inner life by an authorial voice and, second, the rendering of a character's thought in its own idiom while maintaining third-person narration.[2] In *See Under: Love* these techniques allow Grossman to maintain the child's perspective and also the organizational control of a mature narrator. Focalization is restricted to Momik's thoughts and perceptions. It is the child's experience that orients the story, but the text is far more articulate than any version of events a nine-year-old could either recount to an audience or sustain internally to himself. The work therefore clearly depends on a grown-up artist who provides the point from which all is retrospective and makes the tale tellable, but voice here shifts and glides between that of the implied narrator and that of the protagonist. Indeed, childlike vocabulary and intonations are heard much more clearly here than in *The Painted Bird* or *The Age of Wonders,* and, through varied kinds of speech representation, the narrative gains flexibility in imagining the consciousness of the child character. Conveying thoughts more inchoate than rational verbalization, the text also records other thoughts that are informed by language. In addition it reports words clearly registered in Momik's mind as they have been spoken by the boy himself or by others.

In the following scene, for instance, as Momik watches his parents eat, several levels of narrative voice put into evidence several degrees of inwardness in the boy's thinking.

[1] Dinner.

[2] It goes like this: first Mother and Momik quickly arrange the table, and Mother warms up the big pots from the fridge and then brings the dishes. [3] This is when the danger begins. [4] Mother and Father eat with all their strength. [5] They begin to sweat and then their eyes begin to bulge. [6] Momik pretends to eat but all the while watches them carefully and wonders how such a fat woman as his mother could have come out of Grandma Henny and how a scarecrow of a kid like himself could have come out of the two of them. [7] He tastes just a little on the end of his fork, but the food sticks in his throat from all the tension, and that's how it is. [8] His parents have to eat lots of food every night in order to be strong. Once already they managed to escape from death, but the second time, for sure, it wouldn't let them go.[3]

ארוחת ערב.

זה הולך ככה: קודם כל אמא ומומיק מסדרים מהר מהר את השולחן,
ואמא מחממת את הסירים הגדולים מהמקרר, ואחר–כך מביאה את
המנות. מהרגע הזה בעצם מתחילה הסכנה. אבא ואמא אוכלים בכל
הכוח שלהם. הם מתחילים להזיע, ואחר כך העיניים שלהם מתחילות
לבלוט. מומיק עושה את עצמו אוכל, וכל הזמן מציץ בהם בזהירות,
וחושב איך יצאה מסבתא הני אשה כל–כך שמנה כמו אמא, ואיך בכלל
יצא לשניהם ילד כל–כך דחלילי וקטן כמוהו. הוא טועם רק בקצה
המזלג, אבל האוכל נתקע לו בגרון מרוב שהוא מתוח, וזה ככה,
שההורים שלו מוכרחים לאכול כל ערב המון אוכל בשביל להיות חזקים.
פעם אחת הם כבר הצליחו לברוח מהמוות, אבל בפעם השנייה הוא כבר
בטח לא יוותר להם. (46)

Though the parents never divulge details of their past, the son is highly aware of the fear and terrible memories of hunger that torment them even now. The first two sentences present events as Momik perceives them, but which he doesn't necessarily articulate.[4] At the same time the prose is tinged with verbal patterns and colloquialisms that might be ascribed to a child (e.g., *zeh holekh kakha; maher maher*). Such stylistic contagion helps create a closeness between author and fictional figure as it melds their voices together. The second, third, and fourth sentences introduce more distinct dissonance. The word "danger" belongs decidedly to the vocabulary of the author but signals observations peculiar to the boy's domain. The internal contradiction sets off ironic resonance. From the adult view "danger" is an exaggeration or a misnomer. This perspective casts the parents' eating habits as abnormal or damaged behavior determined by the trauma of the war. Because of such words as "bulge" and "sweat" the actions of the mother and father seem pathetic or comically grotesque. For the boy, nonetheless, the concept implied by the word "danger" is apt. The son sees the scene in an idealized way, and he elevates the same actions into the terms of an ongoing struggle (indicated by the phrase "all their strength"). Within this framework bulging and sweating take on a different connotation as titanic effort.

That Momik inscribes his parents in a heroic code is made more explicit in the last two sentences of the passage. It is not the mature narrator who suggests that overeating builds strength and staves off death. Instead, it is the child who sees the meal as part of a fateful battle. The narrated monologue used to convey this opinion employs words that could be entirely the boy's except for the personal pronouns, and the preceding line (6, "he wonders," *hu hoshev*) has prepared the reader for just such a shift that can orient the passage to the child's utterances. As the indirect discourse presents a summary of Momik's thoughts, it provides a minimal but perceptible transition signaling that the boy is struggling to crystallize, perhaps put into words, his awareness of the situation. By line 8 the reader can accept the final pronouncements as Momik's evaluation of affairs, and at the same time the prose evades forcing the issue of whether or not a child would actually pronounce such a sentence to himself. The effect of the last line therefore is to make Momik's voice more pronounced and independent while also assuring that the actual text will fall short of direct quotation.[5]

Because the boy's words are retained within the voice of the narrator, his immature thoughts cannot be readily dismissed as childish prattle. The presentation of a child's view within the cogent narrative of someone older imputes seriousness to the character's inner world. As a result, the conclusions Momik reaches may be inadequate or comically distorted, and his innocence may raise smiles, but the passage insists on the impressive sensitivity and complexity of his mental life. Momik, in short, has discovered a profound truth: that his parents are perpetually engaged in a conflict of monumental proportions. The tensions that drive them are phantasmatic but undeniably compelling. The parents' compulsions therefore strenuously resist being judged by the standard norms of the society, which sees them as pitiful victims. Momik's interpretation is at once misguided and somehow appropriate. Eerily in accord with the intensity of the parents' suffering, his understanding shifts heroism onto them, and a double-edged irony emerges. Working for and against Momik's views, it is created through the superimposition of voices that allows the narrator to exercise both distance from and identification with the character.

Because this strategy effectively shows discrepancies between adult and child views while also promoting empathy with the young character, narrated monologue is used throughout the "Momik" section to reveal exceptional insights on the youngster's part. The boy, for instance, has responsibility for helping Anshel bathe, and he is fascinated by the number on the old man's arm. When, despite insistent trying, he cannot wash it off with soap and water, the child speculates that the marks must be inscribed from within. As a result he is "even more sure that maybe there really was someone inside of grandpa, and maybe inside the others too, and they were calling for help that way" (21). The tentativeness of these lines ("even more sure that maybe there really was") suggests a groping toward new understandings. Though the hypothesis arrived at is patently childish and silly, it expresses in a graphic and immediate way a true circumstance that grown-ups would only state more abstractly, were they willing to express it at all: namely, that the survivors are trapped in an inner life that is largely inaccessible to others.

That this narrative approach helps accord the child's voice a privileged status becomes even more evident by contrast with those occasions when Momik does speak up within the plot actions themselves. At those times either the adults try to silence his questions and observations, or his words demonstrate the gap between the profundity of his inner life and the superficial way his parents and neighbors are prepared to understand him. At night, for example, Mother and Father come to stand by his bed. Momik pretends to be asleep, while in actuality he anticipates with dread the screams they routinely produce during their nightmares. Hoping to spare them additional pain, the son wants his parents to see him as a healthy, contented child who smiles all the time:

> Sometimes he has ideas, he's a real Einstein and he says, for example, as if he were asleep, kick it to me Joey, we'll win today Danny, and other things to make them happy, and once, when it was an especially hard day . . . he sang to them as if in his sleep *etkohol ʿod belevav pehenihima* and from all the excitement wet himself, and all this so they'd see that they don't have to worry about him at all.

> לפעמים וש לו רעיונות של איינשטיין ממש, והוא אומר ככה, כאילו
> משינה, תבעט אלי יוסי, אנחנו ננצח היום, דני, ועוד כאלה דברים
> בשביל לשמח אותם, ופעם, כשהיה יום קשה במיוחד, וסבא רצה לצאת
> אחרי הארוחה בערב, והיה צריך ממש לנעול אותו בחדר שלו, והוא
> התחיל לצעוק שם, ואמא בכתה, ביום הקשה הזה מומיק שר להם כאילו
> מתוך שינה את כֹּהוֹל עוד בלבב פֶּהְנִיהִימה ומרוב שהתרגש מעצמו
> הוא הרטיב, וכל זה בשביל שיראו שבכלל לא צריך לדאג לו... (47–48)

Momik's rendition of the *Hatikvah* anthem, which is convincingly childlike as it suggests scores of unreflecting repetitions, is perceived by the parents through their own emotional distortions as a sign of social adjustment. The reader, of course, having been privy to Momik's inner life, brings a very different knowledge to the events and can interpret his words as a sign of genuine danger. Portrayed here is a child acting overly protective of his parents at the cost of his own need to be understood.[6]

On each of these occasions the author creates the impression of a smooth, continuous narrative surface. Psychonarration approaches narrated monologue and vice versa as the two incorporate into themselves varying amounts of the child character's idiolect. This quality of the prose complements and amplifies one of the peculiar properties of narrated monologue itself. As a technique of storytelling that blurs distinctions between *who sees* and *who tells,* it discourages disentanglement of focalizations and utterances. The resulting conflation of perspectives allows subtle modulations that favor emphasis on either child or adult views. In this respect Grossman's novel differs significantly from the approaches of, for example, Appelfeld and Orlev. In *The Age of Wonders* the grown-up narrator reminiscing back on his own childhood allows the text to maintain the restricted scope of a youngster's understanding, but retains a decidedly adult voice and vocabulary. He can therefore recount his story with an amazement ascribable to a child, even as the narrative disallows joyous naiveté. The entire telling of the tale is suffused with the gravity of mourning and trauma that comes later in the narrated events, after the fact of innocence lost. Orlev sometimes follows a similar pattern, presenting actions through adult vocabulary while recording the fragmentary perceptions a child might entertain. At other times this author more decisively separates the child and adult dimensions of the narrative to maximize the gap between perspectives. What is genuinely a child's speech arises briefly in dialogue, but entirely adult intervention brings admonishments from the narrator that the readers should not confuse their own sensibilities with those of the protagonist.[7]

See Under: Love attempts a much more ambitious integration of child and adult expression. To be sure, the text does not constitute a dramatically innovative mimesis of children's language. Grossman takes fewer risks than many authors in terms of recreating genuine syntactic patterns or the odd vocabulary of young speech. *See Under: Love* is less daring at reproducing inner speech than, for example, Henry Roth's *Call It Sleep.* Taking advantage of narrative techniques familiar in many modern literatures, Grossman is more discursive and less experimental than Roth.[8] Still, his novel is notable for its insightful application of these approaches to the treatment of the Shoah and for the supple use of colloquial idiom in his prose. Grammatical mistakes and childish phrases deliciously capture the new Hebrew of the streets and depart from the stilted, elevated diction that till recently has predominated in Hebrew fiction. The exceptional history of Hebrew, the holy tongue, which in the past century underwent extraordinary rebirth as a modern vernacular, has exerted pressure in highbrow literature against reliance on spoken language. In *See Under: Love,* however, Momik uses such slang as *"betaḥ"* and *"hamon okhel"* (during the dinner scene); at other times he makes childish oaths (*"af pa'am, af pa'am, ḥut barzel,"* 62) and expresses himself with exaggerations of typically childish formulation. In Momik's eyes, Anshel is "the oldest man in the world" (*"ha'ish hakhi zaqen ba'olam,"* 9). Grammatical mistakes, particularly regarding *smikhut*, are also indicative of the child's voice: for instance, *"hashlo-shah hazqenim ha'elah"* (12). Grossman's sensitivity to various registers of the language and his integration of low diction into high art is a sign of Hebrew's increasing maturity as a living language and as an artistic medium in a modern secular literature. They indicate, too, the prominence and worth accorded to the child's outlook and his fresh interpretations of the world around him.

In its narration this fiction struggles with two separate frames of reference, that of the adult narrator and that of the child character, in order to show how the young figure within the plot action struggles with a parallel set of problems: his own transition from one immature frame of reference to another, more mature one. Momik's semiotic initiation is turned to explicit thematic focus, for this is a text preoccupied with a child's attempts to understand his elders. While the narrator allows a young voice into his text, it is the child who, by internalizing the words of grown-ups, allows the largely suppressed perspective of his parents to surface in his own imagination. He thereby grants them admittance to the forefront of the text as a whole and so to the reader's attention.

There is a notable intercalation of adult language in the child's articulate thoughts thanks to the boy's imitation of certain formulaic phrases. The youngster's first rudimentary attempts at absorbing his parents' code of understanding occurs as he copies their speech patterns and the peculiar blend of Hebrew and Yiddish used by the refugees he knows. Whenever Nazis are mentioned, for instance, he tags on the expression *"yemaḥ shemam"* (may their name be blotted out). Similarly, Momik calls himself an *"alter kop,"* that is, "old head" or wise fellow, to congratulate himself on his own intelligence and maturity. In both cases the phrases are inappropriate for a child's speech but an accurate report of what the adults say. Again echoing his parents' and neighbors' parlance, he refers to the world of their past as *erets sham*, the land of THERE. For the grown-ups the one word "there" overflows with significance. Momik adopts their usage naively as if they came from a country literally called THERE.

This use of mimicry in the prose offers psycholinguistic authenticity, for children are capable of repeating many things without fully comprehending them. Perception is commonly a territory staked out ahead of time by more narrowly linguistic knowledge. Momik's parroting of grown-up locutions, in particular, is plausible because he is an exceptionally precocious child with an almost photographic memory. In addition, there is an artistic benefit from this narrative procedure, as it provides a window onto the adult frame of reference never directly evinced outside of Momik's vision. In this way the narrative affords the reader valuable information about the milieu and social background of the family: the parents' Eastern European roots, their bitterness toward the Nazis, and the mystery in which they shroud their past. Momik's direct citation of others also allows the introduction of substantial amounts of Yiddish into the text without making overly cumbersome use of a second language. Somewhat bilingual, but not entirely fluent in Yiddish, the child latches onto some expressions and translates them immediately into Hebrew. Such simultaneous translations make the prose understandable for that sizable portion of the Israeli reading public which would not otherwise know enough Yiddish to follow. The author thus develops a clever device for bringing to life a mode of speech, the language of the European refugees, never before captured so effectively in Hebrew fiction. Altogether, the integration of mature and youthful planes contributes to a successful depiction of child language, while the text also makes successful use of child language for other artistic ends.

A further meeting of adult language and child's inner world occurs when longer statements, spoken by other characters, are absorbed into Momik's thoughts. Early in the novel, for example, the boy reflects on Bella, the owner of a grocery store who is losing all her customers to a recently established supermarket:

> That all her clients were leaving her didn't matter to Bella (so she said) and also that rich now she'd never be, so what, does Rockefeller eat two lunches? Does Rothschild sleep in two beds?

אבל זה שעזבו אותה ככה כל הקליינטים לא אכפת לח (ככה בלה
אומרת),וגם זה שעשירה היא כבר לא תהיה, מה יש, רוקפלר אוכל
שתי ארוחות–צהריים? רוטשילד ישן על שתי מיטות? (16)

As Momik incorporates Bella's modes of thinking and expression into his own (including syntax more appropriate to Yiddish than Hebrew), the text creates a narrated monologue twice removed from the original speaker. Bella's words are filtered through Momik's thoughts and then through the narrator's prose. It is hard to say here if she speaks an awkward Hebrew that suffers interference from Yiddish, or if Grossman takes features of the Yiddish Bella speaks and superimposes them onto his Hebrew writing. Either way, this internalization of adult speech by Momik fosters an interlingual and conceptual montage that works in the interest of representational vividness.[9]

More important, though, than verisimilitude in capturing the linguistic milieu is the way this child processes the information he acquires from the grown-ups, the way in which he assimilates, reevaluates, and transforms the words of others, making them his own. Here he takes in uncritically what Bella has to say. The most dynamic intersection of adult and child discourse comes about as he later begins to question the adults' pronouncements and to think for himself. In many instances he neatly demonstrates Bakhtin's conviction that independent thinking occurs not as a smooth process but as a strenuous effort at liberating oneself from received opinion.

These matters are engagingly dramatized in an early passage that introduces a secondary character, Hannah Zitrin. She is one of a group of survivors who live on Momik's block, who are unable to function sanely, and who first catch the boy's notice after Sabba Anshel's arrival. Not surprisingly, since these figures are so frightening and inaccessible, most of the more sane characters attempt to marginalize them and to dismiss them from consciousness. Momik's reading of Hannah is significant, as it shows him at first reacting to her with scorn, othering her through stereotype, and then reconsidering. Clearly recognizing that she is different, and an Other within Israeli society, he nonetheless arrives at a new respect for her as a victim.

> Here, too, came Hannah Zitrin, whose husband the tailor abandoned her and ran off, *yemah shemo*, and left her a living widow, as she was always screaming in a loud voice, and it was lucky the reparations money came, because otherwise she would have died of hunger here, God forbid, because the tailor *pishakrev*, dog's blood, didn't leave them even so much as what's under a fingernail, everything he took with him, may a cholera take him, and Mrs. Zitrin is really a good woman but also a slut who screws around with shvartzim, *a shvarts yor af ir*, a black year upon her, as mother always says when she passes by, and Mrs. Zitrin definitely does that word with Sasson Sasson, who's a backfielder on the soccer team, Hapoel Yerushalayim, and with Victor Arusi, who's a taxi driver, and also with Azura who has a butcher shop at the shopping center and whose hair is always full of feathers, and actually he looks like a good man and not like one who would go around whoring but everyone knows that he is. And at first Momik hated Hannah with a black hatred, and swore to himself that he would marry only a girl of fine, upstanding family, like in the advertisements of Esther Levin the matchmaker, one like that who would love him because of his fine looks and his wisdom and his modesty, and would by no means be a whore, but when he said something once about Hannah Zitrin to Bella, Bella got angry and started to say what a poor woman Hannah is, and that she needs compassion just like everyone else, and Momik doesn't know every-

thing about what happened to Hannah THERE, and when she was born she surely never dreamed that she would end up like this, everyone has a lot of dreams and hopes at the beginning, that's what Bella said, *nu,* and then Momik started to look at Hannah a little bit differently and saw that she was actually very kind of pretty, she has a big blonde wig, like Marilyn Monroe's hair, and she has swollen legs wrapped in a bunch of bandages and she's really sort of OK, only that she hates her body, and all the time scratches it with her nails and calls it my oven and my disaster.

ובאה גם הגברת חנה ציטרין, שבעלה החייט עזב אותה וברח ימח–שמו, והשאיר אותה אלמנה חיה, ככה היא היתה צועקת תמיד בקולי קולות, ומזל שבאו השילומים, כי אחרת היא היתה מתה פה ברעב, חס וחלילה, כי החייט, פשאקרב, דם–כלבים, לא השאיר להם אפילן מה שיש מתחת לציפורן, הכל לקח אתו, חולירע שתיקח אותו, והגברת ציטרין היא אשה באמת טובה, אבל היא גם זונה ומזדווגת עם שווארצים, א שווארץ יאר אויף איר, שנה שחורה עליה, כמו שאמא אומרת תמיד כשהיא עוברת, וגברת ציטרין בפירוש עושה את המלה הזאת עם ששון ששון, שהוא בק בהפועל–ירושלים, ועם ויקטור ערוסי שהוא נהג טקסי, וגם עם עזורא שיש לו אטליז במרכז המסחרי, והשערות שלו תמיד מלאות נוצות, והוא דווקא נראה איש טוב ולא מזדווג, אבל כולם יודעים שהוא כן. ובהתחלה מומיק שנא את חנה שנאה שחורה, ונשבע לעצמו שהוא יתחתן רק עם בחורה ממשפחה עדינה ומפורסמת, כמו במודעות של אסתר לוין השדכנית, אחת כזאת שתאהב אותו בגלל יופיו וחוכמתו וביישנותו, ובשום אופן לא תהיה מזדווגת, אבל כשאמר פעם משהו על חנה ציטרין לבלה, בלה התרגזה עליו והתחילה לומר כמה חנה היא אשה מסכנה, ושצריך לרחם עליה, כמו שצריך לרחם על כל אחד, ולא הכל מומיק יודע על מה שקרה לחנה שם, וכשהיא נולדה היא בטח לא חלמה שתיגמר ככה, לכולם יש הרבה חלומות ותקוות בהתחלה, ככה בלה אמרה, נו, ואז מומיק כבר התחיל להסתכל על חנה קצת אחרת, וראה שהיא בעצם אשה מאוד די יפה, יש לה פארוקה בלונדינית גדולה, כמו השערות של מרילין מונרו, ופנים אדומים וגדולים עם שפמפם קטן נחמד, ויש לה רגליים נפוחות ועטופות המון תחבושות, והיא בעצם די בסדר, ורק שהיא שונאת את הגוף שלה, וכל הזמן שורטת אותו בציפורניים, וקוראת לו התנור שלי והאסון שלי. (18)

Hannah is presented here prominently through what is reported about her by other characters in the story. Mother, in a highly opinionated way, calls her a whore who fornicates with *"shvartsim."* Not only does she attach her negative judgment of Hannah to a denigrating stereotype, she also overtly employs a derogatory ethnic epithet to refer to the woman's dark-skinned sex partners. Immediately Mother reinforces the negative associations of the word "black" by tagging onto her condemnation the formulation "a black year upon her." Momik latches onto these expressions of disgust and hates Hannah with a black, that is, intense hatred (*"sin'ah sheḥorah"*). The reiteration of the word *black,* yet again, underscores the rigidity of his stance. Shortly thereafter the passage comments quite openly on the force of convention and the tyranny of stereotypic thinking. Azura the butcher looks to Momik like a nice guy but, the boy hastens to observe, everyone knows the opposite. This means that the child is capable of seeing things afresh but is none-theless clearly influenced and swayed by the opinions and preconcep-tions voiced by his family and friends. He then further demonstrates his acceptance of Mother's views by announcing to himself that he will marry only a girl from a fine, upstanding, and well-known family (*"mish-paḥa ʿadinah umefursemet"*). This phrase is significant, because it is memorized from an announcement in the newspaper for a matchmak-ing service. In other words, it is media hype, a simple advertising slogan, but one that Momik in his naiveté takes literally as he incorporates it into his own thinking. With these words the text shows how the boy moves from one reified, rigid formulation to another rather than to original or creative thought.

This direction in his thinking is later interrupted thanks to Bella, the figure in the novel who consistently brings more kindness than fear to her relations with her neighbors. Pointing out that the old woman is more to be pitied than condemned, Bella upsets Momik's assumptions, suggests a new interpretation of Hannah, and so undermines the pre-vailing code of understanding that the boy had previously absorbed. Her comments imply that people are complex (they all have "dreams and hopes, at first") and that Momik has been unaware of Hannah's complexity. The boy takes these cautionary remarks quite seriously, and the impact of Bella's words subsequently leads to an amusing reorgani-zation and reshuffling of paradigms for understanding. The little boy abandons his previous evaluation of Mrs. Zitrin and goes back to take another look at her. Deautomatizing his responses to this woman, he attempts to redefine what he sees in a way that will account for more of the information now available to him.

What he finds is that Hannah is not so bad after all. Specifically, he uses the phrase *"me'od dey beseder,"* really sort of OK. The tentative formulation suggests a wavering between two possibilities. Having broken down the usual conventions with which he previously viewed her, Momik is not quite ready to endorse a new vision. Still unable to choose entirely between two frames of interpretation, he enumerates reasons why he has changed his mind. According to Momik, Hannah turns out to be all right because she is quite an attractive woman, with a big red face, a blonde wig, a mustache, and swollen legs wrapped in bandages. Here the passage turns comic, because the new attempt at devising a code yields results that clash with the assumptions of the implied reader and narrator, both of them adults who inevitably will see the child's reaction in an ironic light. While Hannah may be appealing to

Momik, she cannot be to the reader in the same naive way. Grown-ups can empathize with the child's ability to see differently than adults do, and they can appreciate the child's capacity to perceive physical beauty in unconventional places. Indeed, the description here is effective because it is not entirely distasteful and leaves room for some identification between reader and character. All the same, the audience must finally take exception to Momik's conclusions. The bandages, a highly grotesque detail, color the impact of earlier observations. It is possible to find big red faces on women pretty, but the wig is a more pointedly ambivalent item. While it is Hannah's most positive attribute, the blonde hair is also fake and inappropriate, perhaps even downright ludicrous for an aging woman. Furthermore, it is the product of another era's standards of beauty, several decades outdated at the time the novel was published. Momik finds it attractive because it resembles the hairstyle of Marilyn Monroe, one that at this late date is evidently exposed as convention rather than as inherently beautiful.

As this passage demonstrates Momik's reevaluations of Hannah and his renewed vision, which depends on a shifting and breakdown of conventions and consensus, the text in a number of ways very deliberately calls attention to its preoccupation with codes. The many uses of *k* (like or as) in this short passage bring out a preoccupation with thinking according to a model. (It appears in various forms: as a preposition, *kemo,* four times; as an adverb, *kakha,* three times; and as an adjective, *kazot,* once.) It is not just that the boy relies on adult formulations to define his world (quoting his elders and noting, "as Mother says," "as Bella says," "as Hannah is always screaming"). In addition, when comparing Hannah to Marilyn Monroe, Momik shows that he has put aside one set of criteria for judging Mrs. Zitrin but has immediately inscribed her in yet another set of conventions. When Bella says that Hannah never dreamt she would end up "like that" (*"kakha"*), she similarly relies on a cultural shorthand. She invokes a consensus about how Hannah is, rather than elaborating, explaining, or describing the woman's condition. Such phrases put into relief how much various paradigms govern the characters' thinking.

The end of the passage, in a move that calls attention to much the same issue, reinforces attention to the child's struggle with codes and his function as an agent of defamiliarization. It happens this way: Momik repeats once more that Hannah is OK, but he qualifies his remark by adding that she hates her body. The text notes specifically that she calls it her "oven" and her "disaster." In other words, she interprets it, codifies it according to her own set of criteria, which are other than those by which the child judges her. The explicit statement *"hi kor'et lo"* underscores that the value of the body here depends on someone's perception and reception of it. Evidently, Hannah has internalized the horror of her experiences in the Shoah and directs her anger and anguish against herself. She acts out her emotional disturbance in her sexual licentious-ness and then in her own revilement against herself. (Later in the narra-tive it becomes clear that she has had to serve as a prostitute to avoid being murdered by the Nazis.) It is significant of course that she refers to her body with the words *ason* and *tanur,* two highly charged words in literature concerning the Holocaust. Much fiction on this topic has developed a code of its own, and in that writing words such as *smoke, train,* and *oven* cannot be used neutrally. They always carry a heavy burden of association.[10] Here, by counting on the adult reader's famil-iarity with such connotations, Grossman highlights that Momik is inno-cent of much of the grown-ups' understandings and experience. The author also emphasizes that this passage is about codes, even as he conversely admits the possibility of freeing them up to allow a readjust-ment of understandings.

It is the naive consciousness of the child that becomes the arena for this activity of discovery, and it is through Momik's reactions that the reader can garner insights not available to the older figures in the fiction-al world. In this connection it is noteworthy that Hannah's complexities escape not only her neighbors but her own estimation of herself. She, too, relies on oversimplifications to describe her life. Like a broken record she continually blames her husband for leaving her in poverty. Only later, after Momik's revisioning of her, can the reader see her demeanor anew, and the ending of the passage intensifies the possibility of reinterpretation as the final line reinscribes familiar signs into a new code, transforming the image of Hannah. At the beginning she com-plains of her terror that she would be left with nothing, not even what is under her nails. At the end it becomes clear that what is under her nails is precisely what she cannot accept and what terrifies her the most: her very flesh and existence. She wants at the same time to live and not to live. The nails are what she uses to destroy herself by constantly tearing at her body. This kind of complexity defies the simplistic view of her own circumstance, which she espoused at first, even as this conclusion also challenges the neighbors' put-downs of her. If, before, she came across as a spiteful, self-pitying *kvetch,* who, at this juncture, can fault her? Who can see her purely with contempt and not with compassion?

The prominence accorded to a variety of voices in the passage provides a neat illustration of Bakhtinian dialogue. Psychic life here clearly consists of a complex amalgam of discourses spoken by others and selectively appropriated by the individual. As this text incorporates diverse speakers, representing different social strata and beliefs, it shows how the self—far from being an atomized, private entity—is a social phenomenon constituted in polyphony. Momik, however, does arrive at genuinely creative thought. Though he never relinquishes dependence on external codes, he does come to a new synthesis, a new combination of ideas and fresh personal observations of nonverbal phenomena. Some of Momik's convictions remain laughable—for instance, that Hannah is beautiful. More fundamentally, the notion that beauty in appearance is constitutive of good and bad is, in itself, childish. But Momik is also wiser than his mother in recognizing goodness in Hannah. Without penetrating to her inner life, he has made an important first move away from the rigid, preconceived perceptions he had incorporated from the words of those around him, and toward more independent thinking.

The bivocality of narrated monologue adds further to the unsettling of assumptions, for the perspective of the adult narrator sometimes challenges the child's views. The presence of the adult narrator makes itself felt, for instance, in the choice of the name Bella for the caring, compassionate individual. This authorial estimation of her as a lovely individual contrasts with the child character's misguided valuation of physical beauty. As part of Grossman's overall artistic design, this touch puts Momik in ironic light even as Momik challenges the conventional wisdom about Hannah. From the adult perspective, too, the word *"beferush"* acquires polysemous echoes and deconstructs itself. Momik uses it to mean "definitely," that is, there is no doubt about Hannah's behavior with Azura, Victor, and Sasson. The etymology of the word, however, has to do with interpretation, that which is explicit because it has been explicated. In the context of Momik's undoing of presupposition, the alleged certainty about Mrs. Zitrin comes to seem mainly conventional and not so certain. His "definitely" is no longer definitive, as it depends on Mother's questionable definitions of Hannah. As a result of such ironies, the adult narration evokes creative response on the part of the reader, even as the clashing of voices at the level of narrated events also gives rise to creative synthesis of ideas in the mind of the character, Momik. Readers are not offered a unitary, calcified understanding of the individuals in the fictional world. Instead, they receive a series of conflicting views, free from explicit instruction (dictated from above by the narrator) about what to think. Each reader must absorb those various pieces of information and reach a new understanding of the situation, arriving in his or her own measure at laughter, horror, or pity, identification with the child or distance from him.

The plot of *See Under: Love* moves forward as the little boy attempts to deal more and more specifically with the Shoah. He wants passionately to enter into the grown-ups' discourse in order to decode that secret past he knows has affected Hannah, Anshel, and his parents.

Wavering between his ingrained admiration for strength and his new-found concern for victims, Momik imagines that gathering information and insight will help him save the survivors from their suffering.

He undertakes this mission by patching together impressions of the war era he has received from overheard conversations, taciturn comments, and a variety of texts to which he assigns his own meaning. When, for instance, he hears about "the Nazi beast," *haḥaya hanatsit*, he assumes that the phrase refers to some kind of animal. Subsequently, he begins to collect stray cats, birds, and other creatures to see if he can't identify the wicked one and exorcise the evil out of it. Compounding his confusion is mention in the papers and radio broadcasts about the noted Nazi hunter Simon Wiesenthal. Imagining Wiesenthal's home as a big game hunter's trophy room, Momik determines to write to this man and engage his help in tracking the beast. At least, he figures, he might ask for some tips: do the animals congregate in large herds? what kind of prey do they pursue? and so on. By trapping and overcoming the evil, he feels, he can restore his parents to wholeness and their former power. Momik is convinced, for example, that his father was a kind of emperor and a war hero. He knows that his parents have been in camps, but he interprets this fact in a way commensurate with his own understanding, supposing that the adults he knows from THERE all lived together at a military base training for glorious exploits. Momik is puzzled by the knowledge that there were trains at the camps, but he surmises that the scene must have resembled Westerns in which Indians attack the mail train and settlers defend their railroad.

Adult awareness of historical events after the fact allows the reader to appreciate the humor and irony and to feel compassion for the child's efforts to understand. The narrative avoids excessive cuteness because Momik's inner life is at once engagingly imaginative and intelligent, and because this character makes such an earnest effort to come to terms with a phenomenon the reader knows to be terrifying. The distance between child character and adult narrator disallows pathos. At times, even so, the narrative can lead precipitously from comic twists to heart-rending anguish. With the choice of particularly grisly details, for instance, Momik's interpretations cease to be amusing, and it becomes clear that the child's innocence cannot alter or explain away stark historical facts. When the boy overhears the word *Sondercommando*, he assumes that his father, the brave warrior, had an assistant with the strange name of Sonder. He does not recognize, as the reader painfully must, the German term for those prisoners in concentration camps responsible for operating the gas chambers and crematoria.

As is suggested by the trains, which make sense to Momik only in connection with Westerns, a fundamental aspect of the character's maturation and linguistic experience is his interpretation of reality according to received literary models. This entrance into textuality is based on the stories and heroes of childhood reading and movies (products, of course, of the adult imagination), which are within his comprehension and which can form a bridge to his understanding of the adult code. They constitute for him a first, inadequate step which he must go beyond in order to begin to grasp what happened in the Shoah. Numerous texts have influential impact on the boy: Bible tales learned at school, accounts of heroic deeds performed by Israeli soldiers, the works of Jules Verne and Arthur Conan Doyle, above all the stories written by Anshel Wasserman years ago, before the war, about "The Children of the Heart." These are a troupe of youngsters united in their fight for good against evil, and Wasserman's fiction presents an odd mixture of science fiction, boys' adventure tales, and quaintly outdated Haskalah Hebrew. From this heady mixture the child culls his notions of right and wrong, courage and weakness, the traditional Jewish past, ancient glories, and—he hopes—eventually an explanation of the hidden world his parents refuse to disclose. For instance, conflating fairy tales and the biblical account of Joseph in Egypt, Momik devises an imaginary scenario of orphanhood along classically Freudian lines. Fantasizing that his real parents are royalty from whom he was separated at birth, he speculates that he will return to them later as their savior, like the gloriously successful Joseph reunited with his brothers and his father, Jacob. This fiction corresponds to Momik's need to feel powerful and it reflects, too, the force of secrecy in his life. The little boy is aware that something has been concealed from him, and he wishes that it be something good.

Life lived in imitation of bookish models, the reading of reality according to internalized literary norms, is a theme widely pursued in the history of the novel and one that reaches back to Cervantes' *Don Quixote* and beyond. Here, however, an old pattern takes on new depth in its psycholinguistic verisimilitude as a compelling cognitive portrait of the power of the intertext. The plausibility of the plot development, again, depends on Momik's personality. His precocious intelligence, his sensitivity, his loneliness, which stems from not having siblings, and the isolation from playmates urged on him by overprotective parents— these have all made him an avid bookworm. A range of texts often converge in shaping Momik's imagination. Consider the following scene in which the child daydreams in school about an imaginary friend:

> Bill calls him Johnny and the two of them speak to one another with short remarks and lots of exclamation points like the cleft in Bill's chin. Bill! Good work, Johnny! and so on. Bill has a silver star on his

chest and that means he's a sheriff. Momik doesn't have a star yet. The two of them have a horse they call Blacky. Blacky understands every word and he loves to gallop wildly in the fields, but always at the end he comes back and rubs his head on Momik's chest and that feels really good, and just then Netta the teacher asks him why are you smiling Shlomo Neuman, and Momik has to hide Blacky quickly. He sometimes takes sugar from the kitchen and tries experiments to turn it into cubes like Blacky loves, but it isn't going so well, and the encyclopedia doesn't go up as far as sugar yet and Momik is sure that if it did it would probably say "see under: cubes," and in the meantime he has to find a way to feed that horse, doesn't he? In the wadi by Ein Kerem they go riding at least three times a week, returning children who have disappeared or whose parents have lost them and making an ambush like Orde Wingate for train robbers. Sometimes when Momik lies on his belly and waits, he sees over Mt. Herzl the high chimney of the new building that they're building there and calling by the funny name Yad Vashem and says to himself that it's the smokestack of a ship floating by, full of illegal immigrants from THERE who nobody wants to accept, like in the days of the British Mandate *pishakrev* and he'll save them too, somehow, with Blacky or Bill or his thoughts or his animals or the atomic reactor or Grandpa Anshel's stories about the Children of the Heart or something, and when he asked the old people what the chimney was they looked at one another and finally Munin said, it's a kind of museum and Ahron Marcus, who hadn't been out of his house already for several years, asked if it was an art museum and Hannah Zitrin laughed a crooked laugh and said art, sure, human art, that's what for art they have there.

ביל קורא לו ג׳והני, ושניהם מדברים ביניהם דיבורים מאוד קצרים עם
הרבה סימני קריאה, כמו הלום בו בסנטרו, ביל!! מלאכה יפה, ג׳והני!!
ועוד כאלה. לביל יש כוכב כסף על החזה, וזה סימן שהוא שריף.
למומיק עוד אין שום כוכב. לשניהם יחד יש סוס שקוראים לו בלקי.
בלקי מבין מבין כל מלה, והוא אוהב לדהור פראי בשדות, אבל תמיד בסוף
הוא חוזר ומגרד את הראש בחזה של מומיק, וזה ממש תענוג, ואז
בדיוק המורה נטע שואלת מה עכשיו החיוך הזה, שלמה נוימן, ומומיק
מחביא מהר את בְּלקי. הוא סוחב סוכר מהמטבח ועושה המון ניסויים
בשביל להפוך אותו לקוביות כמו שבלקי אוהב, אבל זה לא כל–כך
הולך לו, והאנציקלופדיה העברית עוד לא הגיעה לסוכר, ומומיק בטוח
שאם היא בכלל תגיע, היא תשלח אותו לעיין ערך קוביות, ובינתיים
צריך למצוא דרך להאכיל את הסוס הזה, נכון? בוואדי של עין–כרם
המ דוהרים לפחות שלוש פעמים בשבוע, מחזירים ילדים שנעלמו או
שההורים שלהם איבדו אותם, ושמים אמבוש של אורד וינגייט לשודדי
הרכבות. לפעמים, כשמומיק שוכב על הבטן ואורב, הוא רואה מעל הר
הרצל את הארובה הגבוהה של הבניין החדש שבנו שם, וקראו לו בשם
המצחיק ״יד ושם״, ואומר לעצמו שהנה זאת ארובה של אונייה ששטה
פה, והיא מלאה מעפילים משם שאף אחד לא רוצה לקבל אותם, כמו
בימי המנדט הבריטי פְּשָׁאקְרֶב, וגם אותם הוא יושיע איכשהו, עם בלקי

או עם ביל או עם המחשבות שלו או עם החיות שלו או עם הכור
האטומי או עם הסיפור של סבא אנשל וילדי הלב או עם משהו,
וכששאל את הזקנים שלו מה זאת הארובה הם הסתכלו אחד על השני
ובסוף מונין אמר ששם יש מין מוזיאון כזה, ואהרון מרכוס, שכבר כמה
שנים לא יצא מהבית, שאל אם זה מוזיאון של אמנות, וחנה ציטרין
צחקה צחוק עקום ואמרה אמנות, בטח, אמנות הבנאדם, זה מה שאמנות
שם. (50–51)

Momik here conjures for himself a friend modeled after the cowboys he idolizes, and he mixes a Western setting with exemplary tales of brave illegal immigrants to Israel. To this conglomeration of ideas and allusions the boy also adds a Polish intertext—his parents' favorite curse, *pishakrev*—as well as reference to the Hebrew encyclopedia. This last text is one Momik once considered an authoritative source of knowledge about adult affairs. Now he finds it inadequate, because incomplete (it is being bought in installments), and because it divides the world into categories of significance that strike him as artificial. From these converging contexts he forges a reality of his own: an ocean in Jerusalem, the setting for a scenario of courageous rescue that might realize his dream of liberating his parents from their perennial fears. The fantasy concludes with an abrupt entrance of the grown-up frame of reference, which for Momik is not yet meaningful, but which for the reader seals the episode with a bitter reminder of atrocities lying beyond the child's knowledge. In this new context the star on Sheriff Bill's chest differs from, yet sadly and ironically recalls, the yellow stars Momik's parents must once have worn on their clothing.

Of particular importance among Momik's literary models is Sholem Aleichem's *Mottel.* Written at the turn of the century, this novel presents a series of adventures undertaken by a young boy from Eastern Europe as he grows up in a traditional Jewish milieu. When that world suffers economic and spiritual decline, Mottel and his family immigrate to America. Momik is fascinated by this work and by the images of small-town life in Poland. The bath house, the market, the synagogue: these for him are wondrous, because inaccessible, and because he associates them with his parents' past in the Old World. When the mother and father begin to open up and talk at length about shtetl life because of their fond memories of Sholem Aleichem's books, Momik feels he has found a key not just to information but to their hearts. He pursues the subject even more in the hope of drawing them closer to him. The parents, however, become alarmed and view his interest as an unhealthy preoccupation with Diaspora weakness. Momik, precisely because he is anxious to explore a past largely repressed by Israeli society, embraces Mottel and plays earnestly at being a Jew in the old Diaspora sense.

With this move the novel effects a marvelous reversal of earlier stories about childhood in Hebrew and Yiddish literature, such as Mendele's *Of Bygone Days*, Bialik's *Aftergrowth*, and a host of others. In the world of traditional Jewish life in Europe children from the age of three were immersed in reading the holy books. Continual study of ancestral glories and ideals helped the Jews hold onto a sense of refinement, spirituality, and chosenness despite hardship and oppression. Steeped in ancient texts and exposed to a spiritual realm far removed from the poverty and degradation of their own social circumstances, the child characters in many pieces of nineteenth-century Jewish fiction find the legends and heroes of the Bible and the geography of the Holy Land a more immediate reality than their actual surroundings.[11] In the case of Grossman's protagonist, recovery of the past through textual study is still vital, but the situation has turned about. Seeking out the culture of exile, Momik takes maps of Israel and replaces the names of Israeli cities with the names of Polish towns. The past he feels he must revive in order to understand himself is the very realm of humiliation, suffering, and eventual annihilation that his earlier counterparts in Jewish literature were intent on escaping.

Momik's absorption in Sholem Aleichem, however, signals the beginning of the breakdown that finally overcomes him. As preoccupation verges on obsession, his involvement with this text signals that he is being dominated by, and absorbed into, the discourse of the past rather than correcting it or reinventing it himself. Momik here has begun a descent into an abyss where he will be less and less in control, more and more overwhelmed by the past he had hoped to tame. Feeling driven to seek out more and more facts about the Holocaust, he consults Bella, who is also a survivor but not so unwilling to speak about the Nazis. Through his conversations with her and through research at the library, the boy comes closer to a detailed picture of the Shoah. In this way he approaches the adult field of knowledge, but the collapsing of the two spheres of understanding, his and theirs, leads finally to Momik's emotional collapse.

First, he discovers that the truth he sought is not one that can be mastered rationally. Momik set out with the conviction that by sheer intelligence and orderly, methodical strategy he would unravel all the mysteries and trap the Nazi beast. To this end he kept a notebook, recording all his spying activities and his information about the land of THERE. Having decided to be a writer like Grandpa Anshel, he also determined to compose an encyclopedia (that is, a comprehensive, exhaustive account) of all significant facts about the secret world. Matters evolve to the contrary, though. As this character begins to get inklings of the horror the Shoah wrought, he himself starts to act more and more irrational. Profoundly disturbed, he stops eating, stops sleeping, and start to abuse the animals in his cellar. Denying them food and water, he aims to infuriate them and so force the Nazi beast to reveal itself.

In this process he makes another important discovery. Momik finds that he, like his parents' persecutors, is capable of cruelty in the name of an allegedly higher purpose (here, to find answers to his questions and to save his family). As a result he experiences the troubled relationship of victimizers to victims. He fears the creatures he torments, for their great hatred and anger toward him imbues them with strength. Afraid of them, he has in effect become a captive of his own cruelty. This development enhances and complicates the undoing of normative assumptions brought out in earlier segments of the text through the child's defamiliarizing vision. Before, by naively imputing heroism to his parents, he endowed the national Other, the victim, with the very quality valued by the majority. By losing his scorn for Hannah Zitrin, Momik learned to see victims as figures deserving of respect in their own right, in their suffering. Later, attempting to right the wrongs of the past, he ascribes strength and beauty to survivors. Then, opening the floodgates of knowledge about the Shoah, he cannot help but admit the awful victimization they have suffered. Their weakness and humiliation cannot be denied, minimized, or glibly rectified. In addition, Momik must accept weakness as part of his own history, and so he begins to shake off the once firm sense that Israeliness is separate from Jewishness. Coming to question the use of force in the basement, he finally arrives at an understanding that undermines any rigid opposition whatever between strength and weakness. In Momik's coercion of the animals pure ends become tainted by violent means, and cruelty leads to a fear that saps strength. The concern with these matters in the plot action is congruent with the adult author's preoccupations in the present of the text's composition. A disillusionment with military prowess, widespread in Israel in the wake of the 1982 Lebanon war, has fermented also in public debate about continuing occupation of the territories that fell to Israel in 1967. These are issues very much at the fore of Grossman's journalistic work, *The Yellow Wind* (1987) and his first novel, *The Smile of the Lamb* (1985). The child character of *See Under: Love* serves as an instrument for further meditation on themes of power and powerlessness.

At the end of the narrative Momik goes beyond unsettling familiar reasoning and beyond the deconstructive stance that dislodges long-standing categories of values. At this point his efforts to understand the Shoah do not respond any more to reason or scientific procedure. Driving himself to physical ill health, no longer making sound judgments, Momik decides to precipitate a climax by bringing the beast its favorite prey: authentic Jews from THERE. Luring the poor, half-crazed survivors from the neighborhood down to his secret lair, the boy hopes to spark a confrontation and finally force his adversary into the open. The bewildered old people find the walls covered with pictures Momik has drawn of death trains, hangings, mass graves, and crematoria. There, amidst the animals crying out, flapping, and beating at their cages, the survivors dimly surmise the terrible battle Momik has been fighting within himself. They can only murmur with inarticulate pity while the boy falls to the floor and in a strange, wordless, inhuman scream urges the beast to come out.

In this moment of breakdown it is not words but pictures, silence, and desperate acts that prevail. This denouement portrays a failure of language and rationality. The ultimate rapprochement of child and adult perception results, moreover, in the annihilation of the child's voice. Only a single paragraph remains in this section of the novel, and it is one restricted almost entirely to authorial reportage. The passage informs the reader that the family sends Momik to a school for troubled children and that Sabba Anshel wanders off one day, never to return. With this, both the narrated events and the narration are finished. The narrative's prime object of scrutiny, the child as a voice of innocence, is gone, and the narrative itself as a superimposition of voices also comes to a close.

This ending, which emphasizes speechlessness at the level of plot, is not itself a failed discourse. It reenacts and so alerts the reader to an essential problem facing the author from the outset at the level of story-telling: how to make sense of the Holocaust, how to give articulate expression to something so overwhelmingly horrific that it threatens to consume any who contemplate it too directly. Confronting the horror proves too much for the character in the story, but the adult writer in a sense succeeds. Of necessity he cannot fully convey the terrors of the Nazi period nor impose meaning on what happened then, but he does dramatize what is so problematic about his role as an artist. The first section in this way serves as the point of departure for the rest of the novel, which grows out of this initial formulation of artistic dilemma. The remaining sections of the work, in various experimental ways, wrestle with the issue of mimesis and representing the Holocaust. Momik becomes a writer, and all that follows can be seen as emerging out of his early experience. At this juncture the narrative shifts away from the childhood of the protagonist and from attempts to capture a child's voice, yet the later sections all explore ramifications of issues raised in chapter 1 and bear the imprint of Momik's early encounters with Sabba Anshel and the Nazi beast.

In chapter 2 the protagonist, now grown up and called Shlomo, spins a yarn about the Polish-Jewish writer Bruno Schulz. In this tale

Bruno is not murdered by the Nazis, as has been recorded by historical accounts. Instead, he is transformed into a fish in the depths of the sea. Such a fiction reflects the artist's wish to discover a world of imagination that will allow survival beyond death and so an escape from the brutal facts of atrocity. Significantly, at a critical moment in the sea, Shlomo envisages Bruno as a curious child/man, ever capable of the fantasy and wonder usually associated only with the very young. Chapter 2 then presents an imaginative recreation of Anshel Wasserman's experience in the concentration camp. In this avowedly fictional version of his life Anshel cannot die. Gas cannot harm him, bullets do not destroy him, and Wasserman spends his time recounting adventure tales about the Children of the Heart to an SS officer. Eventually the hardened Nazi is moved by these stories to a new and humane compassion. The final section of *See Under: Love* is set up as an encyclopedia that documents the twenty-four-hour life of a baby, a character out of Wasserman's stories. An outgrowth of Momik's early project, his planned encyclopedia, this last chapter also turns to children and the world of childhood. It does so, like the preceding chapters, as a way of introducing speculation on the power of the imagination to grapple with the unimaginable, to combat it, understand it, survive it, transform it, or produce from it renewed artistic vision.

Each section creates a complicated new set of quandaries related to these issues and raises questions about the connections between the four disjunct chapters of the novel.[12] All four sections, however, revolve about a central set of fundamental tensions—innocence/brutality, wonder/knowledge of evil—and chapter 1 is instrumental in laying the groundwork for the later perorations on these matters. "Momik" provides the dramatic framework that lends the other narratives coherence, since they are all to be understood as texts produced by the writer Shlomo, a man still haunted in adulthood by the preoccupation with the Shoah that marked his younger days. Chapter 1 likewise sets out the first fundamental opposition between naiveté and horror, and it is this section that presents, for the first time, the inquiring mind that tries to overcome silence and to find new ways of speaking about the gruesome past in order to penetrate its mystery. Finally, the artistic experimentation of the last sections (each of which deserves detailed scrutiny in its own right), together with the very disjunction of these texts, suggests effort. It is not easy to write about the Holocaust. Amassing and abandoning a spectrum of narrative possibilities, the author strains to reach beyond more ordinary fictional strategies. These efforts attest to a basic conviction that conventional language can respond only inadequately to the tragedy. This matter of language is the very issue brought out so forcefully in the opening chapter of *See Under: Love*. There Grossman struggles with the artifice of imagined child language and dualities of narrative stance—in short, with the whole problem of narratability in text featuring a child's inner life—to confront and put into relief another all-pervasive issue informing his novel as a whole: the difficulty of narration and of adopting an interpretive stance in fictional treatments of the Holocaust.

CONCLUSIONS

9 THE IMAGINATION OF THE CHILD IN LITERARY TEXTS

On the other side of the poem there is a path
as thin as a hairline cut,
and someone lost in time
is treading the path barefoot, without a sound.

On the other side of the poem amazing things may
    happen,
even on this overcast day,
this wounded hour
that breathes its fevered longing in the windowpane.

On the other side of the poem my mother may appear
and stand in the doorway for a while lost in thought
and then call me home as she used to call me home
    long ago:
Enough play, Rokhl. Don't you see it's night?

—Rokhl Korn, "On the Other Side of the Poem"

Orphanhood looms large as a preoccupation in the narratives examined in this study. Sholem Aleichem's Mottel gleefully announces, "Hoorah, I'm an orphan," thereby severing himself from responsibility to study Torah. Throughout Bialik's *Aftergrowth* orphanhood serves as a trope for the poverty of the protagonist's early environment. Indicating both material deprivation and also an emotional emptiness attributed to the absence of attentive parents, it calls for compensation through a romantic valorization of the imagination. In *Call It Sleep* the child fabricates parental loss. Davey's false account of his mother's death eases his psychic wrestling with issues of power and powerlessness. In this way the boy gives expression to his anxieties about Gentile/Jewish relations as they are welded into his private oedipal conflicts. Kosinski's Boy, in his turn, begins his arduous journey when abandoned by his parents. Between this event and the time they return for him he has faced too much hardship alone, and so he no longer recognizes them as his father and mother. Appelfeld's orphanhood is a collective one, signaling the disenfranchisement and dislocation of an entire world destroyed in the Holocaust. Finally, Grossman's

See Under: Love poses an imagined and temporary orphaning; the child fantasizes that he has been born to more heroic parents who will rediscover him one day after years of inglorious hiding.

To some degree, no doubt, this recurrent attention to orphanhood is a matter of coincidence. However, the topic surfaces repeatedly because the texts share a fundamental common feature expressed through this unlikely thematic congruence. Thanks to a real or posited disengagement from adult direction, each child character acquires freedom from the dominant values and outlook of his milieu. This phenomenon differs significantly from the preponderance of orphaned protagonists in the Bildungsroman—a staple feature of that genre. Orphanhood there permits young heroes to elect a patrimony, to choose their own mentors who may guide them into acceptance by society. In the narratives of childhood, by contrast, parentlessness is more closely allied with the unsupervised imagination, the child who, left alone, must fall back on his own resources. Accordingly, these texts emphasize the primacy of the child's consciousness and so make for the production of a pointedly defamiliarizing vision. The manifestations of this novel outlook are variegated and range from a gleefully unknowing stance to wonder or to keen perception of the sublime. In connection with the Holocaust, taking a more sinister turn, the same novelty of perspective presents itself as magical thinking, amazement that wavers between interpretation and incomprehension, or a naiveté that leads to ingenious observations. In each case, it should be noted, the singularity of the child's perception is related to a detachment from ordinary language. Whether through ties to allegedly prelinguistic and mystical experience, through buoyant vitality that refuses to be co-opted into adults' woeful quarrels, or through terror so overwhelming that the characters succumb to silence or profound mistrust of words, these young figures all stand outside of conventional expression in their milieu. Theirs is a marginal position which, together with their resilience, endows them with special capacity to recast the world and recontextualize its meanings in unusual ways.

At the same time, the child functions as more than just an intimate stranger capable of seeing the ordinary in extraordinary ways. The artifice of imagining a child's consciousness, which always supposes a composite of mature and immature perceptions, leads to an intersection of discourse. While the voice of the child may be a voice of nonconformity, nascent possibility, or even deconstructive oddity, it is also a highly, inescapably mediated one never detached from the adult author who constructs it, nor ever entirely separate from the adult characters whose words it absorbs, appropriates, or rejects. In both narrated events and the narration of the tale, the child character consists of overlapping impulses that allow the author to put into relief conflicting claims. As such, the imagined child is a peculiarly apt conduit for bringing the past and the future, or the old and the new, into contact with each other. These narratives, then, share a built-in pressure against the solipsism or kookiness to which the search for an innovative point of view might otherwise lend itself. This structural quality fosters an exceptional perspective but also holds it in check, and so the child figure readily serves as a prism that refracts collective issues without distorting them beyond recognition.

Few authors, of course, write about childhood for the sake of aesthetic experiment. The preponderance of texts about children in Jewish fiction stems fundamentally from the given that new worlds belong to new generations. In an immigrant population, for instance, it is much more likely that children, rather than adults, will adapt to a new language; there is then a distinct likelihood that those youngsters will grow up to write fiction in that language and recall their youth. Other writers, not referring to their own childhood, can clearly appreciate thematic possibilities in this area. Sholem Aleichem, for instance, did not write of his own early years in *Mottel* but recognized how he could mold the appealing congruence between new, young lives and new lands into a successful narrative. In short, a variety of demographic and conceptual reasons account for the popularity of childhood as a theme among the Jewish writers discussed in this study. Still, concern with the imagination and with inner life *is* a prime motivating factor that brought these authors to representations of consciousness, and an understanding of narrative voice contributes substantially to an understanding of the richness of these texts and to the ways in which the formal qualities of this art animate and enhance the thematic emphases. Above all, this approach underscores how a contraction or restriction of viewpoint (with an insistence on unknowing, ignorance, or naiveté) leads to a polysemous abundance of meaning or to multiple perspectives. Therein lies much of the energy of these texts and their achievement as works of art.

There are distinct limitations as well as advantages to this brand of narrative. The child's perspective does not foster sociohistorical overviews, exposition of broad collective circumstances, or temporal panoramas. These authors do not offer portraits of individuals who have resolved issues of destruction and rebuilding. By the same token, the very young can reconcile modern individualism with traditional values only on a temporary basis. They are destined to outgrow, quickly, any equilibrium at which they may arrive. They may also achieve such reconciliation only in a realm of the imagination (if they are characters conceived as unchanging metaphors or symbols of cultural values). These novels therefore are not crucibles of consequence; they do not show lives unfolding into maturity as a result of making certain choices. In this connection it is noteworthy that all of these narratives feature inconclusive endings. *Mottel*, written in installments for publication in the popular press, remained unfinished at the time of Sholem Aleichem's death. The final chapters find the main character, now in America, more or less the same as before. An unchanging sprite, he continues to engage in by-now familiar pranks, suffering the misadventures of making a living and filled with amusement at the clash of cultures and expectations that the New World brings. *Aftergrowth* similarly lacks an ending. Appended to chapter 4 is a narrative fragment depicting Shmulik at age seventeen. Still daydreaming and impractical, he is locked in conflict with his father over his plans for the future. Roth's beautifully ambivalent ending, which emphasizes "strangest triumph, strangest acquiescence," distinctly does not explicate how Davey moves on with his life. This indecisiveness has elicited critical speculation about what Davey's life would be like were he to grow up. While such speculation may be misplaced (the text is too fully bound up with childhood to invite a sequel), the point is nonetheless noteworthy as an indication of the open-ended quality brought to the resolution of the novel.

Kosinski, Appelfeld, and Grossman also emphasize inconclusiveness. *The Painted Bird* prevaricates about the value of language and the possibilities of communication, leaving the reader to wonder whether or not the protagonist would be able to reestablish humane contact with others. Appelfeld's plot, sharply curtailed, prevents his narrative from becoming a Bildungsroman, and Grossman closes the crucial first chapter of *See Under: Love* with his character's emotional paralysis. In addition, as Grandfather Anshel wanders off at the end of the "Momik" section, his disappearance creates unease and a sense that the issues raised cannot be resolved. For Mother, not knowing Anshel's whereabouts or what has become of him is harder to accept than his death would be. In each of these fictions the ending is appropriate: a culminating insistence on the ambivalence emphasized throughout the narrative and a final acknowledgment of incompleteness in the protagonist's life. There is, however, an element of risk in the decision not to move beyond earliness. Entrance into the child's inner life and personal world or misunderstandings may constitute an evasion of collective moral questions. At an extreme the result is an overprivatization of the issues, a dissatisfying universalization or political blindness—particularly with regard to the Holocaust.

Take, for instance, Kosinski. As a result of his reliance on the child's ignorance about political events, the author ends up with a tale of universal evil. In *The Notes of the Author* Kosinski disclaims any pretension to accurate reportage on the behavior of particular groups of people in a particular spot; instead, he generalizes about the human propensity for hatred and violence. Moreover, as the novel uses the child's under-standings to blur distinctions between the real and the unreal, Kosinski also creates a world in which Jewishness is a fiction: merely a condition fabricated by enemies of the Jews, but without substance or traditions of its own. Readers impatient with this approach might legitimately ask, does this narrative sidestep the historical specificity of the Holocaust, the Jewishness of the tragedy and of the cultural loss sustained in the mass deaths of the time?

Appelfeld's narrative, for its part, also evolves around the blind-ness of the child. Concerned with self-hatred, the internalizing of anti-Semitism, and various flights from Jewishness, this text does not discuss Nazis at all. Only the people with whom the child has immediate con-tact come under close scrutiny . Though the author assumes that the reader has some knowledge of the Shoah, the historical circumstances in which the family lives are not spelled out. This kind of composition is found in much of Appelfeld's work, and some readers have seen it as a refusal to dignify the Nazis. They applaud Appelfeld for not humanizing the villains by turning them into full-fledged characters.[1] The same quality, though, might be read as casting undue attention on Jewish shortcomings amidst silence about the oppressors. A brilliant narrative approach, one that effectively registers grief, loss, incomprehension, and a sense of displacement, Appelfeld's unique style nonetheless gives rise to ambivalence. His is a tremendous artistic accomplishment, but the social implications of his writing are not always clear. Especially in *The Age of Wonders* the author's reliance on the child as a figure of misper-ception leaves much that is unsaid, much that is uncertain.

Grossman presents a particularly interesting problem. As narra-tion of the child's thoughts undermines the Israeli ideal of heroism, the text also puts into relief Momik's increasing capacity to become an oppressor. Written in a climate of protest against Israeli policy on the West Bank, *See Under: Love* must be read in light of Grossman's uneasi-ness about the contemporary uses of military force in his society. Some readers will object to this aspect of the novel, as it recalls the vexed comparisons between Nazis and Israelis that were so visibly in vogue during the 1980s in the press and in ideological harangues of different stripes. To be sure, *See Under: Love* should not be construed narrowly as a political parable nor a *roman à clef*. A child mistreating a cellar full of animals bears little resemblance to the systematic murder of millions, or, for that matter, to twenty years of occupation, and it would be preposterous to read these episodes reductively as an equivalent of ei-ther. The province of this novel is the personal, far reaches of inner life, and the capacity of the individual person to behave inhumanely. This,

however, is precisely the problem. A touching portrayal of a boy's excruciating sensitivity and a riveting depiction of innocence awakening to an
awareness of violence, this novel grapples with moral conundrums that
stand in uncertain relation to Grossman's political convictions. The
myopia of the child does not make for public policy nor constitute a call
for collective action. Readers who respond seriously to the dilemmas
posed in this novel will be asked to think about what a heavy price
hatred exacts in those who hate, and how cruelty affects those who
exercise it. They will find little basis here, though, to speculate on the
extent to which humaneness, compassion, and abhorrence for violence
might carry over into mature consideration of political crisis: when, for
example, where, and in what measure it makes sense to use military
might, and when it is naive or childish not to. The Momik narrative,
however, beautifully poses another major question more firmly
grounded in social actuality: how to educate the next generations about
the Holocaust. Individuals from each point on the political spectrum
will inevitably respond to this question and interpret this novel in di-
vergent ways. Once again, the narrative of childhood proves startlingly
rich, more in the questions it raises than in any answers it may establish.
The unsettling of certainties, together with the inconclusiveness brought
about through the child's inchoate understandings of issues, proves to
be the exceptional strength of this brand of writing.

The achievement of these narratives becomes clearer when compared to a novel that shares many of the same themes and motivations
but differs in its treatment of youthful perspective. Albert Memmi's *La
statue de sel* (*The Pillar of Salt*, 1954) puts into relief the limits of the
childhood novel as a subgenre of the Bildungsroman.[2] Memmi's text,
for instance, concerns multilingual childhood and a young protagonist's
struggle with Jewish identity in a period of social upheaval. However,
the narrative also moves beyond the framework of the child's experience
to a focus on adolescence and preoccupations more proper to the education novel, that is, an entrance into society. In addition, a marked disso-
nance throughout between adult narration and the child character sets
this text apart from *Mottel, Aftergrowth, Call It Sleep, The Painted
Bird, The Age of Wonders,* and *See Under: Love.* Nowhere does the
child's voice reign or appropriate that of adults. The adult author recounts adventures of childhood but shies away from illuminating that
perspective from within or letting the child speak. As a result, Memmi
provides a story of growing up, which, much like Abraham Cahan's
paradigmatic *The Rise of David Levinsky,* makes a suitable forum for
discussion of Jewish cultural adaptation, generational differences, and
pressures toward assimilation. However, *The Pillar of Salt* aims for

emphases distinct from those of novels that home in on a child's unusual viewpoint.

Raised in the Jewish ghetto of Tunis in the 1920s, the protagonist in *The Pillar of Salt* finds himself caught painfully between three cultures. A Jew in a predominantly Arab society, a native African in a French colony, and the son of a poor family aspiring to leave poverty behind him through a middle-class education, this character never succeeds in reconciling conflicting pulls on his sense of allegiance. From early happiness and unquestioning acceptance of family love and custom, he moves to an infatuation with French culture. This development then leads to a contempt for his parents' Jewishness and the primitive superstition he associates with it. Later he feels hatred for the hypocrisies and timorous respectability of the middle class, which hesitates to accept him, and, as a result, he is attracted to Marxist politics. Eventually he is disillusioned by this course as well, for the brave radical rhetoric of the socialists fails to denounce the pogroms and anti-Semitism that form an ongoing part of Tunisian life. Finally, as a young man, he takes up the pen to recover and integrate all the pieces of his past by writing an autobiographical text.

It is significant that this tale of failed assimilation is told entirely within the discourse of the social realm the character has adopted. Mastering the language of power and prestige, the young writer composes his memoirs in French. This is not the orphaned idiom of a youngster left to his own devices: Davey's "alligay walligay" or Mottel's wordless "nature song." Instead, it is a choice that, in its disavowal of the boy's heritage, adopts the discourse of the teachers the protagonist admires, the mentors he emulates even as he rejects his parents' life and tries to dissociate himself from them. In this way the character repeats the trajectory traveled by Albert Memmi himself, who similarly grew up in Tunis and moved between Jewish, Arab, and European environments.[3] The choice has important implications even after the protagonist/narrator becomes impatient with assimilation. Though he yearns for a wholeness that will accommodate his Jewish background and his secular, Francophone aspirations, and though he goes about writing his memoirs and pondering his Jewish identity, this individual erases from his prose almost all traces of the languages other than French that contributed to his upbringing.

For example, his references to the importance of tradition in the ghetto are explicit and expository, but there is pointed and deliberate omission of Judaeo-Arabic and Hebrew intertexts in the novel. By the same token the character's *bar mitzvah* is referred to as "ma première communion." Casting one culture in the language of another, the author explains Jewishness not from within the framework of its own terms—covenant, commandments, or customs—but from without. Telling, for instance, is the treatment of Jewish education. The chapter on the *kouttab* (the Jewish elementary school, counterpart to the *heder*) is not recounted in chronological order, before an account of the boy's primary instruction at an Alliance school. Rather, it is inserted as part of the narrator's commentary on adolescent rebellion against religion. This means that the school appears less as a formative experience than as an afterthought, important primarily because of the redefinition of Jewishness that the teenaged character or the adult narrator has arrived at belatedly. In addition, virtually no mention is made of study that goes on in the school. Instead, the episode concentrates on a cruel game of mock circumcision that the little boys play one day when the rabbi has left the room. Judaism, consequently, is viewed here in terms of primitive violence and sacrifice, a fascinating but terrible antithesis of all things French or genteel. The narration has reordered events in such a way that the retrospective rejection of Judaism becomes paramount, and retelling privileges the values of the adopted culture over those of the protagonist's origins.

Memmi's narrative strategy in this regard differs markedly from that of Bialik and Roth, who chart a rich dialogue with the authoritative word of a traditional world, even as they depict rebellion against religion. Bialik and Roth also write in a language not native to them, but they use their artistic idiom to make aspects of the past more accessible. Bialik's Hebrew is a natural for animating scenes of *heder* study; Roth's inventive translations and transliterations celebrate the expressive capacities of Yiddish. (Even Kosinski and Appelfeld, writing in adopted languages, cultivate their own brand of dialogue. Their texts are not concerned with reworking or reacting to sacred tradition, but they create a special intimacy with the past. By fostering closeness between the narrator's present and the characters' present, they produce a realm of imagination and memory where both adult and child voice reign.) *The Pillar of Salt*, as the title suggests, depends more on distance. In this work of fiction looking backward will paralyze. The narrator's longings for his Jewish origins stop his march toward assimilation, but he does not retreat very far toward his beginnings. Thematically he indicates the desire to remember, but his highly de-Judaized format indicates that his acclimatization to French values and modes of expression still pulls him in the opposite direction, away from the past.

As is consistent with this emphasis of the text, the narrative never gives the child's voice free rein. The highly occasional instances of direct discourse never fully endorse the primacy of earliness, for they are always framed by self-exegesis and exposition. For instance, when the boy first discovers that the language he knows from home is not the language of the Alliance classroom, his trauma serves as the stimulus for this explication:

> I faced an abyss, without any means of communicating with the far side of it. The instructor spoke only French and I spoke only dialect: how would we ever be able to meet?
>
> These childish anxieties may now seem futile and my position is surely not unique. Millions of men have had to lose their basic unity, no longer recognizing themselves and still seeking in vain their identity. But I also say to myself that this confrontation has nothing reassuring about it; that others try to reassemble, without ever managing it, their scattered limbs. This mere fact confirms me in my awareness of the split in myself. (31)

> J'étais devant un gouffre, sans moyen de communication avec l'autre bord. Le maître ne parlait que français, je ne parlais que patois; comment pourrions nous jamais nous rencontrer?
>
> Ces angoisses enfantines peuvent paraître futiles; ma situation n'est assurément pas unique: des millions d'hommes ont perdu leur unité fondamentale, ils ne se reconnaissent plus et se cherchent en vain. Mais je me dis aussi que cette rencontre n'a rien de rassurant; que d'autres essayent de recoller leurs membres épars sans y parvenir jamais me confirme au contraire dans ce déchirement. (43–44)

This presentation of a distressing bilingualism shows no trace of the child's native tongue. What dialogue can be found here is geared toward an adult listener; there is no orientation toward the boy's first language, no interaction between it and the language of composition. Hidden polemic—that sidelong glance at the audience that anticipates objections or approval—is clearly evident in such phrases as "these childish anxieties may now seem futile" and "millions of men have had to lose their basic unity." This last generalization, along with the counter-argument ("But I also say to myself"), shows the narrator to be quarreling explicitly with himself in expectation of some attack from without. In each case this authorial voice relates less to his object of reference (the multilingual childhood itself) than to the reactions he surmises will come from readers.[4] To be sure, in *Aftergrowth* Bialik's narrator performs much the same kind of self-justification. There, however, the caveats and disclaimers serve as preparation for a self-imposed impossible mission: the attempt to recall a prelinguistic, nonverbal consciousness. Memmi, by contrast, does not use his comments to preface a daring artistic move into defamiliarization or into representation of the unrepresentable. This passage is marked by self-consciousness about language but exhibits no contrapuntal combination of clashing voices that might mutually modify child and adult discourse.

In short, rather than inhabiting the otherness of the child, Memmi's narrative comes to a mature recognition of, and highly articulated realizations about, the child's otherness. Observation of the child from a distance yields a philosophical monologue or a novel of ideas more than a revisioning of the world through the eyes of a child. Indeed, Memmi builds on an understanding of the child as Other to develop an explicit meditation on the marginality of the Jews. The text makes clear that the protagonist will meet with prejudice and social barriers everywhere. Despite his ambition and hard work the world will not open to him, and he will always be seen as a Jew, an alien. In this scheme of things, the child's difference consists largely in his very lack of awareness. That is, his outlook is strange, unconventional, naive, precisely because it rests on his expectations that success will await him regardless of his ethnicity.

Memmi's novel offers an explicit commentary on these semiotic issues. An awareness that context confers belonging and meaning, which comes as the character leaves childhood for adolescence, serves as an important impetus for his maturation and the beginnings of his self-definition. He becomes increasingly conscious of how he fits into a social system, a network of values and understandings, and he sees how his origins define his place in society. It is, for instance, only at this juncture—in the second of three parts of the novel—that he mentions his own name: Alexandre Mordekhai Benillouche. The late introduction of this information suggests that now, for the first time, it has become significant. The boy, after he begins to attend a lycée, suddenly realizes that his name is not an attribute, identical with himself, but a sign, susceptible to interpretation according to various social codes. "Mordekhai" is unmistakably Jewish, and "Benillouche," a Berber family name. While his parents have always prided themselves on their background, the majority society does not. In the world beyond home the boy's name marks him as a native African and a ghetto Jew, the very classifications he wishes to avoid. To make things worse, the European "Alexandre," with its echoes of Alexander the Great, pretends to grandiosity and so represents incongruous presumptuousness for a lad from such a humble station in life. "How ridiculous," the teenaged Mordekhai concludes, "how revealing" (93).

In his professedly autobiographical treatise, *Portrait of a Jew,* Memmi the sociologist endorses and spells out more discursively the ideas prominent in *The Pillar of Salt.* To be a Jew in the Diaspora means to be defined from without. No matter what the individual's positive characteristics may be nor what the tradition means to that person, non-Jews will see Jews differently and bear toward them hatreds not of their own making. As the Other within the discourse of the non-Jew, the Jew becomes subject to all sorts of accusations, stereotypes, and redefinitions in the words of others.

> Everything about the Jews, in short, is said to be bad, even what at first sight may seem to be a virtue. Is it said that the Jew is intelligent? Can we consider that a virtue? No indeed, he is *too* intelligent, his sagacity is destructive, corrosive. Is he said to have a hunger for knowledge? That means he is afflicted with "intellectual bulimia," with a voracious appetite, as though everything about him that is not already negative is made so through his maleficence. (172)[5]

This line of thinking is turned in the novel to depiction of a specific historical moment and milieu, precisely the kind of temporal overview and situational specificity that are lacking in *The Painted Bird* or *The Age of Wonders*, as those narratives rely on a child's limited knowledge of history. Memmi wrote his novel on the eve of Tunisian independence, at a time when he welcomed an end to colonialism, yet feared for the future of the North African Jewish community because of increasing Moslem nationalist sentiment. Documenting events of the times in the novel, Memmi also expresses insights about the Jew as outsider that form part of his evolving understandings of otherness, later expressed in his most well-recognized work on relations between colonizers and colonized peoples, *The Colonizer and the Colonized*.[6] Integrally tied to his most influential ideas as a social philosopher, the principal themes in *The Pillar of Salt* make for a highly readable, lucid, and engaging novel of cultural transformations, one that provides colorful descriptions of the North African Jewish milieu along with highly sympathetic characters. A work of considerable charm and passion, his novel nonetheless poses challenges distinct from those of a childhood narrative such as *Call It Sleep* or *See Under: Love*. Both of these are motivated by a greater oscillation of perspectives that leaves many uncertainties but generates an intensely vibrant interanimation of conflicting voices.

Because Memmi's text so directly concerns itself with assimilation, it puts into relief with particular clarity how language severs the present from the child's world of years ago. Highly encoded, distanced from the past and the experience to which it refers, writing for Memmi and for Mordekhai at once gestures toward the past yet remains estranged from it. If adult writing always and necessarily entails casting the child as Other, Memmi participates in this artistic mechanism with self-consciousness and without overmuch resistance. He regards the Jewish past with nostalgia, but he does not pit himself against the limitations of adult narration, striving for a composite stance that will admit the voice of the child and so resurrect a bygone time in the realm of fiction. As a result he converts the otherness of childhood into something else again: an adult version of what happened many years before. As in Rokhl Korn's verse, "Yener zayt lied" ("On the Other Side of the Poem"), the magic of the child's world remains on "the other side" of the text. In her poem, literally, as in the narrative of childhood more figuratively, the bottom line is that adult words place constraints on the child's play. Calling them back in at night, the adult author summons the child characters from the world they inhabit to the shared consensus recognized by grown-ups. By contrast, the narrative of childhood distinguishes itself as it fights against this order of things. It strives for peculiarly dynamic and plural intersections of voice, as it attempts to create a fictive as-if realm: the imagination of the child.

10 OTHERS: THE SILENT VOICE

A child is vengeance.
A child is a missile into the coming generations.
I launched him: I'm still trembling.

A child is something else again: on a rainy spring day
glimpsing the Garden of Eden through the fence,
kissing him in his sleep,
hearing footsteps in the wet pine needles.
A child delivers you from death.
Child, Garden, Rain, Fate.

—Yehuda Amihai, "A Child Is Something Else Again"

Otherness, unavoidably, is an issue that impinges at some level on every depiction of children in adult literary works. No adult, after all, can speak authoritatively in the name of childhood or in a child's voice, for none can fully enter and represent the consciousness of children. As a result, fictive portrayals of childhood often reveal less about the nature and behavior of children than about images and values imposed on children by grown-up narrators. Much the same may be said of women depicted in literature by men, Jews in writing by Gentiles, Arabs in Israeli fiction, and so on, through all the other Others of literature. Children, though, present a special case, since in an especially intense way, physically and psychically, they are a part of their parents as well as apart from them. Consequently, they are often the objects on whom adults foist their highest hopes and deepest fears and insecurities. Children, in addition, live an accelerated process of growth and change, and their changes constantly defy and challenge any fixed ideas their elders may adopt about them. For these reasons child figures in narrative may serve to put into relief the limited understandings, feelings, and perceptions of those who attempt to describe them.

These are matters that come to bear acutely on two novellas, *A Poet's Continuing Silence,* by A. B. Yehoshua, and *The Cannibal Galaxy,* by Cynthia Ozick.[1] Neither attempts to inhabit the unusual perspective of the child, to illuminate a young character's world from within. However, these texts provide for interesting comparison, as both feature a child, silenced, whose absence of voice itself comes to speak volumes. Yehoshua focuses on a retarded boy, whose impaired ability to speak borders on muteness. Ozick presents a dull-witted, withdrawn girl whose insights elude verbal formulation. These two characters, then, share a radical otherness. They are marginalized outsiders, but as such they also expose the blindness and cultural bias of the older generation. The younger generation represents a voice not properly heard by the grown-ups, and as this voice also resists absorption into or definition within preconceived standards, the way that grown-ups react to the children shows a great deal about their values. Subsequently, as the young characters grow, their voices assert a new power. Eventually, erupting into the adult discourse, their spectral presence directly unsettles the assumptions and frameworks of understanding that previously obtained, and it throws the adults' interpretations of the world into question. This fiction therefore aptly illustrates the principle that Bakhtin considers predominant in the novel and expresses as "the process of coming to know one's own language as it is perceived in someone else's language, coming to know one's own belief system in someone else's system."[2] Even as they eschew representations of the child's consciousness and present the child as a highly subdued voice, the narratives by Ozick and Yehoshua help elucidate how the imagination of the child in fiction may foster dialogic interactions and modify one discourse through another. These two novellas also demonstrate how the literary treatment of childhood has been used to highlight shifting cultural contexts and transformations in Jewish self-conception.

A. B. Yehoshua, A Poet's Continuing Silence

A Poet's Continuing Silence offers an account of an aging poet, his retarded son, and the evolving tensions of their relationship. The narrator, the father, has failed to maintain his creative energies and has ceased not only to write but to desire life itself. As the author underscores by playing on the two meanings of the verb *lishtoq,* to be silent and to be paralyzed, this character's silence constitutes a virtual psychological paralysis.[3] The son suffers a comparable disabling incapacity to function and to express himself. Unable to read or write, he can barely sustain a conversation. It seems that the father's lack of productivity, which expresses itself from day to day as silence and inaction, has transmitted itself to the son and manifested itself in very concrete and exaggerated fashion as a physical malfunction. Since he embodies and materializes the old man's spiritual predicament, the son serves as the shadow of his father, paralleling his shortcomings and calling attention to a shared failure at communication.

However, the son acts not only as a blemished reproduction, an exaggeratedly flawed duplication of the old man. In addition, he exposes the father's rigidities precisely because of his blankness, onto which the father projects various interpretations. In this fashion the older man inadvertently makes known a number of his own crucial assumptions and personal values. Most importantly, because the narrator wants to give up on life, he gravely underestimates his son's vitality. He sees the boy as something less than human and as one who can never change. This assessment in actuality stems from his own weakness and stalled professional progress.

A remarkable illustration of the father's inadequacies comes early on in the narrative when the child is six years old. Following the death of his mother, the son cuts up photographs of her and buries them in the garden. The father, surprised, explains his reaction and the reaction of his two daughters this way: "For the first time our eyes opened and we saw before us a little human being" (13). In saying this, the father admits that until this time he has dismissed or disregarded his son's thoughts and feelings. He notes, too, that on this occasion he beat his son soundly, blaming him for malevolent destruction of property and a willed desecration of the mother's memory. The second part of the explanation therefore undermines the first. Even as the passage claims to report the father's newfound realization of his son's humanity, it in effect underscores the man's continuing blindness. It is evident to the reader that the son, who has been excluded from participating in the mother's funeral, here seeks out a way to express his grief. His manner of mourning is anomalous but genuine, sincere, and entirely human, and the father has failed to grasp this basic idea. Ironically, the son's mute voice has succeeding in speaking, but both his intentions and his forms of expression are misperceived in someone else's language. The boy's capacity for life and for feeling uncovers the father's exhaustion and his lack of insight and foresight.

Contrary to the father's expectations, the son does later undergo significant changes. Though he does not grow intellectually, his body becomes tall and powerful, and his will becomes strong. The father, aging and now physically ailing, abdicates control over the household affairs to the son he always viewed as disabled. Usurping the role of strength, the boy also comes to appropriate the father's interest in poetry. When he decides to try his hand at writing, the son compiles fragments of the old man's unfinished poems, which have been lying about the house, and manages to create from them a new text: "crazy, without meter, twisted, lines needlessly cut off, baffling repetition, arbitrary punctuation" (52). Signing his father's name to this piece, he publishes it in the newspaper, and the story concludes as the father discovers the poem with a shock of recognition. It is eerily both his own and not his own, a pathetic and grotesque deformation of poetry labeled with his name as if to magnify the very incompleteness and inadequacy of his life's work, making them visible for all to see.[4]

Playing on the root *sh.u.v.* as it recurs persistently throughout the story with varied meanings—repetition, return, and response—Yehoshua calls attention to these plot developments as dialogic interaction.[5] The text emphasizes the awakening of the son's ability to answer, reciprocate, or react to another's words. For example, at the start this character serves (literally) as a marginal figure. He relates to others and expresses himself chiefly through subservience: to his father and sisters as the family servant, to his classmates as perpetual monitor of the class and companion of the janitor, to the guests at his birthday party as shoeshine boy. Later, as he develops an interest in poetry, he begins both to question and to answer. Significantly, it is when he learns in school about his father's well-known poetry that he pays attention to class discussion for the first time. Only then, moreover, does the narrative record direct discourse dialogue for the boy, indicating that some real exchange takes place between father and son. The boy asks, "What do you do?" (29), and with increasingly irrepressible excitement and anxiety asks his father about poetry, about resumption of the discarded literary career, about how to write and spell. Finally, the son encourages the father to take up writing again. The boy hopes to revive in him his former vigor and deliver him from that yearning for death which plagues so many of Yehoshua's characters. The old poet, for his part, is unmoved. The son then answers his father's obstinate refusal to live by doing it for him. Imitating the old man's work, he creates a disturbing echo of a text. More than simply a substitution, this act is also an independent response, a disquieting one that finalizes a transition of roles and a transfer of energy from the older to the younger generation.

This scenario yields a pointed case of interpenetrated discourse, that is, of one character's language filtered through another's. Taking his father's words, the son incorporates them into his own context and so breathes new life into them. With this move he demonstrates the principle Bakhtin explains in this way:

> The speech of another, once enclosed in a context is—no matter how accurately transmitted—always subject to certain semantic changes. The context embracing another's word is responsible for its dialogizing background, whose influence can be very great. Given the appropriate methods for framing, one may bring about fundamental changes even in another's utterance accurately quoted. Any sly and ill-disposed polemicist knows very well which dialogizing backdrop he should bring to bear on the accurately quoted words of his opponent, in order to distort their sense.[6]

Although the son attempts to compose poetry as a fulfillment of the father, the awkward, incoherent, and ungainly poem instead mirrors the old man's failures and mocks him with them. As this poem builds itself out of the father's very words, rearranged, it also exemplifies the capacity of language for unceasing acquisition of meaning. In this way it poignantly dramatizes the personal issues at stake. An abundance of meaning subverts the narrator's attempt to stop producing meaning. He rejects change, afraid both to live and to die, but life nonetheless continues. Meaninglessness itself perpetually gains new dimensions. The silence with which the story began has become multifaceted, a dysfunctional voice continuing from one generation to the next. Ironically, therefore, but aptly, muteness serves as the chief vehicle of expression for the characters, even as the emptiness of the protagonist's lives proves to be a paradoxically rich barrenness, constantly generating new manifestations of itself.

The upshot of this denouement is that some tables have been decisively turned. By the end of the text the indictment of the father is complete. While the narrator frequently calls his son a "border case," indicating the boy's mental incapacities, the reader is exposed to ever more parallels between the two figures. These indicate that the father himself also approaches the limits of rational behavior. For many years he has perched precariously, disastrously, on a threshold between death and life, sleep and waking, dreaming and consciousness.

Now, as this fiction directs itself to portraying inner worlds and psychological conflicts of more or less universal appeal, does it also address specifically Israeli issues? It is hard to say, for this novella stands stylistically between the author's earlier, allegorical work and his later attention to particularizing, realistic detail. The events of this narrative take place in Israel, but not at a specifiable time, and the characters remain anonymous. While both the earlier and later fiction of the author have clear social implications—and, indeed, it is impossible to distinguish between personal and national issues in them—narration in *Continuing Silence* hovers on the border between introspective vision and external description. This narrative strategy leaves the reader with referential doubt and gnawing uncertainty over whether or not individual lives reveal collective values in an identifiable context.[7]

Given these difficulties, it is profitable to read *Continuing Silence* against Gershon Shaked's analysis that much of Yehoshua's early writing alludes to an Israel tired of war, eager to surrender to dissipation in sleep and death.[8] Certainly, on one level *Continuing Silence* presents an example of a weary older generation that doubts the future and a second generation that—unable to live up to the glory of its heroic parents, the founders of the state—seems misbegotten even in its most fervent efforts. The reading of this text as social parable, grotesque and exaggerated as it may be, is compatible with a psychological reading that likewise revolves around limits. From both the communal and the personal perspective, the grotesquerie derives in part from the son's limitations but importantly, too, from the father's shortcomings: his inability to recognize the boy as an individual and his unwillingness to adapt to the changing contours of the other's identity, expectations, and needs. Having reached his full capacity for accomplishment within his old framework of viewing things, the father must create a new set of goals, a new context in which to generate meaning, or yield to the next generation the right to do so. All of this fits in with well-known trends in Israeli literature of the sixties, when many writers began to question the founding myths of Zionism and to contrast ideological ideals with the complex problems and harsh realities of actual statehood.

In his later fiction Yehoshua moves beyond this early sense of impasse. He presents a new flexibility on the part of both older and younger characters, and in his own approaches to composition he exhibits a new and complex openness to opposing points of view. Indeed, one of the most applauded features of his subsequent novels, *The Lover* and *Late Divorce*, respectively, is the adoption of a child's voice in the monologues of Naim and Gadi.[9] This structural innovation accompanies a shake-up in social outlook, and the young are of crucial importance, for they are symptomatic of a break with previously prevailing, rigid preconceptions. While failures of communication and misunderstanding remain Yehoshua's central preoccupations in these novels, the author moves toward a patently dialogic structure in his narrative and so opens up the possibility of debate. He introduces multiple monologues that, much like those in Faulkner's *As I Lay Dying*, cast variegated readings of a single situation. Sometimes they echo and sometimes even deliberately interpret one another as various characters mull over what has been said between them in conversation.[10] In doing this, the author attempts to view Israeli circumstances from the perspective of any number of figures once underrepresented in Hebrew fiction. The Palmah generation writers concentrated on the young war hero, the fearless, self-reliant sabra, and so defined as marginal other kinds of individuals who did not fit this central, self-conceived image of Israeli ideals. *The Lover* and *Late Divorce*, by contrast, admit as major characters not only children but also Arabs, *sephardim, yordim,* the ultra-Orthodox, and the insane. No longer portraying a generation stalled and stymied by trying to imitate and compete with an older ideal, Yehoshua in his later fiction responds to the complexities of Israeli society after thirty years of statehood. In this way his texts challenge simplistic earlier symbols of the Zionist dream even as they foreground the polyphonic dimensions of their own narration. The child character, once the embodiment of a potent, growing, but only dimly surmised and troubling future, gives way to the child figure who has come into its own. The future has arrived, and this voice is clearly heard among other new voices that have been recognized as an integral part of a rapidly changing Israel.

Cynthia Ozick, The Cannibal Galaxy

Much as was the case with Yehoshua's *Continuing Silence,* the otherness of the child is central to Cynthia Ozick's comic look at contemporary Jewish education in America, *The Cannibal Galaxy* (1984). This novel features an elusive, uncommunicative child character who, by dint of her enigmatic qualities, serves mainly to show how the rest of the world responds to her. In this way she is instrumental in Ozick's satire, alerting the reader to the assumptions and norms of her environment and magnifying the attitudes prevalent in her social setting. At the same time, the child, Beulah Lilt, catalyzes a series of upheavals and revelations, raising the issue of otherness to the fore of the text and so making of the narrative far more than a caricature or burlesque. To be sure, Ozick lampoons human foibles long the stock in trade of satire: pretension, narrowmindedness, laziness, and rigidity. Her characters, presenting prime examples of these traits, include the schoolmaster oblivious of his own ignorance, the pedant who delights in lists and not in insight or conceptual knowledge, the teacher who assigns marks without having read the students' work. The enigmatic child, though, as she draws attention to these follies, challenges the people who commit them and confounds the world they inhabit, turning the text into a semiotic fable and a study of communication and miscommunication.

Daughter of an intellectually high-powered mother of some renown in academic and philosophical circles, Beulah has no easily definable nature of her own. Unresponsive, described as dim, dull-witted, stony, mute, she is more a silence or an absence than a voice or presence, and she is relegated by her peers and her elders to the margins of every activity. Because of the ways they assimilate her into their own patterns of thinking, this girl reveals much about the rest of the characters: Joseph Brill, the principal of the school she attends, the society of children at the school, the beliefs and ideas of her mother, and later the wider world of arts and the media in which Beulah gains surprising, extraordinary success as a painter.

Brill, whose name suggests truncated brilliance, was once a promising astronomer. Now intellectually spent and emotionally wearied, he has become headmaster of a mediocre Jewish day school in the American Midwest. As the text notes, his is an institution of the middle and in

the middle, middling at best in its quality. His notion of a Dual Curricu-
lum, which combines attention to the masterpieces of Western culture
and also to Jewish heritage, seems to him wasted on the ordinariness of
his pupils and their milieu. Because of Beulah's brilliant mother, Brill
hopes to find in the girl budding genius, and he is sorely disappointed.
Thus, Beulah, the vacant one, is in Brill's view clearly a failure, and a
galling one at that. The headmaster suffers delusions of intellectual
grandeur, and this dull, apathetic girl thwarts his fantasy of fostering
lofty and noble scholarship.

To the mother, though, Beulah is all possibility. Indeed, she is the
probable basis for elaborate theories about emergent genius. At the
local university, for instance, Hester lectures on the shortsightedness of
educators who predict a child's ability only on the basis of early performance. Rabbi Akiva, she recalls from the midrash, laughed when he saw
foxes running on the ruined temple mount. While other sages mourned
the devastation, Akiva rejoiced, for he saw in the destruction a fulfillment of Uriah's prophecy and therefore a sure indication that
Zechariah's prophecy of redemption would also be fulfilled. Lilt concludes that we should judge not from the first text, but the second; in
education, not from the earliest but from the latest piece of evidence.
Teachers, she argues, should not place children in unstimulating ped-
agogical pigeonholes and so stifle their capacity to surprise their elders.

In the meantime, as the mother engages in these intellectual la-
bors, which bolster her conviction that Beulah has exceptional talent,
Beulah to her classmates is something else entirely. She is the outsider
who allows them to define their own power as insiders. Brill notes this
sarcastically, in a letter composed but never sent, to the mother of one of
the successful girls at the school. Corinna, he remarks, acquires her so-
called popularity through exclusion. "She blesses those whom she
blesses. The rest are discards. I believe this is what they term a clique"
(79). Beulah, then, in this circumstance, is yet again seen not as a being
in her own right but as the Other, merely a factor in someone else's
scheme of things. In this instance, she functions as a cipher in the political calculations of the preadolescent in-crowd.

The mother would seem to be the cleverest of the lot, for her
estimations of her child's worth appear fulfilled with Beulah's reap-
pearance, years later, as a celebrated painter. Once more, though, there
is ambivalence about the daughter's true nature. Now she is successful,
but the reader still knows nothing substantive about her or her work per
se. The art critics laud her and promote her art as they spin their various
interpretations of her work. She, for her part, simply denies their approximations. Never making a positive assertion of her own, she says
only that she is not what they think: not a theorist, not the leader of a

new movement in painting, not a product of her mother's thinking or of her upbringing. The reader is left mainly with uncertainty. Is her work great, or is it simply appealing in the eyes of the shallow, effete aesthetes who appraise it in the press? They, after all, have their own job to do, and that is to seek out a story, to create a sensation, to entertain, to discuss. Open doubt, in addition, is cast on the worth of Beulah's art by the reaction of Brill's wife. Iris, attracted largely to all things trendy and kitsch, is nonetheless endearingly forthright in her opinions. Her evaluation of Beulah's painting is unequivocal: "Boring," she pronounces, "Bor-*ing*" (44). Does the truth lie with her or the critics, perhaps somewhere in between, or elsewhere altogether?

Brill's own troubled response provides the most insight. Unable to accept the high-blown assessments of the professionals, he finds in Beulah's art not "the latency of Idea," an "indisputable subject" (146), but a puzzlement pure and simple. Unsure whether the paintings are too abstract or not abstract enough, he finds himself reflecting: "You could fancy amazing scenes in them: but when you approached, it was only paint, bleak here, brilliant here, in shapes sometimes nearly stately, sometimes like gyres. The purity of babble inconceivable in the vale of interpretation" (147–48).

Brill, in short, has no way to process this information. The paintings lie, for him, on the margin of intelligibility. In effect they present a limit case that disrupts his whole sense of order and hierarchy of values. He cannot decide whether Beulah's work is brilliant or empty. If the former, the canvases invert his sense of his own intelligence, for he is unable to appreciate this art and has erred egregiously in his estimation of Beulah. If the latter, the paintings equally disrupt his sense of worth, which is staked on his respect for and identification with the heights of cultural achievement. As a celebration of emptiness, the world of the arts would prove a disappointing sham. Brill, consequently, cannot classify this work according to his usual distinctions of intelligence/stupidity, quick/dull, refined/boorish, and cultivated/ignorant, and his confusion makes clear how limited are his definitions of success. The impasses of meaning threaten to dismantle the binary oppositions that ordinarily guide the headmaster's thinking, and so, much as the retarded son challenged the outlook of the aging poet in Yehoshua's tale, Beulah collapses Brill's customary categories and forces him to rethink his values. The principal, to his credit, acknowledges that he needs new ideas to accommodate this anomalous phenomenon. Though embittered by defeat, he institutes at the school a prize for the student of most creative potential, regardless of class standing.

The enigmatic child of *The Cannibal Galaxy* illustrates the basic semiotic tenet that there is no such phenomenon as preinterpretive

meaning in discourse.[11] Her worth is not intrinsic, identical with herself; rather, she becomes meaningful only within codes of understanding and shared values, based on the presuppositions of those who view
her. Because signs are iterable by definition, because they can be repro-
duced in differing contexts and so come to signify in different ways, their
meaning can never be inherent but relies on the preconceptions brought
to any interpretation. Dramatizing the sign, this child figure helps turn
interpretation into the central theme of the text. Hester Lilt's keynote
speech, a grievance against the headmaster couched in terms of signs,
supports a reading of the text as semiotic fable. In this central passage
she claims that he has not learned properly to decode the world and so
obtusely misinterprets his students:

> The hoax is when the pedagogue stops too soon. To stop at Uriah
> without expectation of Zechariah is to stop too soon. And when the
> pedagogue stops too soon, he *misreads every sign,* and thinks the
> place of the priest is by rights the place of the fox, and takes the fox for
> all its qualities to be right, proper, and permanent; and takes ag-
> gressiveness for intelligence, and thoughtfulness for stupidity, and
> diffidence for dimness, and arrogance for popularity and dreamers for
> blockheads, and brazenness for the mark of a lively personality. (68,
> emphasis added)

While promoting her own interpretive authority, Lilt makes explicit that
the novella is preoccupied with context as it affects the process of signification.

The child character serves another function as well. She does not
appear merely as a blankness onto whom interpretations are foisted, for
she creates a discourse that gradually comes to up-end Brill's own.
Beulah's paintings are her voice. The headmaster underestimates her
abilities and sees in her a deaf-mute, an "absence of language" symptomatic of "America the vulgar" whose children have only jabber (84–
85). On various occasions during her childhood he notes that she is fond
of drawing, but pooh-poohs her interest in artwork. However, that
Beulah offers a language not understood by Brill is made clear at the end
of the novel:

> The forms, the colors, the glow, the defined darkness, above all the
> form of things, all these were thought to be a kind of language. She
> spoke. The world took her for an astonishment. . . . [Brill] felt embit-
> tered by her language; he could assimilate it even less than her moth-
> er's. The light and the dark, the colors, the transmogrification of
> forms: strange, violent, quick tongues, she could talk! (156)

It is true that Beulah's artistic expression is revealed only very
partially through the filter of Brill's and others' opinions. Neither the

reader nor the characters are drawn into her discourse about the world. She is drawn into theirs, remaining herself primarily an Other. But it is in its marginality that this voice takes on its particular strength. Its potent dialogic capacity, its ability to expose the limits of Brill's understanding, comes from its near-silence.

Assigned new meanings in new contexts, Beulah suggests how language may be populated by the intentions of others. As her own language begins to assert itself, much as was the case with the poet's son, Beulah's life has also served to show that unceasing acquisition of meaning is an inevitable part of the dynamic, pluralistic nature of language. This function of hers helps illuminate the phrase "the purity of babble inconceivable in the vale of interpretation." Those words are originally Hester Lilt's, in a philosophical tract that bewilders Brill. Lilt's point, succinctly put, is that there is no such thing as non-sense. Given the human rage to interpret, to grant phenomena significance in accordance with one's own needs and self-interests, even babble may take on the importance that individuals perceive in it (and even if that perceived meaning should be only that something is without cogent meaning within current schemes of understanding). With a changing context Lilt's statement of inconceivability itself takes on conceivable definition and makes itself clear to Joseph Brill. For the headmaster, in the moment of impasse he reaches with Beulah's paintings, the self-contradictory phrase appropriately designates the contradiction he himself faces. Babble has become concrete. And, far from meaningless, it has been imparted significance and worth by the very intellectual elite Brill admires.

How is the reader to assess Beulah's new significance? To begin, her development confirms the author's belief in the redemptive qualities of human potential for change. The freedom to change one's life, Ozick has argued, is the essence of the Judaic ethic. In her essays, as she celebrates the possibilities of moral and spiritual growth, this author invokes the ideal of *teshuva* to speak of the energy of creative renewal.[12] This concept, meaning "turning" or "return," stems from that same root, *sh.u.v.*, so prominent in Yehoshua's *Continuing Silence*. The final turn of events in *The Cannibal Galaxy* constitutes a celebration of underestimated human potential: Beulah's, as she is redeemed from neglect, and Brill's, as the headmaster develops a new capacity to understand the error of his ways.

Beulah's evolution also contrasts with and so puts into relief developments in Brill's own life. The girl acquires remarkable new significance in proliferating contexts, while the headmaster remains without a context, without a communal forum that might grant his ideas lasting power or meaningful debate and dissemination. Indeed, a large portion of the novella is devoted to documenting his dislocation. Many of Brill's defeats do not arise simply from an inability to achieve (as the former astronomer puts it, to reach for the heights), nor even from his rigidities and his narrow expectations that others should approach and interpret the world just as he himself would. These are shortcomings that become crippling, because he is faced repeatedly with the dilemma of not belonging. During his youth in France, Brill's is a classic story of failed assimilation. This character is at home neither with Jews nor with non-Jews. Then, as a refugee from Nazi domination, he discovers that he cannot make his peace with American culture. His life-project, the Edmond Fleg Primary School, grows out of the headmaster's fragmented life and suffers the same limitations as he. It aspires to patrician, refined intellectuality, a fusion of twin antiquities ("King David's heel caught in Victor Hugo's lyre," 57), but it finally serves only the needs of a suburban community fundamentally unconcerned with either. The school amounts to neither a yeshiva nor a mock-Sorbonne, for its clientele is preoccupied with money, success, the pettiness and squabbling of local personalities, and (as Brill perceives it), "myriad meetings of the mothers' groups . . . bazaars, lotteries, all the kitsch of their coffee and cake, hairdos, exercise classes, tennis camps, and oh God the rest of it" (75). Therefore, as Brill attempts to synthesize a new world from the scattered, heterogeneous cultural baggage brought with him from his youth, his educational utopia exists in his mind alone.

The school, in effect, can only reproduce its own values and cannot challenge anyone, like Beulah, who reaches beyond the mores of a very limited milieu. Beulah's success in the art world demonstrates that Brill has been unable to enter into sustained, mutually productive dialogue with real talent. However, this state of affairs reflects badly not only on Brill. Given Ozick's abiding preoccupations with Judaism and art, the girl's triumph itself is troubling. An original altogether, something other than her training could make of her, Beulah grows up in alienation from Jewish education and identification. The headmaster's notions of Jewishness may be narrow and rigid, while she symbolizes the vitality and brilliance of ongoing interpretation, but her work exhibits no binding ties to Judaism at all.

The pervasive concern in the text with belonging and contextuality therefore proves to be an extension of themes dwelt on elsewhere by Ozick in her essays: the enduring difficulty of maintaining a cohesive Jewish life in Dispersion, the challenge of combining Jewish commitment with the enormous impact Western culture has had on the Jews since the era of Emancipation. In a world of Exile and of cultural displacements multiplied many times over, questions of what Jews can and cannot meaningfully share as a people take on paramount importance. In *The Cannibal Galaxy* the semiotic model, with its concerted attention to matters of inclusion, exclusion, redefinitions, and changes of meaning determined by community consensus, is aptly turned to fictional explorations of cultural displacement, and especially of what can be handed on to children and what not.

In her essay "Bialik's Hint," Ozick sums up her views by turning explicitly to the issue of contextuality and noting that "it was the Enlightenment, in letting Jews 'in,' that defined them as having been 'out'" (25). Of course, they *were* outsiders, politically and economically speaking, but, Ozick argues, their intellectual life was extensive, a literate culture long flourishing in an illiterate Europe, yet one dismissed or distorted by the majority cultures. Ozick urges American Jews no longer to be outsiders or accept the status of the Other, vulnerable to misinterpretation, stereotyping, and unjust accusation. She calls on them to define a center of their own, to create a new cultural context in which Jewish values will hold their own together with Western ones. To do this means to blend "enlightenment ideas of skepticism, originality, individuality, and the assertiveness of the imagination" with the Jewish values of "restraint, sobriety, collective conscience, [and] moral seriousness." Ozick sees this task as requiring extraordinary genius, "the brilliance of the unexpected, the explosive hope of fresh form."[13]

Brill arouses particular interest in this debate, because he is not simply an unquestioning member of the school community. He resents those aspects of the academy that are closely aligned with the superficial, partial, local ethnicity that Ozick has often lamented and that she thinks serves for many American Jews as an all-too-frequent substitute for an understanding of Judaism in its essential obligations and fundamental principles. Brill, moreover, has also repudiated as misguided and immature the adoration of beauty and artistic greatness that he pursued in his youth at the expense of Jewish commitment. This "religion of Art," Ozick has related, was an error of her own youth as well, and she subsequently came to see it in opposition to, if not always inimical to, Judaism. Cautioning against the danger of idolatry in the practice and pursuit of art, she has turned frequently in both fiction and nonfiction to the idea that too much appreciation for art or nature may result in worshiping creation, rather than the Creator.[14]

Brill, in effect, like Ozick, has a vision of synthesizing genuine Jewish cultural richness with Western thought; so why is he the main object of her satiric attack? The answer must be because he has settled for too little, and so belittled a cherished dream of the author's. (Hester Lilt takes him to task a number of times, telling him he has stopped too soon with his ideas.) He has failed to see that interpretation cannot be foreclosed without turning into narcissistic idolatry, and he has failed to create a community that can engage in dynamic interpretation. The goal of creating a new cultural synthesis remains a problematic one, however, for Ozick as well, because the two kinds of values are seen as being in opposition to each other. The author herself has offered few concrete proposals to accomplish the dream other than issuing vague calls for communal commitment and a moral imagination that will initiate in America a new Yavneh, a center for Jewish cultural regeneration. And, while Ozick's own work is known for its erudition, its densely textured prose laden with allusion to Jewish and non-Jewish texts, her fiction has also often turned on a contradiction; as it excoriates literature, viewing imaginative writing as idolatry, this literary endeavor undercuts its own worth.[15] *The Cannibal Galaxy,* for its part, does not prescribe solutions. Hester Lilt, as she applies midrash to her own scholarly work, recalls Ozick's prescription for titanic intellectual efforts, which, drawing on Jewish sources, may forge an inventive discourse hitherto unknown in America. Her work, though, remains idiosyncratic. She creates a context of her own, but her creative appropriation of the tradition remains a lonely enterprise. It is one to which not only lesser talents but also the daughter, Beulah, is lost. The novel, when all is said and done, criticizes Jewish education with biting comedy but endorses no certainties and so serves primarily as a gesture of dissatisfaction with many forms of American Jewish cultural expression.

The otherness of the child serves an indispensable role in all of this. It is not just that Beulah catalyzes the plot, setting Brill to think about his failures. She is pivotal, too, as she introduces new forms of expression he does not understand. In several ways her existence disrupts Brill's complacent attitudes. In the process, the author's imagining of the child also introduces key concepts of contextuality and consensus that generate much of the primary tension of the narrative. Beulah's plight as an outsider exposes Brill's own outsider status and so also calls attention to the lot of the Jews as a people in the throes of cultural transition and as a minority in continuing adaptation to the majority culture around them.

As in Yehoshua's *Continuing Silence,* the child takes on this importance for several reasons: because this figure is radically silent, because of the inevitability of the child's growth, and because of the plenitude of imagination imputed to the main characters. Both the retarded son and Beulah are figured as artists. The imaginative forces alive within them are the ones that most challenge accepted, conventional formulations of values and that produce a new language, however misbegotten. The child is not simply a symbol of the new, nor representative of changed values, but an instrument of innovation who turns the text to a dynamic process of appropriating, questioning, or discrediting established outlooks. A lively, unpredictable unknown, this figure makes for an ideal narrative device to highlight shifting currents in Jewish life.

Each text was composed at what the authors perceived as a moment of collective impasse, and each poses (unanswered) questions about what will come next. The marginal outsider, coming into his or her own, does not provide definitive predictions but certainly points to the volatility and mutability of changing margins.

The child characters in both *Continuing Silence* and *The Cannibal Galaxy* represent what Bakhtin describes as the "muted discourse that usually rages beyond the boundaries of the dominant cultural universe and defines the range of that universe."[16] These are peculiarly refined examples, stripped to the bare essentials, of the alien word that makes for a rejoinder to the prevailing wisdom and that shapes it or redefines it through dialogic interaction. Otherness in Ozick's tale is reinforced further by the fact that the child character is female. Her femininity endows her with an additional alien quality for the consistently misogynistic Brill. In view of Ozick's feminist inclinations, this figure may be read doubly as a symbol of untapped potential.[17] Beulah stands as a reminder that earlier Jewish fiction concerned with childhood and religious education focused almost exclusively on boys and neglected or marginalized girlhood. Creating young characters who embody the active, creative power of improvisation and change, both Yehoshua's novella and Ozick's present a neat illustration of the child as a revolutionary voice, and both bring to fictional life Bakhtin's premise that it is the most marginalized discourse that can most fully transform established opinion.

NOTES

Chapter One. Fictive Voices: The Discourse of Childhood

1. Yehuda Amihai's poem appears in *Shalvah gedola* (Jerusalem: Schocken Books, 1980), 33. The English translation is by Chana Bloch in *The Selected Poetry of Yehuda Amihai* (New York: Harper and Row, 1986), 133–34.

2. A session of the 1987 MLA Convention was devoted to "*Infans:* Representing the Language of the Child." I am indebted to Mark Heberle, organizer of the session, for his helpful formulation of significant literary issues to be addressed in connection with child language and the child as Other in the discourse of adults.

3. For salient examples, see the essays collected in *Race, Writing, and Difference,* ed. Henry Louis Gates, Jr. (Chicago: University of Chicago Press, 1986).

4. Critics who have promoted this approach include, for example, E. M. Forster, *Aspects of the Novel* (New York: Harcourt, Brace, 1927); Käte Hamburger, *The Logic of Literature,* trans. Marilynn J. Rose (Bloomington: Indiana University Press, 1973); Wayne Booth, *The Rhetoric of Fiction* (Chicago: University of Chicago Press, 1961); Robert Humphrey, *Stream of Consciousness in the Modern Novel* (Berkeley: University of California Press, 1955); Melvin Friedman, *Stream of Consciousness: A Study in Literary Method* (New Haven: Yale University Press, 1955); Dorrit Cohn, *Transparent Minds: Narrative Modes for Presenting Consciousness in Fiction* (Princeton: Princeton University Press, 1978).

That literary art has a valuable role as a supplement and corrective to psychological studies of children is Robert Coles's premise in *Irony in the Mind's Life: Essays on Novels by James Agee, Elizabeth Bowen, and George Eliot.* Of special interest are pages 56–106, on Agee's *A Death in the Family.*

5. Philippe Ariès, *L'enfant et la vie familiale sous l'Ancien Régime* (Paris: Librairie Plon, 1960). This study appeared in English, translated by Robert Baldick, in 1962 (New York: Random House).

6. Among those who challenge Ariès's work are Lloyd de Mause, ed., *The History of Childhood* (New York: Psychohistory Press, 1974), and Linda Pollock, *Forgotten Children: Parent-Child Relations from 1500 to 1900* (New York: Cambridge University Press, 1983). While de Mause cautions that too little has been done by historians in the research of childhood, his volume contains informative and extensive bibliographies of work that has been published on this topic. Two studies that deftly combine documentation of changing attitudes toward childrearing or childhood with analysis of fiction are Albert Stone's *The Innocent Eye: Childhood in Mark Twain's Imagination* (New

Haven: Yale University Press, 1961) and Andrew Wachtel's *The Battle for Childhood: Creation of a Russian Myth* (Stanford: Stanford University Press, 1990).

7. To gauge that interest, see George Boas's *The Cult of Childhood* (London: Warburg Institute, University of London, 1966); Reinhard Kuhn's *Corruption in Paradise: The Child in Western Literature* (Hanover, N.H.: University Press of New England, 1982); Peter Coveney's *The Image of Childhood: The Individual and Society; A Study of the Theme in English Literature* (Baltimore: Penguin Books, 1967); and William Walsh's *The Use of Imagination: Educational Thought and the Literary Mind* (Harmondsworth: Penguin Books, 1959).

8. Kuhn, *Corruption in Paradise*, 16–64.

9. Sander Gilman explains this psychological phenomenon in *Difference and Pathology: Stereotypes of Sexuality, Race, and Madness* (Ithaca: Cornell University Press, 1985), and *Jewish Self-Hatred: Anti-Semitism and the Hidden Language of the Jews* (Baltimore: Johns Hopkins University Press, 1986).

10. Laurence Ricou, *Everyday Magic: Child Languages in Canadian Literature* (Vancouver: University of British Columbia Press, 1987).

11. See Ricou, *Everyday Magic*, 8–13.

12. Richard Coe has explored this topic at length in *When the Grass Was Taller: Autobiography and the Experience of Childhood* (New Haven: Yale University Press, 1984). While the border between fiction and nonfiction must remain tentative, imaginative writing leaves more leeway for experiment than do texts purportedly factual in nature and which are geared toward exegesis, after the events, by a cognizant, more informed adult perspective. Also of interest are Coe's comments in *Reminiscences of Childhood: An Approach to Comparative Mythology,* in *Proceedings of the Leeds Philosophical and Historical Society,* vol. 19, no. 6, 1984. These essays note the numerous instances of Jewish writers who have composed autobiographies concerned primarily with childhood and adolescence, and Coe's studies are indispensable as a source of bibliography.

13. Patricia Meyer Spacks documents changing definitions of adolescence in *The Adolescent Idea: Myths of Youth and the Adult Imagination* (New York: Basic Books, 1981).

14. See, for example, accounts by Sam B. Girgus, *The New Covenant: Jewish Writers and the American Idea* (Chapel Hill: University of North Carolina Press, 1984); Bernard Sherman, *The Invention of the Jew: Jewish American Education Novels, 1916–1964* (New York: Thomas Yoseloff, 1969); Irving Malin, ed., *Contemporary American Jewish Literature* (Bloomington: Indiana University Press, 1973); and Gershon Shaked, *Im tishkaḥ ei-pa'am: 'iyyunim besifrut yehudit amerika'it* (Tel Aviv: Eked, 1971).

15. Discussions include Gershon Shaked, *Gal ḥadash basipporet ha'ivrit* (Merhavia: Hakibbutz Hameuchad, 1970), 71–86; Gideon Telpaz, *Israeli Childhood Stories of the Sixties* (Providence: Scholars Press, 1983); and Yael Feldman, "In Pursuit of Things Past: David Shahar and the Autobiography in Current Israeli Fiction," *Hebrew Studies* 24 (1983): 99–106.

16. S. Y. Abramovitch (Mendele the Bookseller), *Of Bygone Days*. This narrative appeared in various stages written in both Yiddish (titled *Shloyme reb*

Khayims) and Hebrew (titled *Bayamim hahem*). The introduction was published in Hebrew in 1894, and the book took complete form between then and 1911. English citations are from the translation by Raymond Scheindlin, *Of Bygone Days*, as it appears in *A Shtetl and Other Yiddish Novellas*, ed. Ruth R. Wisse (Detroit: Wayne State University Press, 1986), 251–359; here, 330.

17. For a popular description of traditional Jewish childrearing and education in this part of the world, including the role of the *melamed*, see Mark Zborowski and Elizabeth Herzog, *Life Is with People: The Jewish Little Town of Eastern Europe* (New York: International Universities Press, 1952). For recent scholarship on traditional Jewish schooling, see David Kraemer, "Images of Childhood and Adolescence in Talmudic Literature," in *The Jewish Family: Metaphor and Memory*, ed. David Kraemer (New York: Oxford University Press, 1990), 65–80; and, in that same volume, Gershon Hundert, "Jewish Children and Childhood in Early Modern East Central Europe," 81–94. Also of interest by Hundert is an essay on "Approaches to the History of the Jewish Family in Early Modern Poland-Lithuania," in *The Jewish Family: Myths and Reality*, ed. Steven M. Cohen and Paula E. Hyman (New York: Holmes and Meier, 1986), 17–28.

18. Abramovitch, *Of Bygone Days*, 303. David Patterson discusses the matter in connection with a range of fictional narratives in *The Hebrew Novel in Czarist Russia* (Edinburgh: Edinburgh University Press, 1964).

19. Shaul Stampfer, "Patterns of Marriage in Eastern European Jewry." (Lecture, Jewish Studies Colloquium Series, University of Washington, Seattle, Wash., 28 April 1987.)

In "Childhood, Marriage, and the Family in the Eastern European Jewish Enlightenment" (Cohen and Hyman, *The Jewish Family*, 45–61), David Biale amasses evidence of misery in traditional Jewish childhood and also provides a review of research and autobiographical sources on the topic. This discussion in effect shows, however, that many problems occurred less because the child was considered an adult than because of the uneasy blend of responsibilities and dependence imposed on youngsters. *Heder* education and early marriage put the minor at the mercy of adults (the *melamed* and the in-laws) less concerned for his well-being than his own parents might have been. By the same token, part of the sexual maladjustment stemmed from a lack of instruction and guidance.

20. Yekhiel Shtern, "A Kheyder in Tyszowce (Tishevits)," *YIVO Annual of Jewish Social Science* 5 (1950): 142–70. This account maintains that children worked individually with the teacher for a few minutes each day. The rest of the time was divided between recitation, games, and a range of amusements.

21. For instance, parents celebrated the first day of lessons with cakes so that the child would associate learning with sweetness. Part of the didactic effectiveness of the Passover *hagadah* came from its inclusion of counting songs, riddles, child characters, and questions for children to ask.

22. Although her book is finally more of a parenting manual than a historical study, Shoshana Matzmer-Bekerman provides informative detail on Orthodox Jewish stances toward childrearing in *The Jewish Child: Halakhic Perspectives* (New York: KTAV, 1984).

23. For discussion of the absorption of the child into sacred text as a theme in Agnon's fiction, see Anne Golomb Hoffman, "Housing the Past: Agnon's *A Guest for the Night*," *Prooftexts* 2 (September 1982): 265–82.

24. For discussion of introspection and representations of consciousness as an innovation in Hebrew literature, see, for instance, Dan Miron's *Bo'ah laylah: Hasifrut ha'ivrit bein higayon le'igayon bemifneh hame'ah ha'esrim* (Tel Aviv: Dvir, 1987) and Robert Alter's *The Invention of Hebrew Prose: Modern Fiction and the Language of Realism* (Seattle: University of Washington Press, 1988).

25. Alan Mintz, *Banished from Their Father's Table: Loss of Faith and Hebrew Autobiography* (Bloomington: Indiana University Press, 1989), especially 57–88, and "Mordechai Ze'ev Feierberg and the Reveries of Redemption," *AJS Review* 2 (1977): 171–99.

26. S. Ben Zion, *Kol kitvei S. Ben Tsion* (Tel Aviv: Dvir, 1943), 31.

27. These are all Ashkenazi childhoods. Lev Hakak presents a survey of Sephardi childhoods and religious schooling as depicted in Hebrew short fiction, in *Yerudim vena'alim* (Jerusalem: Kiryat Sefer, 1981). The experience of the girl child deserves a full discussion of its own. Since females were excluded from studying the holy tongue, they do not often receive prominent attention in this thematic realm. Anne Lapidus Lerner begins investigation of this topic in "Lost Childhood in Eastern European Hebrew Literature," in Kraemer, *The Jewish Family*, 95–112. This essay compares traditional Jewish boyhood and girlhood as depicted in the fiction of Isaac Dov Berkowitz and Devorah Baron. It would be of interest to compare texts written in Yiddish (for example, Bella Chagall's memoir, *Burning Lights—Brenendike likht*) and accounts written in Hebrew (for instance, by Baron, one of the exceptions who did achieve a Hebrew education usually reserved for boys).

28. See Elie Wiesel's *Night* (New York: Hill and Wang, 1960), published first in French as *La nuit* (Paris: Editions de Minuit, 1958).

29. A number of studies have commented on these works individually, but none has discussed them collectively or explored childhood perspectives and voices as a general phenomenon prevalent in literary treatments of the Holocaust. Lawrence Langer examines Aichinger's novel in *The Holocaust and the Literary Imagination* (New Haven: Yale University Press, 1975), 124–65; Alan Mintz provides a perceptive analysis of Appelfeld in *Ḥurban: Responses to Catastrophe in Hebrew Literature* (New York: Columbia University Press, 1984). His discussion touches on child characters in the author's early fiction but mentions *The Age of Wonders* only tangentially. Sidra Ezrahi briefly considers childhood and the Holocaust in *By Words Alone: The Holocaust in Literature* (Chicago: University of Chicago Press, 1980), 157–58. In *Indelible Shadows: Film and the Holocaust* (New York: Random House, 1983), 69–79, Annette Insdorf notes a number of movies that, portraying Jews as children during the Holocaust, associate Jews with special vulnerability. This discussion, however, does not distinguish clearly between children and adolescence, nor does it devote attention to the inner lives of children.

In a related but distinct area of inquiry that does not explicitly concern the representation of consciousness in fiction, several studies have pointed out a pervasive preoccupation in Hebrew literature with returning to the past, after the Holocaust, to reckon with loss and lost childhood. See, for instance, Robert Alter, *After the Tradition: Essays on Modern Jewish Writing* (New York: Dutton, 1969), 163–80; Edward Alexander, *The Resonance of Dust: Essays on Holocaust Literature and Jewish Fate* (Columbus: Ohio State University Press, 1979), 73–120; and, especially, Shaked, *Gal ḥadash,* 82–86. There is a considerable (and growing) body of scholarship on literary responses to the Holocaust, touching on the issue of combating silence. In addition to the titles mentioned above, see, for instance, George Steiner, *Language and Silence: Essays on Language, Literature, and the Inhuman* (New York: Atheneum, 1967); David Roskies, *Against the Apocalypse: Responses to Catastrophe in Modern Jewish Culture* (Cambridge, Mass.: Harvard University Press, 1984); and James Young, *Writing and Rewriting the Holocaust: Narrative and the Consequences of Interpretation* (Bloomington: Indiana University Press, 1988).

30. George Eisen, *Children and Play in the Holocaust* (Amherst: University of Massachusetts Press, 1988). See also Debórah Dwork, *Children with a Star: Jewish Youth in Nazi Europe* (New Haven: Yale University Press, 1991).

31. *I Never Saw Another Butterfly,* ed. Hana Volavková, trans. Jeanne Němcová (New York: McGraw-Hill, 1976).

Chapter Two. Narrative Voice and the Language of the Child

1. Among Bakhtin's publications, the most important for this discussion is *The Dialogic Imagination: Four Essays,* trans. Caryl Emerson and Michael Holquist (Austin: University of Texas Press, 1981). Also crucial is the volume called *Le marxism et la philosophie du langage* (Paris: Editions de Minuit, 1977), published under the name I. L. Voloshinov. For biographical background on Bakhtin and for an overview of his work, including an explanation of why many scholars ascribe the Voloshinov text to Bakhtin, see Katerina Clark and Michael Holquist, *Mikhail Bakhtin* (Cambridge, Mass.: Harvard University Press, 1984). Another survey is provided by Tzvetan Todorov in *Mikhail Bakhtin: The Dialogical Principle,* trans. Wlad Godzich (Minneapolis: University of Minnesota Press, 1984). I. M. Ivanov, *The Significance of Baxtin's Ideas on Sign, Utterance, and Dialogue for Modern Semiotics* (Tel Aviv: Papers on Poetics and Semiotics, Porter Institute, 1976), outlines the novelty of Bakhtin's thinking and traces developments within the field of semiotics which Bakhtin anticipated or on which he exerted seminal influence.

2. This omission in Bakhtin's theory has been the stimulus for ongoing debate within the field of feminist criticism about women's discourse and expressivity. See, for instance, Patricia Yaeger's "Eudora Welty and the Dialogic Imagination," *PMLA* 99 (October 1984): 955–73, and her book-length study, *Honey-Mad Women: Emancipatory Strategies in Writing by Women* (New York: Columbia University Press, 1987), along with Wayne Booth's "Freedom of Interpretation: Bakhtin and the Challenge of Feminist Criticism," in *Bakhtin: Essays and Dialogues on His Work,* ed. Gary Saul Morson (Chicago: University

of Chicago Press, 1986), 145–76. The issue of female voices bears special importance for my comments on Cynthia Ozick, in Chapter 10.

3. This is also, of course, a standard strategy for comedy, including the television sitcom variety.

4. Yaeger provides useful discussion of revolutionary discourse and Benjamin's ideas in *Honey-Mad Women,* 220–21.

5. For a study of that genre and a description of its distinguishing features, see Jerome Buckley, *Seasons of Youth: The Bildungsroman from Dickens to Golding* (Cambridge, Mass.: Harvard University Press, 1974).

6. For discussion of the concept of defamiliarization, see Lee T. Lemon and Marion J. Reis, *Russian Formalist Criticism: Four Essays* (Lincoln: University of Nebraska Press, 1965). On ways to reduce the strangeness of literature and to restore the communicative function of fictional texts, see the chapter on convention and naturalization in Jonathan Culler's *Structuralist Poetics: Structuralism, Linguistics, and the Study of Literature* (Ithaca: Cornell University Press, 1975), 131–60. Richard Coe structures extensive discussion around the idea of the child possessing a magical, alternative view of the world in *When the Grass Was Taller.*

7. The phrase "the inchoate as literary strategy" is borrowed from a paper by Elizabeth Goodenough, "The Visionary Child in Virginia Woolf," presented at the 1987 MLA convention.

8. The phrase "making strange" is a favorite term of the Russian Formalists. Robert Pattison's *The Child Figure in English Literature* (Athens, Ga.: University of Georgia Press, 1978) comments at some length on the child's unusual perceptions, which are often naive, yet more insightful than the perceptions of adults. However, this study is primarily concerned with a narrowly thematic approach to literary treatments of original sin, and so neglects the wide variety of purposes that the myopia of childhood has served as a narrative strategy.

9. The inventiveness and the limitations of Bakhtin's formulations as analytical tools are discussed by Brian McHale in "Free Indirect Discourse: A Survey of Recent Accounts," *Poetics and Theory of Literature* 3 (1978): 249–87.

10. Gerard Genette, *Figures III* (Paris: Editions du Seuil, 1972); in English, *Narrative Discourse: An Essay in Method,* trans. Jane E. Lewin (Ithaca: Cornell University Press, 1980). Seymour Chatman's *Story and Discourse: Narrative Structure in Fiction and Film* (Ithaca: Cornell University Press, 1978) presents a synthesis of various theories of narrative and refines the concept of focalization by discussing distinctions between literature and film. In *Narrative Fiction: Contemporary Poetics* (London: Methuen, 1983), Shlomith Rimmon-Kenan offers a summary of Genette's ideas and also surveys the terms other theorists have espoused to approach focalization and narration.

11. For instance, Rimmon-Kenan mentions Joyce's *Portrait of the Artist,* Henry James's *What Maisie Knew,* and Charles Dickens's *Great Expectations,* pressing all three into the service of illustrating her points about focalization (72–76).

12. Cohn, *Transparent Minds,* 11–18.

13. There exists a voluminous psycholinguistic literature on child language. Sources of information on this growing body of research include Adele Abrahamsen, *Child Language: An Interdisciplinary Guide to Theory and Research* (Baltimore: University Park Press, 1977), and two annual bibliographies: *Child Development Abstracts and Bibliography* (University of Chicago Press) and *Language and Language Behavior Abstracts* (ed. University of Michigan; since 1985, titled *Linguistics and Language Behavior Abstracts*). My discussion will refer to psycholinguistic models primarily in connection with Henry Roth's *Call It Sleep* (Chapter 5, below).

Carole Peterson and Alyssa McCabe have done descriptive psycholinguistic research into the ways children actually do tell stories, in *Developmental Psycholinguistics: Three Ways of Looking at a Child's Narrative* (New York: Plenum, 1983). Also of interest is Mary Jane Hurst's application of psycholinguistic insights to her readings of American fiction: *The Voice of the Child in American Literature: Linguistic Approaches to Fictional Child Language* (Lexington: University Press of Kentucky, 1990).

14. McHale elucidates these possibilities in "Free Indirect Discourse." His synopsis of work on free indirect discourse available since 1957 covers studies by Stephen Ullman, Ann Banfield, and I. L. Voloshinov (presumed to be a pen name of Bakhtin or to voice Bakhtin's ideas). For thorough discussion of earlier debate, see Roy Pascal's *The Dual Voice* (Manchester: Manchester University Press, 1977). An issue of a journal devoted to this topic, *Poetics Today* 2, no. 2 (1981), includes articles by Mieke Bal, Ann Banfield, and Moshe Ron, among others. It provides discussion of the history and development of pertinent critical terminology, associated modes of narration, and their relation to mimesis.

15. My remarks here draw on the fine discussion by Laurence Ricou in *Everyday Magic*, 34–36.

16. Brian McHale, "Speaking as a Child in *U.S.A.*: A Problem in the Mimesis of Speech," *Language and Style* 17, no. 4 (1984): 352–70.

17. "Restricted code" is Basil Bernstein's term, used primarily to refer to lower-class speech patterns. Speakers of restricted code assume that their audience shares a frame of reference with them, and so they do not articulate definitions of their operative terms as speakers of elaborate code are more wont to do. "Language and Socialization," in *Children and Language: Readings in Early Language and Socialization*, ed. Sinclair Rogers, 329–45 (London: Oxford University Press, 1975). For more extended discussion of research into this topic, see Bernstein, *Class, Codes, and Control: Theoretical Studies toward a Sociology of Language* (New York: Schocken Books, 1974).

18. Kaja Silverman offers a lucid overview of these issues in *The Subject of Semiotics* (New York: Oxford University Press, 1983).

19. Compare, for instance, Bakhtin's dialogics with Julia Kristeva's insistence that every text consists of the absorption and transformation of another, such that intertextuality can replace the notion of intersubjectivity: *Desire in Language: A Semiotic Approach to Literature and Art,* ed. Leon S. Roudiez, trans. Thomas Gora, Alice Jardine, and Leon S. Roudiez (New York: Columbia University Press, 1980). Jonathan Culler cogently discusses the problem of de-

fining intertextuality and its limits in *The Pursuit of Signs: Semiotics, Literature, Deconstruction* (Ithaca: Cornell University Press, 1981), chapter 2.

20. Robert Alter, *Motives For Fiction* (Cambridge, Mass.: Harvard University Press, 1984), 10. Terry Eagleton also critiques overextension of the concept of textuality in his *Introduction to Literary Theory* (Minneapolis: University of Minnesota Press, 1983). For background, see Terence Hawkes, *Structuralism and Semiotics* (Berkeley: University of California Press, 1977).

21. Meir Sternberg, "Polylingualism as Reality and Translation as Mimesis," in *Poetics Today* 2, no. 4 (1981): 221–39.

Chapter Three. *Sholem Aleichem*—Mottel, The Cantor's Son

1. Abramovitch, *Of Bygone Days,* 268.

2. Alan Mintz comments on the invention of a new language, *"safah aheret,"* in Bialik's "Habrekha" ("The Pool") and in M. Z. Feierberg's "Whither"; see "Mordechai Ze'ev Feierberg."

3. For example, Peretz's "Lag B'omer" and Sholem Aleichem's *Yosele Solovey.* S. Niger discusses these matters in his study of Sholem Aleichem, in *Geklibene Shriftn* (New York: Idischer Kultur Farlang, 1928), 77–89.

4. Niger, 88, contrasts the treatment of nature by these two authors.

5. *Motl Peyse dem khazns.* All quotations here are taken from the Yiddishe Buchfarlag edition (Warsaw, 1953). An English translation exists as *Adventures of Mottel the Cantor's Son,* done by Tamara Kahana (New York: H. Schuman, 1953). My quotations draw on this version but significantly modify it at times.

6. For example, Niger insists on Mottel's carefree innocence as it stands in sharp opposition to the woe and travails of his elders. In contrast, Maurice Samuel insists on a consonance between Mottel and his elders; his book, *The World of Sholem Aleichem* (New York: Knopf, 1943), argues that Mottel is a perfect little Kasrilevker, i.e., one who only has to "see the world in the proper way and all is well" (191). Whether or not they see Mottel as an unusually optimistic character or one who is typically so, both see the breakdown of the shtetl as a tragedy. Dan Miron's study of Mottel, discussed below, suggests that the narrative has quite a different emphasis, a celebratory farewell to the old and welcome of the new.

7. Dan Miron, "Bouncing Back: Destruction and Recovery in Sholem Aleykhem's *Motl Peyse dem khazns,"* YIVO *Annual of Jewish Social Science* 17 (1978): 119–84. Miron also provides a review of earlier scholarship (by M. Viner, Y. Y. Trunk, and S. Niger), pointing out that previous criticism failed to address in depth such matters as composition, structuring, and stylistics.

8. Khone Shmeruk documents the evolution of the text through its various versions in "Sippurei Mottl ben hahazan leShalom Aleikhem: hasituatsiah ha'epit vetoldotav shel hasefer," *Siman Kri'ah* 12/13 (1981): 310–26.

9. See ibid., 314.

10. In "Dekonstruktsiah shel dibur: Shalom Aleikhem vehasemiotika shel hafolklor hayehudi," the afterword to *Tevye hehalban umonologim* (Tel

Aviv: Simon Kri'ah and Hakibbutz Hameuchad, 1983), 195–212, H. Benyamin (Benjamin Hrushovsky) comments on the representation of spoken discourse in Sholem Aleichem's art, which in some ways resembles the fiction of Dostoevsky. Much as that novelist introduces varied voices through ideological harangues, Sholem Aleichem admits multiple speakers through the conversations of his garrulous characters. Both writers are intensely concerned with the transmission and assessment of the speech of others. Consequently, the issue of reported discourse surfaces here as in Dostoevsky's fiction, which stimulated and has been illuminated by one of Bakhtin's major works, *Problems of Dostoevsky's Poetics*, available in English translation by Caryl Emerson (Minneapolis: University of Minnesota Press, 1984). Any number of critics have commented on the talkativeness of Sholem Aleichem's characters. See, e.g. Ruth Wisse, *Sholem Aleichem and the Art of Communication* (Syracuse: Syracuse University Press, 1979). For commentary on the cacophony of voices that Sholem Aleichem creates in reaction to disaster, see Roskies, *Against the Apocalypse*, 163–94.

    11. Bakhtin, *The Dialogic Imagination*, 332.

    12. Miron, "Bouncing Back," 178. Miron examines the function of the Sholem Aleichem narrator at length in "Sholem Aleykhem: Person, Persona, Presence" (Uriel Weinreich Memorial Lecture 1, New York: YIVO, 1972). Related discussion of Abramovitch's adoption of the Mendele persona is presented in Miron's *A Traveler Disguised: A Study in the Rise of Modern Yiddish Fiction in the Nineteenth Century* (New York: Schocken Books, 1973).

    13. McHale, "Free Indirect Discourse."

    14. For discussion of this kind of humor with relation to other double entendres in Sholem Aleichem, see Rhoda S. Kachuk, "Sholom Aleichem's Humor in English Translation," YIVO *Annual of Jewish Social Science* 11 (1956/57): 39–81. My contention is that this sort of humor is not simply meant to raise a smile but is also fully integrated thematically into the chapter.

    15. On Mottel as a diminutive but less grotesque Menachem Mendel, see Y. Trunk, *Sholem Aleykhem—zayn vezn un zayne verk* (Warsaw, 1937), 313–71.

    16. Roskies, *Against the Apocalypse*, 176, 182–84. Though the narrator in Kipnis's text is twenty-two years old, he exhibits a childlike incredulity. Closer to Mottel's story would be Bialik's "Haḥatsotsra nitbaysha." See the detailed analysis by Gershon Shaked in *'Al arba'a sippurim: perakim bisodot hasippur* (Jerusalem: Jewish Agency, 1963), 94–121. Mottel's innocent reactions to catastrophe make him a precursor also of child characters in fictional treatment of the Holocaust, such as in Appelfeld's *The Age of Wonders* and Grossman's *See Under: Love*. A narrative more contemporaneous with *Mottel*, and one that focuses more specifically on catastrophes of special impact for children in Eastern Europe, is Yehuda Steinberg's *In Those Days* (*Bayamim hahem*, 1905). This text details a boy's conscription into the Russian army and the pain of his separation from family and Jewish custom. The child's naiveté there is cultivated more for purposes of pathos, as a contrast with brutality, than as a way to defuse pathos.

    17. Shmeruk, "Sippurei Mottl," 317.

    18. Bakhtin's well-known discussion of language as a subversive, car-

nivalesque force can be found in *Rabelais and His World* (Bloomington: Indiana University Press, 1984).

19. For more on such verbal exchanges, see Benyamin, "Dekonstruktsiah shel dibur."

20. For a biographical sketch, see Joseph Butwin and Frances Butwin, *Sholem Aleichem* (Boston: G. K. Hall, 1977).

21. This view is compatible with, but extends beyond, Dov Sadan's early observation that Sholem Aleichem's monologues often serve as frames for the typology of a large family. Sadan notes that, often, one individual speaks but focuses attention more on his surrounding milieu than on himself. See "Three Foundations [Sholem Aleichem and the Yiddish Literary Tradition]," trans. David G. Roskies, *Prooftexts* 6 (January 1986): 52–64. (Special issue on Sholem Aleichem, ed. Roskies.) Miron's argument, that *Mottel* does not present genuine monologue, is made on the grounds that the narrator's words are not dramatically situated as authentic child speech in a concrete, believable circumstance. At issue, for my point, is less the verisimilitude of Mottel's utterances than the underlying structural propensity of the text (thanks to the child figure) to admit oscillating perspectives.

22. In "Polylingualism as Reality," Meir Sternberg labels this technique "selective reproduction," as opposed to "vehicular matching," which cites a foreign language at length.

23. Sternberg calls this technique "explicit attribution."

24. Functioning similarly to relativize signification is the phrase *"er meynt"* or *"dos meynt"*; for instance, on pages 121, 122, 127.

25. Ruth Wisse, *The Schlemiel as Modern Hero* (Chicago: University of Chicago Press, 1971), 43. Art and nature as positive, shaping forces of the imagination are discussed by David Roskies in connection with *Mottel,* Sholem Aleichem's autobiographical *Funem Yorid* (*From the Fair*), and Mendele's *Shloyme reb khayims* (*Of Bygone Days*) in an essay called "Unfinished Business: Sholom Aleichem's *From the Fair,*" *Prooftexts* 6 (January 1986): 65–78.

26. Robert Alter, *Rogue's Progress: Studies in the Picaresque Novel* (Cambridge, Mass.: Harvard University Press, 1961).

27. Miron, "Bouncing Back," 148.

28. Butwin and Butwin (*Sholem Aleichem*) discuss the role of orphanhood in connection with the Bildungsroman tradition and Sholem Aleichem's writing.

29. Irving Howe and Eliezer Greenberg, "Introduction" to *A Treasury of Yiddish Stories* (New York: Viking Press, 1974), 1–71.

Chapter Four. Hayim Nahman Bialik—Aftergrowth

1. Bialik's essay "Gilui vekhisui balashon" appears in *Kol kitvei Ḥ. N. Bialik* (Tel Aviv: Dvir, 1953): 191–93. An English translation by Jacob Sloan, *"Revealment and Concealment in Language,"* appears in *Modern Hebrew Literature,* ed. Robert Alter (Philadelphia: Berman House, 1975), 127–37. Zvi Luz has examined at length the notion of *gilui vekhisui* as a generating force in

Bialik's poetry. See *Tashtiot shira: 'ikarim bapoetikah shel Bialik* (Tel Aviv: Sifriat Poalim, 1984). See also Arnold Band, "Hagilui bakhisui: tafkid hametafora bemasot Bialik," *Meḥkarei Yerushalayim besifrut 'ivrit* 10–11 (1987): 189–99.

2. Bialik's grasp of these matters was strengthened by his familiarity with Russian symbolism and exposure to nonliterary writing. He followed the work, for instance, of Potebniah, a linguist in the philosophical-psychological vein whose disciples included Victor Shklovsky of the Russian Formalists. For discussion, see Luz, *Tashtiot shira*, 157–58. Modernism was not the prime source of Bialik's creativity, but the modernist distinction between signifiers and signifieds, sound and sense, found a responsive chord within the Hebrew poet. Hamutal Bar Yosef has called for greater recognition of the impact modernism had on Bialik and other Hebrew writers of his generation. See her essays, "Bialik vehashira harussit," *Moznayim* 64 (1990): 38–46, and "New New Criticism," *Prooftexts* 7 (September 1987): 301–5.

3. Hans Aarsleff, *From Locke to Saussure: Essays on the Study of Language and Intellectual History* (Minneapolis: University of Minnesota Press, 1982), 27.

4. Scholars have offered a variety of explanations for tensions in Bialik's texts between private experience and inadequately expressive public discourse. These tensions have been seen, for example, as resulting from the pressures that Ahad Ha-am and others placed on Bialik. They urged him to gear his work toward national collective issues and so to gloss over highly personal explorations of psychic life. Other explanations have insisted on a psychological struggle, as Bialik wrestled with desires both to hide and to expose private feelings. These matters have been discussed by, among others, Yakov Fichman, Adi Zemah, Dov Sadan, Reuven Shaham, Dan Miron, and Ahron Mazya. For a summary and bibliographical information, see Luz, *Tashtiot shira*, 41–50. While debate about such issues is of much value for an understanding of *Aftergrowth*, it is not central to my purposes and so will not be treated here in depth. My basic stance is that these issues complement, rather than diminish or contradict, the argument that linguistic drama is a prime organizing principle of Bialik's narrative.

5. Prominent examples include Jeffrey Mehlman's *A Structural Study of Autobiography* (Ithaca: Cornell University Press, 1974); Philippe Lejeune, *Le pacte autobiographique* (Paris: Editions du Seuil, 1975); James Olney, *Metaphors of the Self* (Princeton: Princeton University Press, 1972); and W. C. Spengemann, *The Forms of Autobiography* (New Haven: Yale University Press, 1980).

6. Yael Feldman, "Gender In/Difference in Contemporary Hebrew Fictional Autobiography," *Biography* 11 (Summer 1988): 191.

7. Feldman, 191, remarks on loss as a peculiarly concrete and accelerated phenomenon in Hebrew literary circumstance. Bialik's ambivalence toward Jewish tradition has, of course, been the focus of extensive critical debate. His equivocal withdrawal from the religious world of his childhood has been treated, for instance, by Baruch Kurzweil, *Bialik veTshernihovsky* (Jerusalem: Schocken Books, 1961), 3–22, 173–87; Eli Shweid, "Bein she'arey hatehara

vehatum'ah," in *Shalosh eshmorot* (Tel Aviv: Am Oved, 1964), 13–25; Gershon Shaked, "Lamah Bialik 'adayin 'imanu k'an ve'akhshav," in *Hallel leBialik,* ed. H. Weiss and Y. Itzhaki (Ramat Gan: Bar Ilan University, 1989), 17–22, and in English translation, "Bialik Here and Now," *The Shadows Within: Essays on Modern Jewish Writers,* trans. Jeffrey Green, Yael Lotan, and Eleanor Lapin (Philadelphia: Jewish Publication Society, 1989), 123–32. Distance from the simplicity of childhood beliefs in Bialik's fiction is the focus of Shaked's comments on "Haḥatsotsrah nitbaysha" in *'Al arba'a sippurim.*

8. For discussion of this opening as an echo of Sholem Aleichem's narrative, see Dan Miron, "Bouncing Back," 119–23.

9. Citations here come from *Sippurim,* ed. Yizhak Fiksler (Tel Aviv: Dvir, 1963) and the translation by I. M. Lask in *Aftergrowth and Other Stories* (Philadelphia: Jewish Publication Society, 1939).

10. These ideas are found in Jacques Lacan, *Ecrits,* trans. Alan Sheridan (New York: Norton, 1977). For a full bibliography and discussion of Lacan's theories, see Anthony Wilden, *The Language of the Self: The Function of Language in Psychoanalysis* (Baltimore: Johns Hopkins Press, 1968), and Anika Lemaire, *Jacques Lacan* (London: Routledge and Kegan Paul, 1977). Briefer, highly lucid introductions to this often difficult material can be found in Catherine Belsey, *Critical Practice* (London: Routledge and Kegan Paul, 1982), 60–61, 85–86, and Silverman, *The Subject of Semiotics,* 148–93. Silverman carefully explicates Lacan's debt to and rereading of Freud.

11. Kurzweil sees *Aftergrowth* as a crucial text that sums up the concern with orphanhood found throughout Bialik's artistic oeuvre. See *Bialik veTshernihovsky,* 3–7. For further discussion of absence and bereavement as a psychological origin for artistic impulse in Bialik's writing, see David Aberbach, "Bialik veWordsworth: shirat hayaldut," *Moznayim* 45 (July 1977): 102–12; idem, "Loss and Separation in Bialik and Wordsworth," *Prooftexts* 2 (May 1982): 197–208; and idem, *Bialik* (New York: Grove Press, 1988), 89–102, 108–10. Aberbach refers to *Aftergrowth* at some length but does not bring a Lacanian model to his psychological readings.

12. Hillel Barzel discusses the history of the word *safiah* in *Ḥ. N. Bialik, S. Y. Agnon: meḥkar uferush* (Tel Aviv: Yahdav, 1986), 190.

13. This reading runs counter to the analysis by Adi Zemah, which considers the mirror an aperture onto a hidden world of romantic mysteries, *Halavi hamistater: 'iyyunim bitsirato shel Ḥayyim Naḥman Bialik* (Jerusalem: Kiryat Sefer, 1976), 74–75. Zemah associates the mirror with a return to earliest childhood and with erotic desires, i.e., as an escape from the strictures of social convention, whereas a Lacanian reading must view it as a step toward self-definition within a social network.

14. It has been argued that the mirror stage is always culturally determined and so embedded in the symbolic order. The "imaginary" and the "symbolic" coexist in various ways within the adult. For discussion and critique of Lacan's theory, see Silverman, *The Subject of Semiotics,* 156–58.

15. Iconic comparison of the letters was a commonly used mnemonic device in *heder* pedagogy. See Diane Roskies, "Alphabet Instruction in the East European Heder: Some Comparative and Historical Notes," *YIVO Annual of*

Jewish Social Science 17 (1979): 21–53. Bialik, however, does not emphasize the conventionality of the images. Instead, the text emphasizes the visualization as a product of the child's imagination. That is to say, the images take on importance as they take on a life of their own in Shmulik's mind, impeding rather than aiding his learning.

For comparison between *Aftergrowth* and other Jewish fiction that depicts first encounters with religious texts, see Naomi Sokoloff, "Discoveries of Reading: Childhood Stories by Bialik, Shahar, and Roth," *Hebrew Annual Review* 9 (1985): 321–42.

16. Robert Scholes provides a discussion of the freedoms and restraints that semiotic codes impose on language use, in *Semiotics and Interpretation* (New Haven: Yale University Press, 1982), 1–5.

17. Gershon Shaked, "Hamar'ot harishonim—'al Safiaḥ me'et Ḥ. N. Bialik," in *Me'assef mukdash litsirat Ḥayyim Naḥman Bialik,* ed. Hillel Barzel (Ramat Gan: Masada, 1975), 145–61.

For another discussion of the child's transformative vision that fills even the most everyday of items with radiance and beauty, see Leah Goldberg, "Arb'a zekhukhiot," *Kneset, sidra ḥadasha* (Jerusalem: Mosad Bialik, 1960), 81–88. On biblical antecedents for associating the child with wonder, see Kurzweil, *Bialik veTshernihovsky,* 180–85. The theme of appropriating biblical passages was noted even in early critical discussion of *Aftergrowth,* for example, in Yakov Fichman's *Shirat Bialik* (Jerusalem: Mosad Bialik, 1946), but this matter was not integrated into discussion of the overall structure of the narrative.

18. This kind of prose, shaped by unvoiced but expected objections or arguments from others, has been called "hidden polemic" by Mikhail Bakhtin, in *Problems of Dostoevsky's Poetics,* 203–8.

19. Genesis 14:5 and Deuteronomy 2:20.

20. For psychoanalytic readings of this scene, see Shaked, "Hamar'ot harishonim," 155–56, and David Aberbach, "Screen Memories of Freud, Bialik, and Wordsworth," *Midstream* 25 (October 1979): 39–43.

21. Shaked, "Hamar'ot harishonim," 154–55.

22. Bakhtin, "Discourse in the Novel," in *The Dialogic Imagination,* 259–422. See 341–55 for Bakhtin's ideas on how individuals make language "internally persuasive," that is, the ideological becoming of a human being through the process of assimilating the words of others.

23. Dan Miron, *Hapreidah min ha'ani he'ani: mahalakh behitpathut shirato hamukdemet shel Ḥayyim Naḥman Bialik, 1891–1901* (Tel Aviv: Everyman's University, 1986).

24. Fischel Lahover, ed., *Igrot Ḥayyim Naḥman Bialik* (Tel Aviv: Dvir, 1937), 1: 126–27.

25. Miron, *Hapreidah min ha'ani he'ani,* 317–20.

26. For other documentation of Bialik's reliance on Yiddish in his art, see Yizhak Bakon, *Bialik bein 'ivrit leyiddish* (Tel Aviv: Ben Gurion University Press, 1987), and Ziva Shamir, *Hatseratsar meshorer hagalut* (Tel Aviv: Papyrus, 1986). Shamir excavates evidence that Bialik introduced folk elements of Yiddish into his Hebrew poetry and so implemented low mimetic qualities in his work, against the prevailing norms of Hebrew verse that favored highly elevated

diction and modes of writing. It should be noted that, in prose, low mimetic norms drawing on Yiddish were already possible. The overall effect of Bialik's choice to use Hebrew was to suppress the first language of his youth. A full investigation into the underlying Yiddish currents in his prose works remains a desideratum for future research.

Chapter Five. Henry Roth—Call It Sleep

1. Bonnie Lyons makes this assertion as she focuses on the main motifs and plot developments of the novel, such as Davey's fear of the cellar and his association of its dark horrors with sex and death. See *Henry Roth: The Man and His Work* (New York: Cooper Square, 1977). Naomi Diamant insightfully discusses the protagonist's decoding of signs around him and his simultaneous engagement in an encoding process by which his imagination organizes reality into its own idiosyncratic patterns of meaning. See "Linguistic Universes in Henry Roth's *Call It Sleep*," *Contemporary Literature* 27, no. 3 (1986): 337–55.

Shorter commentary on the child's development in the novel has been offered by Sherman, *Invention of the Jew*, 82–92; Girgus, *New Covenant*, 95–108; and Gershon Shaked, *The Shadows Within: Essays on Modern Jewish Writers* (Philadelphia: Jewish Publication Society, 1988), 68–69.

2. For discussion of another author, David Shahar, who has also concentrated on the Jewish child's first encounter with religious texts, see Sokoloff, "Discoveries of Reading."

3. The citations are drawn from the Avon Books edition (New York, 1962).

4. In "The Interior Monologue in *Call It Sleep*," *Studies in American Jewish Literature* 5 (Spring 1979): 2–10, Frances Kleederman illustrates passages representing Davey's inner speech. The texts bear out L. S. Vygotsky's contentions about the forms of inner speech as internalized social exchange. Resemblances between Vygotsky and Bakhtin in their ideas about assimilating the discourse of others are not coincidental. The two were members of the same circle of Russian intellectuals. For details, see Caryl Emerson, "The Outer Word and Inner Speech: Bakhtin, Vygotsky, and the Internalization of Language," in *Bakhtin: Essays and Dialogues on His Work,* ed. Gary Saul Morson (Chicago: University of Chicago Press, 1986), 21–40.

5. The preponderance of conjunction in early speech is documented, for instance, by Roger Brown, *A First Language: The Early Stages* (London: Allen and Unwin, 1973), 30; Keith T. Kernan, "Semantics and Expressive Elaboration in Children's Narratives," in *Child Discourse,* ed. Susan Ervin-Tripp and Claudia Mitchell Kernan (New York: Academic Press, 1977), 99–100; and Ruth Weir, *Language in the Crib* (The Hague: Mouton, 1962), 87, 91.

6. Bakhtin, *The Dialogic Imagination*, 282.

7. There has been considerable research on the topic of verbal mediation in cognition, particularly on ways in which language enhances memory. For an overview, see S. M. Erwin and W. R. Miller, "Language Development," in

Readings in the Sociology of Language, ed. Joshua Fishman (The Hague: Mouton, 1968), 68–98.

8. For useful comments on children's restricted rights and the verbal strategies children favor for taking initiatives in conversation with adults, see George A. Miller, *Spontaneous Apprentices: Children and Language* (New York: Seabury Press, 1977), 132–35.

9. Joseph Church, *Language and the Discovery of Reality: A Developmental Psychology of Cognition* (New York: Random House, 1961), and M. M. Lewis, *Language, Thought, and Personality in Infancy and Childhood* (New York: Basic Books, 1963), comment on the element of recursiveness in a child's speech. They argue that language increasingly becomes an object of action and thoughts for the school-age child. Some research suggests that linguistic self-consciousness begins much earlier. See Thelma Weeks, *Born to Talk* (Rowley, Mass.: Newbury House, 1969). Her work refines and expands on the categories of language use developed by M.A.K. Halliday in *Explorations in the Functions of Language* (London: Edward Arnold, 1973), and she discusses ages at which children acquire skills in manipulating language to different purposes. Diane Nelson Bryen demonstrates how children in contact with varying groups develop increased awareness of social expectations and the appropriate diction for different contexts. See *Inquiries into Child Language* (Boston: Allyn and Bacon, 1982).

10. Davey's attitudes toward his bilingualism range from curiosity to embarrassment about his Yiddish-speaking family. Because of these attitudes, in addition to the linguistic awareness and semiotic sophistication he acquires, his case would be of interest for any thematic study of bilingual characters. He exemplifies many of the points set forth in François Grosjean's *Life with Two Languages: An Introduction to Bilingualism* (Cambridge, Mass.: Harvard University Press, 1982). For a sociolinguistic description of lexical and phonological interference, bilingual puns, and other features of Yiddish and English in contact as presented in *Call It Sleep,* see Frances Kleederman's dissertation, "A Study of Language in Henry Roth's *Call It Sleep*" (New York University, 1974). The novel is a gold mine of examples of such phenomena, which have been defined in, for example, Uriel Weinreich's classic *Languages in Contact: Findings and Problems* (The Hague: Mouton, 1968).

11. George Steiner, *After Babel: Aspects of Language and Translation* (New York: Oxford University Press, 1975), 35.

12. The vague referentiality of the novel's title has occasioned considerable critical discussion. One of the most convincing comments is Wayne Lesser's "A Narrative's Revolutionary Energy: The Example of Henry Roth's *Call It Sleep,*" *Criticism* 23 (Spring 1981): 155–76. Lesser regards Davey's semiotic initiation as a discovery of the instability of meaning in language. His study does not discuss the unique features of children's language, but it presents a very informative comparison of this last paragraph of the novel with the opening rhetoric of the prologue. See also T. Mooney, "The Explicable 'It' of Henry Roth's *Call It Sleep,*" *Studies in American Jewish Literature* 5 (Spring 1979): 11–18.

13. Peter A. de Villiers and Jill G. de Villiers, *Early Language* (Cambridge, Mass.: Harvard University Press, 1979). For discussion of these matters in relation to fictional depictions of child language, see Ricou, *Everyday Magic*.

14. Steiner, *After Babel*, 47.

15. Following Bakhtinian models, Hannah Wirth-Nesher details an overlap of Christian and Jewish discourse in *Call It Sleep*, particularly in the passages that represent Davey's thoughts at the moment of the electric shock, which resemble a long polyphonic poem. See "Between Mother Tongue and Native Language: Multilingualism in Henry Roth's *Call It Sleep*," *Prooftexts* 10 (May 1990): 297–312.

Chapter Six. *Jerzy Kosinski*—The Painted Bird

1. Jerzy Kosinski, *Notes of the Author on The Painted Bird* (New York: Scientia-factum, 1967).

2. Ivan Sanders remarks on the preponderance of close-ups over panoramas in "The Gifts of Strangeness: Alienation and Creation in Jerzy Kosinski's Fiction," *Polish Review* 19 (1974): 171–89. See also Daniel J. Cahill's discussion in "Jerzy Kosinski: Retreat from Violence," *Twentieth Century Literature* 18 (April 1972): 121–32.

3. See Sanders, "Gifts of Strangeness." For a comparison with the tradition of naturalism in nineteenth-century writing, see, for example, Erich Auerbach's *Mimesis: The Representation of Reality in Western Literature*, trans. Willard Trask (Princeton: Princeton University Press, 1953), 493–524.

4. Kosinski, *Notes of the Author*, 13.

5. Citations from *The Painted Bird* are drawn from the Bantam Books edition (New York, 1978). The novel was originally published in 1965.

6. Cohn, *Transparent Minds*, 166–72.

7. Stanley Corngold, "Jerzy Kosinski's *The Painted Bird*: Language Lost and Regained," *Mosaic* 4 (Summer 1973): 153–67. This cogent discussion also argues that the novel highlights its own genesis as fiction. In a Proustian fashion, *The Painted Bird* spells out the process that the narrator undergoes in recovering his voice and, thus, in achieving a language suitable for expressing his formative years.

8. In "The Gifts of Strangeness" Ivan Sanders points out crescendo and the accompanying explosion as an important structural element of the novel.

9. See Sternberg's typology of represented speech differences in "Polylingualism as Reality."

10. Sanders, "The Gifts of Strangeness," 179.

11. Kosinski, *Notes of the Author*, 9. For discussion of this aesthetic, see also Corngold, "Kosinski's *Painted Bird*," 162. No doubt, part of the appeal of *The Painted Bird* when it first appeared was that it contributed to the vogue for the violent, the bizarre, and the absurd in American fiction of the sixties. For more lengthy comment, see Barbara Jane Tepa's "Inside the Kaleidoscope: Jerzy Kosinski's Polish and American Contexts" (Ph.D. diss., St. John's University of New York, 1975). However, Kosinski bears special comparison with Alejo Car-

pentier. That writer's fictional world presents a landscape naturally characterized by bizarre incongruity and infused with magic through superstitious beliefs, unlike the blatant artifice and invention of a Barth or a Pynchon.

12. Edmond Jabès, "Song of the Last Jewish Child," trans. Anthony Rudolf, in *Voices within the Ark: The Modern Jewish Poets,* ed. Howard Schwartz and Anthony Rudolf (New York: Avon Books, 1980), 893–94.

13. In "The Structure of *The Painted Bird,*" *Journal of Narrative Technique* 6 (1976): 132–36, R. J. Spendal postulates that the book divides into a symmetrical pattern: two halves of ten chapters apiece. Each half presents parallel events, and individual chapters or episodes find frequent counterparts in the opposing section of the text.

14. Paul Bruss makes this observation in "Kosinski's Early Fiction: The Problem of Language," a chapter from his book *Victims: Textual Strategies in Recent American Fiction* (East Brunswick, N.J.: Associated University Press, 1981), 167–82.

15. Ibid., 170.

16. David Richter, "The Three Denouements of Jerzy Kosinski's *The Painted Bird,*" *Contemporary Literature* 15 (Summer 1974): 370–85.

17. For a discussion of the novel as picaresque, see Patricia K. Meszaros's "Hero with a Thousand Faces, Child with No Name: Kosinski's *The Painted Bird,*" *College Literature* 6 (1979): 232–44.

18. Kosinski, *Notes of the Author,* 21–24.

19. Sidra Ezrahi discusses Kosinski's treatment of the Shoah as an "allegory of the diffusion of evil" in *By Words Alone,* 153–58.

20. Norman Lavers's *Jerzy Kosinski* (Boston: Twayne Publishers, 1982) provides extensive biographical background on the author.

21. For discussion of the psychological motives behind stereotyping, see the introductory chapter to Sander Gilman's *Difference and Pathology,* 15–35.

Chapter Seven. Ahron Appelfeld—The Age of Wonders

1. Ahron Appelfeld, *Masot beguf rishon* (Jerusalem: Hasifriah Hatsionit, 1979), especially 19–26 and 41–51. My citations in English draw from a version of these ideas presented by Appelfeld as "Holocaust Writings: Personal Reflections" (Samuel and Althea Stroum Lectures, University of Washington, Seattle, Wash., 1983).

2. Mintz, *Ḥurban,* 203–38. This perceptive analysis touches on child characters in Appelfeld's early work but mentions *The Age of Wonders* only very briefly.

3. Ibid., 220.

4. Ahron Appelfeld, *Tor hapela'ot* (Jerusalem: Hakibbutz Hameuchad, 1978). An English translation by Dalyah Bilu has appeared as *The Age of Wonders* (New York: Washington Square Press, 1981). Quotations from the novel are taken from these two editions.

5. Several studies have examined this pervasive preoccupation in Hebrew literature with a return to the past, after the Holocaust, to reckon with loss and

lost childhood. See, for instance, Shaked's "Yaldut 'avudah," in *Gal ḥadash,* 71–86; Alter's *After the Tradition,* 163–80; and Alexander's *Resonance of Dust,* especially chapter 3.

6. See, for example, Gershon Shaked's assessment in *Gal ḥadash,* 149–67; Esther Fuchs's "Hahasaḥa hatematit: tashtit mivnit bekitvei Ahron Apelfeld," *Hebrew Studies* 23 (1982): 223–27; and Lily Rattok's *Bayit 'al blimah* (Tel Aviv: Heker, 1989). Rattok includes an extensive bibliography of the Appelfeld criticism surveyed in her monograph.

7. Dan Miron, *Pinkas patuaḥ* (Tel Aviv: Sifriat Poalim, 1979), 49–59.

8. Further examples can be found in the English on pages 67, 69, 71, 73, 74, 75, 80, 85, passim, and in the Hebrew on pages 70, 78, 89, 91, 93, 120, passim.

9. See, for instance, pages 55, 85, 121.

10. Cohn, *Transparent Minds,* 43.

11. Additional examples using *ke* plus the present tense are found in the Hebrew on pages 41, 45, 48, 57.

12. The phrase is Cohn's, *Transparent Minds,* 171.

13. For extended passages of the evocative present, see pages 66–67, 72, and 73 in the Hebrew. This stylistic feature is not maintained in the English.

14. Uri Orlev, *The Lead Soldiers,* was published originally by Sifriat Poalim (Tel Aviv, 1956); quotations here are from the 1983 edition. The English translation, by Hillel Halkin, appeared in 1980 (New York: Taplinger).

15. Bernstein, "Language and Socialization," 329–45.

16. Harold Fisch, *A Remembered Future* (Bloomington: Indiana University Press, 1984).

17. Appelfeld, *Masot beguf rishon,* 9–18.

18. This is the subject of Appelfeld's novel *Mikhvat ha'or* (Tel Aviv: Hakibbutz Hameuchad, 1987).

19. Hillel Barzel, "Zikat Apelfeld leKafka," *Zehut* (May 1981): 112–20.

20. David Jacobson pursues the question of parallels between Kafka and Appelfeld in relation to *Badenheim,* in an essay called "Kill Your Common Sense and Then Perhaps You'll Begin to Understand," *AJS Review* 13 (1988): 129–52. In that novel some characters do futilely rely on common sense in a failed attempt to explain their deteriorating circumstances to themselves. Others, who relinquish common sense, perceive and comprehend more but lose their sanity.

Chapter Eight. David Grossman—See Under: Love

1. For accounts of the initial silence in Hebrew literature on the subject of the Holocaust, see Mintz, *Ḥurban,* 157–64; Ilan Avisar, "The Evolution of the Israeli Attitude toward the Holocaust as Reflected in Modern Hebrew Drama," *Hebrew Annual Review* 9 (1985): 31–52; and Sidra Ezrahi, "Revisioning the Past: The Changing Legacy of the Holocaust in Hebrew Literature," *Salmagundi* 68–69 (1985/86): 245–70.

2. Cohn, *Transparent Minds,* 11–18.

3. Translations of *See Under: Love* here are my own. Pages cited refer to the location of the passage in the original Hebrew, *'Ayen 'erekh: ahavah* (Jerusalem: Hakibbutz Hameuchad, 1986). An English translation by Betsy Rosenberg appeared in 1989 (New York: Farrar, Straus and Giroux).

4. Representing something between reflective and nonreflective consciousness, these lines may be designated, in Cohn's terms, as "narrated perception."

5. As Cohn remarks, "By leaving the relationship between words and thoughts latent, the narrated monologue casts a peculiarly penumbral light on the figural consciousness, suspending it on the threshold of verbalization in a manner that cannot be achieved by direct quotation. This ambiguity is unquestionably one reason why so many writers prefer the less direct technique" (103). This ambiguity is also a particularly important factor in the adaptability of narrated monologue to the depiction of a child's inner life.

6. Momik's desire to protect his parents is typical of children of Holocaust survivors. For a psychological study, see Aaron Hass, *In the Shadow of the Holocaust: The Second Generation* (Ithaca: Cornell University Press, 1990).

7. See Chapter 7, pp. 144–46, for a discussion of Orlev.

8. See comments on Vygotsky and Roth in Chapter 5, n. 4.

9. Meir Sternberg coined the term "verbal transposition" to refer to superimpositions of foreign syntax onto the language of composition ("Polylingualism as Reality").

10. For detailed discussion and a list of some of the more common terms that comprise this Holocaust code, see Hannah Yaoz, *Sipporet hasho'ah be'ivrit* (Tel Aviv: Am Oved, 1980).

11. Mottel in some ways provides a departure from this model, since he rebels against his environment and eagerly leaves the shtetl behind to embrace the New World. For Momik, all the same, Mottel embodies the shtetl experience. He is a throwback to a previous era, and his personal adventurousness does not divest him of cultural association with the past. His spriteliness does allow him an additional entrance into Momik's imagination, though. Grossman's character easily appropriates Sholem Aleichem's into his fantasy life, and Mottel, earlocks flying behind him, joins Bill and Johnny as they gallop across the plains.

12. In his review of *See Under: Love* after the novel first appeared, Gershon Shaked succinctly analyzed the relationship of each of the parts of the text with the central thematic tension between imagination and horror: "Yaldei halev vehamifletset," *Yediot aharonot,* 3 July 1986. An English version of this analysis appeared as "The Children of the Heart and the Monster: *See Under: Love*," *Modern Judaism* 9 (October 1989): 311–23. For a discussion of the second part of *See Under: Love* in comparison with Cynthia Ozick's *The Messiah of Stockholm*, a Jewish-American novel about the second generation to the Holocaust, see Naomi Sokoloff, "Reinventing Bruno Schulz," *AJS Review* 13 (1988): 171–99.

Chapter Nine. The Imagination of the Child in Literary Texts

1. See, for instance, Mintz's *Ḥurban*, 226.

2. Albert Memmi, *La statue de sel*, 1954. Translated by Edouard Roditi, the novel appeared in English in 1955 as *The Pillar of Salt* (New York: Criterion Books). Quotations in French are from the Gallimard edition, 1966.

3. For more background, see Isaac Yétiv, *Le thème de l'aliénation dans le roman maghrébin d'expression française de 1952–56* (Sherbrooke, CELEF, Canada, 1972). For information on how Memmi fits in with the tradition of Tunisian writing and the issue of ethnic minority status, see H. A. Bouraqui, "La littérature maghrébine du dedans and du dehors du champ critique," *Présence francophone: revue littéraire* 11 (Autumn 1975): 3–14.

4. Bakhtin discusses "hidden polemic" in *Problems of Dostoevsky's Poetics*, 196.

5. Albert Memmi, *Portrait d'un Juif* (Paris: Gallimard, 1962); English translation by Elisabeth Abbot (New York: Orion Press, 1962).

6. Albert Memmi, *The Colonizer and the Colonized*, trans. Howard Greenfeld (New York: Orion Press, 1965); originally, *Portrait du colonisé, précédé du portrait du colonisateur* (Paris: Buchet/Chastel, 1957).

Chapter Ten. Others: The Silent Voice

1. Yehoshua's story appeared as *Shetiqa holekhet venimshekhet shel meshorer* in the collection *Mot hazaqqen* (Merhavia and Tel Aviv: Hakibbutz Hameuchad, 1962). Quotes are taken from the English version by Miriam Arad in *Three Days and a Child* (New York: Doubleday, 1980) and from *'Ad ḥoref* (Merhavia: Hakibbutz Hameuchad, 1975). Ozick's novella was published in 1984 (New York: Knopf).

2. Bakhtin, *The Dialogic Imagination*, 282.

3. The narrator remarks, for example, "I feel myself lying there as though paralyzed, half dead" (21); *"hineh ani mutal kemeshutaq, met lamaḥatseh"* (114).

4. This final poem is not produced for the reader to peruse, but samples of the son's poetry can be gleaned from earlier portions of the text. The lines viewed separately, or together as a unit of composition, comment appropriately on the son's incoherence and the father's barren silence:

autumn, rain, gourd
bread, path, ignominy
Oblivion o'ercomes me
This azure sky's the match of man
Futile again before thee
This long slow winter
my lunacy in my pale seed

5. *Lehashiv* signifies *to answer,* for example, *"hu heshiv li bishelila,"* 113 ("he said no," 19). *"Lehashiv"* in the sense of more general response appears elsewhere: *"im ani mevakesh lehashiv lo kigemulo ulesharto af ani, eyn hadavar 'oleh beyaday,"* 118 ("When I wish to reciprocate and wait upon him in turn, nothing comes of it," 26).

For more detailed discussion of tensions between repetition and new beginnings, including commentary on the uses of *sh.u.v.* in this novella, see Naomi Sokoloff, "Contrast, Continuity, and Contradiction: Opening Signals in A. B. Yehoshua's 'A Poet's Continuing Silence,'" *Hebrew Annual Review* 5 (1981): 115–36.

6. Bakhtin, *The Dialogic Imagination,* 340.

7. Gilead Morahg provides an excellent overview of Yehoshua's stylistic evolution in "Reality and Symbol in the Fiction of A. B. Yehoshua," *Prooftexts* 2 (May 1982): 179–98.

8. Shaked, *Gal ḥadash,* 125–48. See also Robert Alter's *Defenses of the Imagination: Jewish Writers and Modern Historical Crisis* (Philadelphia: Jewish Publication Society, 1977), especially "Fiction in a State of Siege," 213–32, and "A Problem of Horizons," 249–62.

9. A. B. Yehoshua, *Hame'ahev* (Tel Aviv: Schocken Books, 1977); an English translation by Philip Simpson of *The Lover* appeared in 1978 (Garden City, N.Y.: Doubleday). *Gerushim meuḥarim* (Merhavia: Hakibbutz Hameuchad, 1982); an English translation by Hillel Halkin appeared in 1984 (New York: Doubleday).

10. See Gilead Morahg, "Affirmative Structure in A. B. Yehoshua's *The Lover,*" *Hebrew Studies* 20, no. 1 (1979–80): 98–106, and compare these comments to those in another of his essays, "Outraged Humanism: The Fiction of A. B. Yehoshua," *Hebrew Annual Review* 3 (1979): 141–55.

11. Naomi Sokoloff's "Interpretation: Cynthia Ozick's *Cannibal Galaxy,*" *Prooftexts* 6 (September 1986): 239–57, further pursues discussion of this aspect of the novel.

12. On the concept of *teshuva* in Ozick's view, see "Innovation and Redemption: What Literature Means," in *Art and Ardor* (New York: Knopf, 1983), 238–48. Bonnie Lyons comments on these matters in "Cynthia Ozick as a Jewish Writer," in "The World of Cynthia Ozick," a special issue of *Studies in American Jewish Literature* 6 (Fall 1987): 13–23.

13. Cynthia Ozick, "Bialik's Hint," *Commentary* 75 (February 1983): 22–28; here, 27. See also "Toward a New Yiddish," in *Art and Ardor,* 151–77.

14. Overdedication to art as youthful folly is the topic, for instance, of Ozick's essay "The Lesson of the Master," in *Art and Ardor,* 291–97. On idolatry, in the same collection of essays see also "The Riddle of the Ordinary," 200–209, and "Literature as Idol: Harold Bloom," 178–99. Fiction revolving around these issues includes "Usurpation," in *Bloodshed and Three Novellas* (New York: Dutton, 1976), 129–78; "The Pagan Rabbi," in *The Pagan Rabbi and Other Stories* (New York: Knopf, 1971), 1–37; and *The Messiah of Stockholm* (New York: Knopf, 1987).

Ozick's attention to this theme has attracted discussion in many of the critical studies of her work, including the book-length studies that have begun to appear: Joseph Lowin, *Cynthia Ozick* (Boston: G. K. Hall, 1988), and Sanford Pinsker, *The Uncompromising Fictions of Cynthia Ozick* (Columbia: University of Missouri Press, 1987).

15. For discussion that deftly demonstrates the allusive layeredness of *The Cannibal Galaxy,* see Elaine Kauvar's "The Dread of Moloch: Idolatry as Metaphor in Cynthia Ozick's Fiction," *Studies in American Jewish Literature* 6 (Fall 1987): 111–28. Also of interest is Elisa New's review essay, "Cynthia Ozick's Timing," *Prooftexts* 9 (September 1989): 288–94.

16. Bakhtin, *The Dialogic Imagination,* 282.

17. See Ozick's "Notes toward Finding the Right Question," in *On Being a Jewish Feminist: A Reader,* ed. Susanna Heschel (New York: Schocken Books, 1983), 120–51.

INDEX

Aberbach, David, 218n. 11
Abramovitch, S. Y. [pseud. Mendele the Bookseller], *Of Bygone Days* (*Bayamim hahem*), 10, 43, 44, 74, 172, 208–9n. 16
Adolescence, 6
Ahad Ha-am. *See* Ginzberg, Asher
Aichinger, Ilse, *Herod's Children* (*Die Grössere Hoffnung*), 15
Alexander, Edward, 211n. 29, 224n. 5
Alter, Robert, 34, 210n. 24, 211n. 29, 223n. 5
Amihai, Yehuda: "A Child Is Something Else Again," 3, 27; *Not of This Time, Not of This Place* (*Lo me'akshav velo mik'an*), 132
Anti-Semitism, 14, 18, 51–52, 61, 96, 111, 117–18, 125–28, 131–32, 141, 148, 154, 183, 185, 188–89
Appelfeld, Ahron: aesthetic principles, 129–31, 133–34; *Badenheim* (*Badenheim 1939*), 224n. 20; compared to Bialik, 129; compared to Grossman, 153; compared to Memmi, 187; essays (*Masot beguf rishon*), 129–30; "Hagerush," 131
—*The Age of Wonders* (*Tor hapela'ot*): child's perspective constructed by adult, 18; compared with *The Lead Soldiers*, 144–46; compared with *Mottel*, 144; ending of, 147, 182; general, 7, 17, 26; incomprehension as theme, 134–40; Kafka in, 148–49; narrative voice, 140–44; political implications, 183; specimen passage commentary, 150–52; structure of, 131–32, 146–47
Arenas, Reinaldo, *Celestino antes del alba*, 6

Ariès, Philippe, 5, 10
Asscher-Pinkhof, Clara, *Star Children* (*Sterrenkinder*), 15
Auerbach, Eric, 222n. 3
Autobiography, 8–9, 17, 66, 84, 104, 181

Bakhtin, Mikhail, and dialogic imagination: definition of theory of, ix–x, 23–25; and history of the novel, 25; modern Jewish literature, 36; narrative voice, 27–28, 89; and otherness, 83; polyphony, 47, 57, 215n. 10; poststructuralist successors, 33, 34; psychic life, 166–67; semiotic thematics, 33–35, 92, 192, 194, 205; subversive qualities of language, 122
Baron, Devorah, 210n. 27
Bar Tov, Hanokh, *Whose Little Boy Are You?* (*Shel mi atah yeled?*), 9
Bar Yosef, Hamutal, 217n. 2
Be'er, Hayim, *Notsot*, 9
Begley, Louis, *Wartime Lies*, 15
Bellow, Saul, *Herzog*, 8
Ben Amotz, Dan, *To Remember, to Forget* (*Lizkor velishkoah*), 132
Benjamin, Walter, 25
Berkowitz, Isaac Dov, 210n. 27
Bernstein, Basil, 146, 213n. 17
Biale, David, 209n. 19
Bialik, H. N.: "Habrekhah," 43; "Hahatsotsrah nitbayshah," 215n. 16; modernism, 65, 83; "Oyf dem hoykhn barg," 85; "Revealment and Concealment in Language" ("Gilui vekhisui balashon"), 65, 67, 80, 83–84, 129–30; romanticism, 65–66, 83; secularization, 83–86
—*Aftergrowth* (*Safiah*), characterization, 19; compared to *The Age of Wonders*, 144; compared to *See Under: Love*, 172; ending of, 182;

229